THIRD EDITION

EXCEL WORKBOOK

160 Exercises with Solutions and Comments

M. Ballerini · A. Clerici
M. C. Debernardi · D. Del Corno
M. De Pra

Copyright © 2015, 2017, 2021 EGEA S.p.A.
Via Salasco, 5 – 20136 Milano
Tel. 02-58365751 – Fax 02-58365753
egea.edizioni@unibocconi.it – www.egeaeditore.it

All rights reserved, including but not limited to translation, total or partial adaptation, reproduction, and communication to the public by any means on any media (including microfilms, films, photocopies, electronic or digital media), as well as electronic information storage and retrieval systems. For more information or permission to use material from this text, see the website www.egeaeditore.it

Given the characteristics of Internet, the publisher is not responsible for any changes of address and contents of the websites mentioned.

Third edition: February 2021

ISBN Domestic Edition 978-88-31322-08-9
ISBN International Edition 978-88-31322-08-9
ISBN Digital International Edition 978-88-31322-09-6

Table of Contents

PREFACE — XV
PLAN OF THE WORKBOOK — XVII

SECTION 1. EXERCISES — 1

UNIT 1. EXCEL BASICS — 3

EXERCISE 1.1 - Quarterly sales	5
EXERCISE 1.2 - Four elections	6
EXERCISE 1.3 - Income	7
EXERCISE 1.4 - Cinema	8
EXERCISE 1.5 - Courses	9
EXERCISE 1.6 - Population by age	10
EXERCISE 1.7 - Sales data	11
EXERCISE 1.8 - Exams	12
EXERCISE 1.9 - Balance sheet	13
EXERCISE 1.10 - TV shows	14
EXERCISE 1.11 - Cigarettes	15
EXERCISE 1.12 - Families	16
EXERCISE 1.13 - Beer and wine	17
EXERCISE 1.14 - Three elections	18
EXERCISE 1.15 - Athletics	19
EXERCISE 1.16 - Bills	20
EXERCISE 1.17 - Turnover analysis	21
EXERCISE 1.18 - US and foreign sales	22
EXERCISE 1.19 - Rainfall	23
EXERCISE 1.20 - UFO	24
EXERCISE 1.21 - Accidents	25
EXERCISE 1.22 - Music sales	27
EXERCISE 1.23 - Seven dwarfs	28

EXERCISE 1.24 - Expenses	29
EXERCISE 1.25 - Three musketeers	30
EXERCISE 1.26 - Murders	32
EXERCISE 1.27 - City council	33
EXERCISE 1.28 - Parliamentary groups	34
EXERCISE 1.29 - Regional chief towns	35
EXERCISE 1.30 - Population (summary exercise)	37
UNIT 2. FROM SIMPLE FUNCTIONS TO NESTED FUNCTIONS	**39**
EXERCISE 2.1 - Home loans	41
EXERCISE 2.2 - Internet users	43
EXERCISE 2.3 - Top sellers	45
EXERCISE 2.4 - Alphabet Inc.	47
EXERCISE 2.5 - Show	49
EXERCISE 2.6 - Productivity	50
EXERCISE 2.7 - Customer care	52
EXERCISE 2.8 - Istat	53
EXERCISE 2.9 - Planets (summary exercise)	55
EXERCISE 2.10 - Home Sweet Home (summary exercise)	58
UNIT 3. MATH FUNCTIONS AND ADVANCED CHARTS	**61**
EXERCISE 3.1 - Drugstores	63
EXERCISE 3.2 - Men at work	64
EXERCISE 3.3 - Car Insurances	65
EXERCISE 3.4 - Exam	67
EXERCISE 3.5 - Clothing Store	69
EXERCISE 3.6 - Beauty Business	70
EXERCISE 3.7 - Cosmetics Shop	72
EXERCISE 3.8 - International Education	74
EXERCISE 3.9 - Dinner with classmates (summary exercise)	76
EXERCISE 3.10 - Wages (summary exercise)	78
UNIT 4. FINANCIAL FUNCTIONS AND WHAT-IF ANALYSIS	**81**
EXERCISE 4.1 - Emerald	83
EXERCISE 4.2 - Smart Courses	84
EXERCISE 4.3 - Credits and debts	85
EXERCISE 4.4 - Cloth Paradise	87
EXERCISE 4.5 - Discount on rates	89
EXERCISE 4.6 - Smart Investments Bank	91
EXERCISE 4.7 - Garden Center (summary exercise)	93
EXERCISE 4.8 - GreenBio (summary exercise)	95
EXERCISE 4.9 - PhotoMagic (summary exercise)	98
EXERCISE 4.10 - Bright Sun (summary exercise)	101

UNIT 5. TEXT FUNCTIONS AND PIVOT TABLES — 105
- EXERCISE 5.1 - IBAN codes — 107
- EXERCISE 5.2 - Names — 108
- EXERCISE 5.3 - Superstore — 109
- EXERCISE 5.4 - Beauty — 110
- EXERCISE 5.5 - Europe sales — 111
- EXERCISE 5.6 - Erasmus — 112
- EXERCISE 5.7 - Vitanic — 114
- EXERCISE 5.8 - Office Line — 115
- EXERCISE 5.9 - Greenwich Village (summary exercise) — 116
- EXERCISE 5.10 - Black-yellow supporters (summary exercise) — 118

UNIT 6. MANAGING DATES AND TIMES — 121
- EXERCISE 6.1 - Two hours — 123
- EXERCISE 6.2 - Timesheet — 124
- EXERCISE 6.3 - Date check — 126
- EXERCISE 6.4 - Linguistic certifications — 128
- EXERCISE 6.5 - Techno Building — 129
- EXERCISE 6.6 - Hotel Booking — 131
- EXERCISE 6.7 - My Friends — 134
- EXERCISE 6.8 - Temporary workers — 136
- EXERCISE 6.9 - Payments (summary exercise) — 138
- EXERCISE 6.10 - Stationery (summary exercise) — 141

UNIT 7. LOOKUP & REFERENCE FUNCTIONS, DATA PROTECTION — 145
- EXERCISE 7.1 - Rocky Sports — 147
- EXERCISE 7.2 - Property Evaluation — 148
- EXERCISE 7.3 - Copy shop — 150
- EXERCISE 7.4 - Paper and related — 152
- EXERCISE 7.5 - Purchasing Department — 153
- EXERCISE 7.6 - DoReMi — 155
- EXERCISE 7.7 - Thinkstore — 156
- EXERCISE 7.8 - Print Service — 158
- EXERCISE 7.9 - European University — 160
- EXERCISE 7.10 - Consulteam — 162
- EXERCISE 7.11 - Candidates selection — 164
- EXERCISE 7.12 - MagicWood — 166
- EXERCISE 7.13 - Phone calls (summary exercise) — 168
- EXERCISE 7.14 - Box Office Star (summary exercise) — 171
- EXERCISE 7.15 - Sunshine Events (summary exercise) — 174

UNIT 8. MACROS AND ELEMENTS OF VBA — 177
- EXERCISE 8.1 - Students — 179

EXERCISE 8.2 - Tickets	180
EXERCISE 8.3 - Product list	181
EXERCISE 8.4 - Stores	182
EXERCISE 8.5 - Household linens	183
EXERCISE 8.6 - Arithmetic	184
EXERCISE 8.7 - Airbnb	185
EXERCISE 8.8 - Filtered data	186
EXERCISE 8.9 - Deliveries	187
EXERCISE 8.10 - Subtotals	188
EXERCISE 8.11 - Table	189
EXERCISE 8.12 - Worksheet protection	190
EXERCISE 8.13 - Chart axis	191
EXERCISE 8.14 - Table template	192
EXERCISE 8.15 - Alternate rows	193
EXERCISE 8.16 - Sales chart	194
EXERCISE 8.17 - Add worksheets	195
EXERCISE 8.18 - Sales pivot	196
EXERCISE 8.19 - Insert rows	197
EXERCISE 8.20 - Stock Exchange (summary exercise)	198
UNIT 9. MORE FUNCTIONS AND SOLVER	**201**
EXERCISE 9.1 - Hot deals	203
EXERCISE 9.2 - Blue Vision	205
EXERCISE 9.3 - Gold	207
EXERCISE 9.4 - Personal loan	209
EXERCISE 9.5 - New car	210
EXERCISE 9.6 - Gluten-free products	211
EXERCISE 9.7 - Condo fees	213
EXERCISE 9.8 - Car purchase	214
EXERCISE 9.9 - Promotional Campaign	216
EXERCISE 9.10 - German course	218
EXERCISE 9.11 - Overtime	219
EXERCISE 9.12 - Home video	220
EXERCISE 9.13 - Hotel Eden (summary exercise)	222
EXERCISE 9.14 - TechMind contest (summary exercise)	225
EXERCISE 9.15 - PluriPlast (summary exercise)	228
UNIT 10. DATABASE FUNCTIONS AND CHART OPTIONS	**231**
EXERCISE 10.1 - Payroll office	233
EXERCISE 10.2 - Sport shoes	234
EXERCISE 10.3 - Budget	235
EXERCISE 10.4 - District competition	236

EXERCISE 10.5 - Admission office	237
EXERCISE 10.6 - Distributors	239
EXERCISE 10.7 - Car dealer	240
EXERCISE 10.8 - Fruit & Vegetables	242
EXERCISE 10.9 - Albert Einstein	244
EXERCISE 10.10 - SEFCO (summary exercise)	246
UNIT 11. FINANCIAL APPLICATIONS	**249**
EXERCISE 11.1 - Premium Bonds	251
EXERCISE 11.2 - Coupon&Coupon	253
EXERCISE 11.3 - FRN	254
EXERCISE 11.4 - Reverse floater	256
EXERCISE 11.5 - Capital budgeting	257
EXERCISE 11.6 - Super Leasing	258
EXERCISE 11.7 - Stock performance	259
EXERCISE 11.8 - Stock analysis	260
EXERCISE 11.9 - Regression	262
EXERCISE 11.10 - Market Analysis (summary exercise)	263
UNIT 12. DATA ANALYSIS AND REPORTING	**265**
EXERCISE 12.1 - Turnover	267
EXERCISE 12.2 - Orders	268
EXERCISE 12.3 - Gifts	269
EXERCISE 12.4 - Product IDs	270
EXERCISE 12.5 - Counties and offices	271
EXERCISE 12.6 - Variable period	272
EXERCISE 12.7 - Choose your category	273
EXERCISE 12.8 - Chart with bands	274
EXERCISE 12.9 - Scroll bar	275
EXERCISE 12.10 - Dashboard (summary exercise)	276
SECTION 2. COMMENTS AND FUNCTIONS	**279**
COMMENTS AND FUNCTIONS UNIT 1	**281**
EXERCISE 1.1 - Quarterly sales (commented)	281
EXERCISE 1.2 - Four elections (commented)	284
EXERCISE 1.3 - Income (commented)	285
EXERCISE 1.4 - Cinema	286
EXERCISE 1.5 - Courses (commented)	286
EXERCISE 1.6 - Population by age (commented)	288
EXERCISE 1.7 - Sales data (commented)	290
EXERCISE 1.8 - Exams (commented)	291
EXERCISE 1.9 - Balance sheet	292

EXERCISE 1.10 - TV shows	292
EXERCISE 1.11 - Cigarettes	292
EXERCISE 1.12 - Families	292
EXERCISE 1.13 - Beer and wine	292
EXERCISE 1.14 - Three elections	293
EXERCISE 1.15 - Athletics (commented)	293
EXERCISE 1.16 - Bills	293
EXERCISE 1.17 - Turnover analysis	293
EXERCISE 1.18 - US and foreign sales (commented)	294
EXERCISE 1.19 - Rainfall (commented)	295
EXERCISE 1.20 - UFO	295
EXERCISE 1.21 - Accidents	295
EXERCISE 1.22 - Music sales (commented)	296
EXERCISE 1.23 - Seven dwarfs	296
EXERCISE 1.24 - Expenses (commented)	296
EXERCISE 1.25 - Three musketeers	297
EXERCISE 1.26 - Murders	297
EXERCISE 1.27 - City council (commented)	297
EXERCISE 1.28 - Parliamentary groups	297
EXERCISE 1.29 - Regional chief towns (commented)	298
EXERCISE 1.30 - Population (commented)	299
COMMENTS AND FUNCTIONS UNIT 2	**303**
EXERCISE 2.1 - Home loans (commented)	303
EXERCISE 2.2 - Internet users (commented)	305
EXERCISE 2.3 - Top sellers (commented)	306
EXERCISE 2.4 - Alphabet Inc.	310
EXERCISE 2.5 - Show	310
EXERCISE 2.6 - Productivity	310
EXERCISE 2.7 - Customer care	310
EXERCISE 2.8 - ISTAT (commented)	310
EXERCISE 2.9 - Planets (commented)	311
EXERCISE 2.10 - Home Sweet Home (commented)	313
COMMENTS AND FUNCTIONS UNIT 3	**315**
EXERCISE 3.1 - Drugstores (commented)	315
EXERCISE 3.2 - Men at work (commented)	317
EXERCISE 3.3 - Car insurances (commented)	319
EXERCISE 3.4 - Exam	321
EXERCISE 3.5 - Clothing Store	321
EXERCISE 3.6 - Beauty Business	321
EXERCISE 3.7 - Cosmetics Shop	321

EXERCISE 3.8 - International Education ... 322
EXERCISE 3.9 - Dinner with classmates (commented) ... 322
EXERCISE 3.10 - Wages (commented) ... 323

COMMENTS AND FUNCTIONS UNIT 4 ... **327**
EXERCISE 4.1 - Emerald (commented) ... 327
EXERCISE 4.2 - Smart Courses (commented) ... 329
EXERCISE 4.3 - Credits and debts (commented) ... 331
EXERCISE 4.4 - Cloth Paradise ... 332
EXERCISE 4.5 - Discount on rates ... 332
EXERCISE 4.6 - Smart Investments Bank ... 333
EXERCISE 4.7 - Garden Center (commented) ... 333
EXERCISE 4.8 - GreenBio ... 334
EXERCISE 4.9 - PhotoMagic (commented) ... 335
EXERCISE 4.10 - Bright Sun ... 336

COMMENTS AND FUNCTIONS UNIT 5 ... **339**
EXERCISE 5.1 - IBAN codes (commented) ... 339
EXERCISE 5.2 - Names (commented) ... 340
EXERCISE 5.3 - Superstore (commented) ... 341
EXERCISE 5.4 - Beauty (commented) ... 342
EXERCISE 5.5 - Europe sales ... 343
EXERCISE 5.6 - Erasmus ... 344
EXERCISE 5.7 - Vitanic ... 344
EXERCISE 5.8 - Office Line ... 344
EXERCISE 5.9 - Greenwich Village ... 344
EXERCISE 5.10 - Black-yellow supporters (commented) ... 344

COMMENTS AND FUNCTIONS UNIT 6 ... **349**
EXERCISE 6.1 - Two hours (commented) ... 349
EXERCISE 6.2 - Timesheet (commented) ... 350
EXERCISE 6.3 - Date check (commented) ... 352
EXERCISE 6.4 - Linguistic Certifications ... 354
EXERCISE 6.5 - Techno Building ... 354
EXERCISE 6.6 - Hotel booking (commented) ... 354
EXERCISE 6.7 - My friends ... 357
EXERCISE 6.8 - Temporary workers (commented) ... 357
EXERCISE 6.9 - Payments (commented) ... 359
EXERCISE 6.10 - Stationery (commented) ... 361

COMMENTS AND FUNCTIONS UNIT 7 ... **365**
EXERCISE 7.1 - Rocky Sports (commented) ... 365
EXERCISE 7.2 - Property evaluation (commented) ... 368
EXERCISE 7.3 - Copy shop ... 370

EXERCISE 7.4 - Paper and related (commented) ... 370
EXERCISE 7.5 - Purchasing Department ... 372
EXERCISE 7.6 - DoReMi ... 372
EXERCISE 7.7 - Thinkstore ... 372
EXERCISE 7.8 - Print Service ... 372
EXERCISE 7.9 - European University ... 373
EXERCISE 7.10 - Consulteam ... 373
EXERCISE 7.11 - Candidates selection ... 373
EXERCISE 7.12 - MagicWood ... 373
EXERCISE 7.13 - Phone calls (commented) ... 373
EXERCISE 7.14 - Box Office Star ... 376
EXERCISE 7.15 - Sunshine Events (commented) ... 376

COMMENTS AND FUNCTIONS UNIT 8 ... 381

EXERCISE 8.1 - Students (commented) ... 381
EXERCISE 8.2 - Tickets (commented) ... 383
EXERCISE 8.3 - Product list (commented) ... 384
EXERCISE 8.4 - Stores (commented) ... 386
EXERCISE 8.5 - Household linens ... 387
EXERCISE 8.6 - Arithmetic (commented) ... 387
EXERCISE 8.7 - Airbnb (commented) ... 389
EXERCISE 8.8 - Filtered data (commented) ... 390
EXERCISE 8.9 - Deliveries (commented) ... 390
EXERCISE 8.10 - Subtotals ... 391
EXERCISE 8.11 - Table (commented) ... 391
EXERCISE 8.12 - Worksheet protection (commented) ... 392
EXERCISE 8.13 - Chart axis (commented) ... 394
EXERCISE 8.14 - Table template (commented) ... 395
EXERCISE 8.15 - Alternate rows (commented) ... 397
EXERCISE 8.16 - Sales chart (commented) ... 399
EXERCISE 8.17 - Add worksheets (commented) ... 401
EXERCISE 8.18 - Sales pivot (commented) ... 404
EXERCISE 8.19 - Insert rows (commented) ... 406
EXERCISE 8.20 - Stock Exchange (commented) ... 409

COMMENTS AND FUNCTIONS UNIT 9 ... 413

EXERCISE 9.1 - Hot deals (commented) ... 413
EXERCISE 9.2 - Blue Vision (commented) ... 414
EXERCISE 9.3 - Gold (comment) ... 415
EXERCISE 9.4 - Personal loan (commented) ... 417
EXERCISE 9.5 - New car ... 418
EXERCISE 9.6 - Gluten-free products ... 418

EXERCISE 9.7 - Condo fees	418
EXERCISE 9.8 - Car purchase	419
EXERCISE 9.9 - Promotional campaign (commented)	419
EXERCISE 9.10 - German course	420
EXERCISE 9.11 - Overtime	420
EXERCISE 9.12 - Home video	420
EXERCISE 9.13 - Hotel Eden (commented)	420
EXERCISE 9.14 - TechMind contest	422
EXERCISE 9.15 - Pluriplast	423
COMMENTS AND FUNCTIONS UNIT 10	**425**
EXERCISE 10.1 - Payroll office (commented)	425
EXERCISE 10.2 - Sport shoes (commented)	425
EXERCISE 10.3 - Budget (commented)	429
EXERCISE 10.4 - District competition (commented)	430
EXERCISE 10.5 - Admission office	430
EXERCISE 10.6 - Distributors	430
EXERCISE 10.7 - Car dealer	431
EXERCISE 10.8 - Fruit and vegetables	431
EXERCISE 10.9 - Albert Einstein	431
EXERCISE 10.10 - SEFCO (commented)	431
COMMENTS AND FUNCTIONS UNIT 11	**435**
EXERCISE 11.1 - Premium Bonds	435
EXERCISE 11.2 - Coupon&Coupon	435
EXERCISE 11.3 - FRN	435
EXERCISE 11.4 - Reverse floater	435
EXERCISE 11.5 - Capital budgeting	436
EXERCISE 11.6 - Super leasing	436
EXERCISE 11.7 - Stock performance (commented)	436
EXERCISE 11.8 - Stock analysis	437
EXERCISE 11.9 - Regression	438
EXERCISE 11.10 - Market Analysis (commented)	438
COMMENTS AND FUNCTIONS UNIT 12	**441**
EXERCISE 12.1 - Turnover	441
EXERCISE 12.2 - Orders	441
EXERCISE 12.3 - Gifts	441
EXERCISE 12.4 - Product IDs	441
EXERCISE 12.5 - Countries and offices	441
EXERCISE 12.6 - Variable period	442
EXERCISE 12.7 - Choose your category	442
EXERCISE 12.8 - Chart with bands	443

EXERCISE 12.9 - Scroll bar 443
EXERCISE 12.10 - Dashboard (commented) 443
AUTHORS **447**

Preface

This workbook derives from many years of experience of the authors in Excel courses. The experience with students of different ages, background and employment status, ranging from first year university students to master students, up to managers and professionals with several years of work experience, has allowed us to understand how Excel is an indispensable tool useful in all kinds of jobs and at all levels, and is as important as poorly known. The majority of users, even those who say or believe they know how to use Excel, actually know and use only a very limited number of features, often in an elementary and ineffective way.

Excel in fact is the most used tool in businesses and offices, and its knowledge is a competitive advantage that college students already have when they need to carry out the first group work: those who know how to use Excel have an edge over the others. This competitive advantage becomes more important when they enter into a business environment. When facing an interview, one of the most feared questions is: "So, you told me that you have a good knowledge of Excel: let's try to build a pivot table to analyze these data..." and here starts a cold sweat and, while you try to draft a response, the belief that the position will be assigned to someone else grows. Employers know that those who have a good knowledge of Excel work more efficiently, and workers know that with a solid Excel foundation one can perform daily work better and more quickly, whether it is a table with a few simple formulas or the analysis of complex data.

This workbook allows putting into practice the use of a wide variety of formulas, functions and features (such as pivot tables, macros, statistical and financial functions, and the Solver add-in) that allow working effectively and professionally with Excel.

This workbook is divided into 12 thematic units. Unit 1 starts with the basics of Excel, and unit after unit the workbook is designed to arrive in a progressive manner to deal with very complex cases. In the dedicate web area at http://mybook.egeaonline.it you can find the digital edition of the book with all the initial and solved files that allow to perform the exercises and test the solutions. Among the 160 exercises available, over 80 are commented, to highlight the basic concepts and the peculiarities, and clarify the most complex tasks.

Plan of the Workbook

Unit 1. Excel Basics
Topics: simple formulas (addition, subtraction, multiplication, division), using absolute and mixed references, calculating a percentage, calculating a percentage variation, SUM, AVERAGE, MAX, MIN, COUNTA, COUNT, IF, ABS functions, formatting, simple sorting, creating and customizing simple charts.
(30 exercises, 15 commented)

Unit 2. From Simple Functions to Nested Functions
Topics: importing data, TRIM, AND, OR, COUNTBLANK functions, nested functions, conditional formatting, sorting on multiple levels, filter, and Paste command options (Values).
(10 exercises, 6 commented)

Unit 3. Math Functions and Advanced Charts
Topics: SUMPRODUCT, COUNTIF, AVERAGEIF, SUMIF functions, conditional formatting with formulas, Subtotal, Remove Duplicates command, linking cells, creating charts with a trend line, and charting mixed charts and with two axes.
(10 exercises, 5 commented)

Unit 4. Financial Functions and What-If Analysis
Topics: financial functions: PMT, FV, naming cell or ranges, Paste command options (Transpose), Scenarios, and Goal Seek.
(10 exercises, 5 commented)

Unit 5. Text Functions and Pivot Tables
Topics: text functions: RIGHT, LEFT, MID, CONCATENATE, UPPER, LOWER, PROPER, LENGTH, SEARCH, statistical functions: COUNTIFS, SUMIFS, AVERAGEIFS, pivot table, pivot chart, data validation.
(10 exercises, 5 commented)

Unit 6. Managing Dates and Times
Topics: formulas with dates and times, normalization of time units, date and time functions: DAY, MONTH, YEAR, HOUR, MINUTE, SECOND, WEEKDAY, DAYS, TODAY, NOW, DATE, DATEDIF, and IFERROR functions.
(10 exercises, 7 commented)

Unit 7. Lookup & Reference Functions, Data Protection
Topics: Lookup & Reference functions: VLOOKUP, MATCH, statistical function RANK.EQ, worksheet protection, workbook protection, file protection, and encryption.
(15 exercises, 5 commented)

Unit 8. Macro and Elements of Visual Basic for Applications (VBA)
Topics: recording a macro in Excel, assigning a macro to a shape or a button, and simple VBA editing.
(20 exercises, 18 commented)

Unit 9. More Functions and Solver
Topics: ROUND, INT, RAND, RANDBETWEEN, HLOOKUP, PPMT, IPMT, RATE, VA, NPV, IRR, TEXT, CONVERT, NETWORKDAYS functions, Data tables, advanced filter, and Solver add-in.
(15 exercises, 6 commented)

Unit 10. Database Functions and Chart Options[1]
Topics: use and creation of templates, SUM function with 3D references, Database functions: DSUM; DMIN; DMAX; DCOUNT; DAVERAGE, commenting, Compare and Merge Workbooks command, and advanced chart options.
(10 exercises, 5 commented)

Unit 11. Financial Applications

---

[1] This unit is specifically dedicated to the preparation of the ECDL/ICDL Advanced Spreadsheets certification.

Topics: Financial functions: YIELD, XIRR, TBILLYIELD, NPV, IRR, XNPV, PPMT, IPMT, date and time functions: COUPPCD, COUPDAYBS, COUPDAYS, COUPNCD statistical functions: MEDIAN, STDEV.S, VAR.S, COVARIANCE.S, CORREL, KURT, SKEW, SLOPE, INTERCEPT, RSQ, and Data analysis add-in.
(10 exercises, 2 commented)

Unit 12. Data Analysis and Reporting
Topics: lookup & reference functions: INDEX, INDIRECT, OFFSET, information function ISNUMBER, data validation, form control setting (checkbox and scroll bar), and options of the Paste command (Paste as linked picture).
(10 exercises, 2 commented)

SECTION 1.

EXERCISES

Unit 1. Excel Basics

Topics of this unit:

Simple formulas (addition, subtraction, multiplication, division), using absolute and mixed references, calculating a percentage, calculating a percentage variation, SUM, AVERAGE, MAX, MIN, COUNTA, COUNT, IF, ABS functions, formatting, simple sorting, and creating and customizing simple charts.

EXERCISE 1.1 - Quarterly sales

The file **Exercise 1.1 - Quarterly sales.xlsx** contains data about the sales of a food company, based in the United States of America but selling its products worldwide, especially in Italy. These data are divided by region and by quarter.

You are asked to:

1. Calculate the totals for each region, for each quarter, and the total for the whole year. Consider that all values correspond to US dollars.
2. Calculate the percentage of each individual region, related to the yearly total. Show at least one decimal figure.
3. Create a pie chart that represents the values of total sales for the three regions. Show the value of each region in a section of the pie.

Apply appropriate formatting and organize the data in a suitable manner to ensure maximum readability, and give a neat and professional appearance to the worksheets.

Save the changes and close the file.

EXERCISE 1.2 - Four elections

Open the file **Exercise 1.2 - Four elections.xlsx**. The file contains the results of four hypothetical elections in a fictional town, for seven different parties.

You are asked to:

1. Calculate the total number of votes for each election in cells **B11:E11**.
2. Create a column chart representing the votes obtained by each party in the elections of 2020.
3. Create a second table, starting at cell **A14**, with the same headings of the one with the votes (names of parties, election years, and party/year). Within this table, calculate the percentage value corresponding to the votes obtained by each party, in respect of each election.

Apply appropriate formatting and organize the data in a suitable manner to ensure maximum readability, and give a neat and professional appearance to the worksheets.

Save the changes and close the file.

EXERCISE 1.3 - Income

Open the file **Exercise 1.3 - Income.xlsx**. The **Income** worksheet shows the average incomes of 12 colleagues, in 10 consecutive years (in US dollars).

You are asked to:

1. Calculate, in row **15** of the **Income** worksheet, the total for each year.
2. Calculate, in column **L**, the minimum value of the income for each individual.
3. Calculate, in column **M**, the maximum income for each individual.
4. Calculate, in column **N**, the average income for each individual.
5. Create a column chart representing the average income of each of the 12 colleagues.
6. Calculate, in cell **B17**, the grand total of the income of the colleagues in the 10 years.
7. Copy into the **Percentages** worksheet the table headers available on the **Income** worksheet (years and names of colleagues).
8. Calculate, in the table of the **Percentages** worksheet, how much each income value of a given year and a given person represents, in terms of percentage, with respect to the grand total calculated above.

Apply appropriate formatting and organize the data in a suitable manner to ensure maximum readability, and give a neat and professional appearance to the worksheets.

Save the changes and close the file.

EXERCISE 1.4 - Cinema

Open the file **Exercise 1.4 - Cinema.xlsx**. The file contains data for tickets and receipts (in US dollars) of the cinema located in Lombardy, in the last year, according to the province.

You are asked to:

1. Sort the table according to the value of the takings, in a descending order.
2. Calculate in row **17** the total number of tickets sold and takings for Lombardy.
3. Calculate the minimum and maximum values and the average of tickets sold and the takings for the provinces of Lombardy.
4. Calculate the number of the provinces of Lombardy.
5. Calculate the average ticket price in Lombardy, using the values calculated at point 2.
6. Calculate in column **D** how much the value of the takings of each province is, as a percentage, compared with the total calculated in step 2.
7. Create a column chart representing the values of the takings of each province.

Apply appropriate formatting and organize the data in a suitable manner to ensure maximum readability, and give a neat and professional appearance to the worksheets.

Save the changes and close the file.

EXERCISE 1.5 - Courses

Open the file **Exercise 1.5 - Courses.xlsx**. The file contains fictitious data relating to students enrolled in the courses of a hypothetical training center.

You are asked to:

1. Calculate in row **11** the total number of students enrolled each of the years considered.
2. Calculate in column **D** the variation in the number of students enrolled last year with respect to the previous one, for each course and for the total annual subscribers.
3. Calculate in column **E** the percentage variation in the number of students enrolled last year with respect to the previous one, for each course and for the total annual subscribers.
4. Transform the percentage variations just calculated into their respective absolute values in column **F**.
5. Calculate in cells **B13:C15** the maximum and minimum values, in addition to the average number of students for each year.
6. Use a function in cell **B17**, which gives the results "Increase" if the number of last year's students is greater than that of the previous year, "Decrease" otherwise.
7. Create a column chart that allows comparing the value of the students enrolled in each course for the two years considered.

Apply appropriate formatting and organize the data in a suitable manner to ensure maximum readability, and give a neat and professional appearance to the worksheets.

Save the changes and close the file.

EXERCISE 1.6 - Population by age

Open the file **Exercise 1.6 - Population by age.xlsx**. The file contains the data taken from the website of Istituto nazionale di statistica (Istat), relative to the Italian population of the decade from 2005 to 2014, broken down by age in completed years (0 years, 1 year etc., up to 100 and more).

You are asked to:

1. Calculate the total population per year in row **106**.
2. Calculate, in column **L**, the percentage variation for each age in 2014 compared with that in 2013.
3. Calculate, in column **M**, the maximum value for each age.
4. Create a column chart that represents the total value of the population from the year 2005 to 2014.
5. Create a line chart that allows comparing the evolution of the population in the years considered, with respect to three specific age classes: 30, 60, and 90 years.

Apply appropriate formatting and organize the data in a suitable manner to ensure maximum readability, and give a neat and professional appearance to the worksheets.

Save the changes and close the file.

EXERCISE 1.7 - Sales data

Open the file **Exercise 1.7 - Sales data.xlsx**. The file contains data on receipts (including VAT) of some branches of a commercial company.

You are asked to:

1. Calculate, in row **15**, the total turnover for each quarter. Consider that values are expressed in US dollars.
2. Calculate in column **D**, for every subsidiary and for the total of all the subsidiaries, the increase in turnover (in US dollars) that occurred in Quarter II compared with Quarter I.
3. Calculate in column **E**, for every subsidiary and for the total, the percentage variation in turnover occurred in Quarter II compared with Quarter I.
4. Calculate, in the following columns, the turnover and the VAT for Quarter II, netting out the receipts (note that receipts = turnover + VAT, assuming a VAT rate of 22%), and the respective totals.
5. Once you have completed all the calculations, sort the list considering the percentage variation in receipts occurred in Quarter II compared with Quarter I, from the highest to the lowest.
6. Create a column chart that allows comparing the receipts for each branch in the two quarters.

Apply appropriate formatting and organize the data in a suitable manner to ensure maximum readability, and give a neat and professional appearance to the worksheets.

Save the changes and close the file.

EXERCISE 1.8 - Exams

Open the file **Exercise 1.8 - Exams.xlsx**. The file contains data related to the study plan of a student, with the list of exams and, for those already passed, the grade obtained.

You are asked to:

1. Give the worksheet the name **Data**.
2. Into another worksheet, edit the following table:

Number of exams in the program	
Number of passed exams	
Number of exams to pass	
Average grade	
Number of exams "cum laude"	
Maximum grade	
Minimum grade	

3. Complete the table with formulas and functions that calculate the required information. Consider that, in the example above, the "laude" does not fall in the average calculation.
4. Create a pie chart that represents the number of exams taken and the ones still to take. Show data labels with the value of each section of the pie chart. Make sure that the two sections of the pie chart are green (that relating to exams) and red (that relating to the exams to take). Add to the chart the title "Road to graduation".
5. Rename the second worksheet as **Calculations**. Delete any other worksheet in the file, except the **Data** and **Calculations** worksheets.

Apply appropriate formatting and organize the data in a suitable manner to ensure maximum readability, and give a neat and professional appearance to the worksheets.

Save the changes and close the file.

EXERCISE 1.9 - Balance sheet

Open the file **Exercise 1.9 - Balance sheet.xlsx**. The file contains data for a simplified financial statement, showing the receipts and expenditures of a hypothetical company for three months (the amounts are stated in terms of US dollars).

You are asked to:

1. Calculate in cells **B5:D5** the profit (or loss) for each month, as the difference between revenues and costs.
2. Calculate in cells **E2**, **E3**, and **E5** the total revenues, costs and profit for the quarter.
3. Use a function in cells **B7:E7** to show as a result the word "Loss" if in the month (or quarter, in the case of cell **E7**) there has been a loss, otherwise the word "Profit".
4. Create a line chart that allows comparing the performance of the revenues and costs during the three months.

Apply appropriate formatting and organize the data in a suitable manner to ensure maximum readability, and give a neat and professional appearance to the worksheets.

Save the changes and close the file.

EXERCISE 1.10 - TV shows

Open the file **Exercise 1.10 - TV shows.xlsx**. The file contains data on some TV shows produced in a year by the major Italian national TV channels.

You are asked to:

1. Calculate in cells **E3:E9** the total broadcast hours for each genre, concerning RAI channels. Do the same in cells **J3:J9** for Mediaset.
2. Calculate in row **11** the total hours of transmission for each channel, and the totals for RAI and Mediaset.
3. Calculate in cells **F3:F9** the value, in percentage terms, of the hours of broadcasting concerning RAI channels for each genre. Do the same in cells **K3:K9** for Mediaset. (Note: If the formula is set correctly in cells **F3:F9**, you can copy it without rewriting it.)
4. Enter a formula in cell **L3:L9**, which shows for each genre the result "RAI" if the broadcast hours of RAI for that specific genre are superior to the broadcast hours of Mediaset, otherwise shows "Mediaset."
5. Create a column chart that allows comparing the percentage of broadcast hours for each genre, for RAI and Mediaset.
6. Create a column chart that allows comparing the total hours of programming for each genre, divided between the three Mediaset channels.

Apply appropriate formatting and organize the data in a suitable manner to ensure maximum readability, and give a neat and professional appearance to the worksheets.

Save the changes and close the file.

EXERCISE 1.11 - Cigarettes

Open the file **Exercise 1.11 - Cigarettes.xlsx**. The file contains data on the consumption of cigarettes per year, broken down by gender, age, and region.

You are asked to:

1. Use a function to calculate the average for men and women for each of the three regions considered, in columns **H** and **O**.
2. Use a function to calculate the average of the three regions considered for each age group for women and men, in row **8**.
3. Use a function to calculate the maximum value of the three regions considered for each age group for women and men, in row **9**.
4. Use a function in cell **B12** to obtain results in "more" if the value of the north for the age group 15–24 in cell **B4** is higher than the Italian average, in cell **B8**, otherwise "less." Use the relative and absolute references properly, so you can copy the formula and get the correct result in cells **B12:G14** and **I12:N14**.
5. Create a column chart that allows you to compare the average consumption for men and women, for the three regions considered (north, center and south).

Apply appropriate formatting and organize the data in a suitable manner to ensure maximum readability, and give a neat and professional appearance to the worksheets.

Save the changes and close the file.

EXERCISE 1.12 - Families

Open the file **Exercise 1.12 - Families.xlsx**. The file contains data on the composition of Italian families by number of members, broken down by region and by the total area of Italy.

You are asked to:

1. Calculate in the rows **31:33** the maximum, minimum, and average for the Italian regions in reference to the average number of members (column **B**) and the percentage composition by number of members (columns **C:H**).
2. Sort the table according to the average number of members in a descending order.
3. Create a column chart that allows comparing the families according to the number of members in the areas of North, Central, South, and Italy.

Apply appropriate formatting and organize the data in a suitable manner to ensure maximum readability, and give a neat and professional appearance to the worksheets.

Save the changes and close the file.

EXERCISE 1.13 - Beer and wine

Open the file **Exercise 1.13 - Beer and wine.xlsx**. The file contains data related to the consumption of beer and wine in Italy, broken down by age, gender, and area.

You are asked to:

1. Calculate, in columns **G** and **M**, the averages for beer and wine for each area of Italy.
2. Calculate, in rows **9** and **14**, the averages for beer and wine for each age group.
3. Calculate, in column **N**, the difference in percentages of men and women of the consumption of wine and beer for each area of Italy (with reference to the average value).
4. Calculate, in rows **16:19**, the prevalence of the consumption of beer or wine for each gender, age group, and area of Italy. The function to be entered in cell **B16**, and then copied in all other cells, should return the result "beer" when beer consumption exceeds the consumption of wine for women aged between 15 and 34 years, living in North area. Otherwise, the function should give the result "wine".
5. Create a column chart that allows comparing the average consumption of wine in Italy, for women and men, in the geographic areas considered (North, Central, South, and Italy).

Apply appropriate formatting and organize the data in a proper manner to ensure maximum readability, and give a neat and professional appearance to the worksheets.

Save the changes and close the file.

EXERCISE 1.14 - Three elections

Open the file **Exercise 1.14 - Three elections.xlsx**. The file contains the votes of three rounds for the 10 parties that have participated in the elections.

You are asked to:
1. Calculate in row **15** the total number of votes recorded in each of the three rounds of election.
2. Insert a column in the worksheet, after the one that contains the data of 2010. In this new column, calculate how much is in percentage terms the number of votes received by each party with respect to the total votes recorded in 2010.
3. Insert a column in the worksheet, after the one that contains the data of 2015. Perform the same calculation of the previous point, referring to the vote in 2015. If you have correctly written the formula at the previous point, simply copy it in the corresponding cells of the new column to get the correct results here.
4. Copy the formula again in the first free column after the one that contains the data of 2020 to obtain the percentages for the votes of 2020.
5. In the following column, calculate the percentage variation in the votes of each party between 2020 and 2015.
6. In the cells of the next column, insert a function that returns as a result "Party on the rise" if the percentage variation calculated at the previous point is greater than zero, otherwise "Declining party".
7. Sort the table according to the votes obtained in the elections of 2020, in a descending order (from the largest to smallest).
8. In column **J**, transform the percentage variations calculated in step 5 in absolute values.
9. Create a line chart that represents the total number of votes recorded in the three rounds of election.

Apply appropriate formatting and organize the data in a suitable manner to ensure maximum readability, and give a neat and professional appearance to the worksheets.

Save the changes and close the file.

EXERCISE 1.15 - Athletics

Open the file **Exercise 1.15 - Athletics.xlsx**. The file contains the measures of the jumps made by several athletes in a long jump race.

You are asked to:

1. Format the cells containing the measures of the jumps to display two decimal places.
2. Insert in cells **E3:E7** a function that shows the best result for each athlete.
3. Enter the new athlete Columbus between Mayer and Petersbourgh, with the following measures: 8.09, 7.86, and 8.15 meters.
4. Insert in cells **F3:F8** a function that, for each athlete, shows the result "Promising athlete!" if the best jump is 8.15 meters or higher, otherwise leave an empty cell.
5. Delete the row **1** of the worksheet.
6. Sort the list by the best jump, from the farthest to shortest.
7. Create a bar chart that shows the measure of the best jump for each athlete. Make sure that the chart shows the data labels, beside each bar, with the measure of the jump.
8. Create a bar chart that allows comparing the measure of three jumps for each athlete.

Apply appropriate formatting and organize the data in a suitable manner, to ensure maximum readability, and give a neat and professional appearance to the worksheets.

Save the changes and close the file.

EXERCISE 1.16 - Bills

Open the file **Exercise 1.16 - Bills.xlsx**. The file contains the expenses of a family for electricity, telephone, and gas in a certain quarter (values in US dollars).

You are asked to:

1. Use a function to calculate, in cells **E4:E6**, the total expenditure for each month.
2. Use a function to calculate, in cells **B8:E8**, the total expenditure for each type of bill.
3. Calculate, in cells **F4:H6**, the percentage represented by each type of bill on the total expenditure for each month. You just need to write a single correct formula in cell **F4**, and then copy it into adjacent cells. Copy the formula also in cells **F8:H8**, to calculate the percentage of the total expenditure for the quarter.
4. Calculate, in cells **B12:D14**, the percentage represented by each bill on the total expenditure for the quarter for each type of bill. You just need to write a single correct formula in cell **B12**, and then copy it into the adjacent cells.
5. Insert a column chart representing the expenses for electricity, telephone, and gas in the three-month period to show the data separated by the type of bill and allow the comparison of the total expenditure for the month.

Apply appropriate formatting and organize the data in a suitable manner, to ensure maximum readability, and give a neat and professional appearance to the worksheets.

Save the changes and close the file.

EXERCISE 1.17 - *Turnover analysis*

Open the file **Exercise 1.17 - Turnover analysis.xlsx**. The file contains the sales data relating to customers of a company operating in the music sector. The values are expressed in US dollars and are for the most recent year ("Turnover" column) and the previous ("Previous year turnover" column).

You are asked to:
1. Insert in the first column available a formula that calculates, for each customer, the variation in the turnover (in US dollars) of the last year with respect to that of the previous year. Make sure that if data of the previous year are not available, as a result the formula returns the text "Not available". Add the heading **Increase** to the column.
2. Insert in the next column available another formula in order to calculate, for each customer, the percentage variation in the turnover that has occurred in the last year with respect to that of the previous one. Even in this case, if the data of the previous year are not available, as a result the formula should return the text "Not available". Add the heading **Increase %** to the column.
3. Place in a further column a formula that allows to highlight with a double asterisk (**) customers whose increase was less than 5%. For other customers nothing should appear. Add the heading **Low increase** to the column.
4. Sort the table, based on the turnover in a descending order.
5. Create a column chart that allows comparing the turnover of the two-year period, for each customer.

Apply appropriate formatting and organize the data in a suitable manner to ensure maximum readability, and give a neat and professional appearance to the worksheets.

Save the changes and close the file.

EXERCISE 1.18 - US and foreign sales

Open the file **Exercise 1.18 - US and foreign sales.xlsx**. The file contains the data of the last six months, regarding the sales of a US company that sells its products mainly in the United States of America, but is trying to expand the business abroad. The data, expressed in US dollars, are divided between the sales in the United States and abroad.

You are asked to:

1. Calculate the total for each month, that is, the total for the United States and abroad, and the grand total.
2. Create optimal charts to communicate each of the following messages:
    a. Highlight the growth of total sales (e.g., with a column chart).
    b. Highlight the strong sales growth in the United States (e.g., with a line chart).
    c. Highlight the growth of the total sales, highlighting the significance of the United States against that of abroad (e.g., with a stacked column chart).
    d. Show, in percentage terms, the share of sales (total of six months) of the United States and abroad, with respect to the grand total (e.g., with a pie chart).
    e. Finally, show how the use of a different scale on the axis of the values can amplify or lessen a phenomenon, creating two similar charts (e.g., in lines):
        i. One that highlights different sales growth between the United States and abroad in the six-month period; and
        ii. One representing the same data, but flattening the difference

Apply appropriate formatting and organize the data in a suitable manner, to ensure maximum readability, and give a neat and professional appearance to the worksheets.

Save the changes and close the file.

EXERCISE 1.19 - Rainfall

Open the file **Exercise 1.19 - Rainfall.xlsx**. The file contains data on rainfall recorded in New York City in each month of a given five-year period.

You are asked to:

1. Calculate, in column **G**, the average of each month for the period considered.
2. Calculate, in row **17**, the total rainfall for each year.
3. Calculate, in cell **B20**, the average rainfall for the five years considered.
4. In cells **B18:F18** enter a function that returns the result "Yes" if the total rainfall of each year is higher than the average rainfall of the five years, otherwise "No".
5. Create in the same worksheet a column chart representing the average monthly rainfall.
6. Rename **Sheet1** with the name **Data** and **Sheet2** with the name **Percentages**.
7. Copy the table headings available in the **Data** worksheet into the **Percentages** worksheet (months and years).
8. Calculate, in the table of the **Percentages** worksheet, the percentage values corresponding to each month of each year, of the total of each year, both available in the **Data** worksheet. To carry out the calculation, write a single formula in the **Percentages** worksheet and copy it to all the other cells.

Apply appropriate formatting and organize the data in a suitable manner, to ensure maximum readability, and give a neat and professional appearance to the worksheets.

Save the changes and close the file.

EXERCISE 1.20 - UFO

Open the file **Exercise 1.20 - UFO.xlsx**. The file contains data on UFO sightings recorded by the police in the State of New Jersey in the months of a particular decade.

You are asked to:

1. Calculate, in column **N**, the total number of sightings per year.
2. Calculate, in column **O**, the maximum number of sightings per year.
3. Calculate, in column **P**, the minimum number of sightings per year.
4. Calculate, in row **15**, the average of the sightings per month.
5. Create in the same worksheet a column chart that represents the total number of sightings per year.
6. Rename **Sheet1** with the name **Data** and **Sheet2** with the name **Percentages**.
7. Copy the table headings (months and years) from **Data** worksheet to **Percentages** worksheet.
8. Calculate, in the table of the **Percentages** worksheet, the percentage values corresponding to each month of each year, of the total of each year, both available in the **Data** worksheet. To carry out the calculation, write a single formula in the **Percentages** worksheet and copy it to all the other cells.

Apply appropriate formatting and organize the data in a suitable manner, to ensure maximum readability, and give a neat and professional appearance to the worksheets.

Save the changes and close the file.

EXERCISE 1.21 - Accidents

Open the file **Exercise 1.21 - Accidents.xlsx**. The file contains data on accidents at work registered in the Member States of the European Union (EU) during the period 1997-2003.

You are asked to:

1. Calculate, in column **I**, the total number of accidents for each country over the period.
2. Calculate, in row **20**, the total number of accidents per year.
3. Calculate, in row **21**, the maximum number of accidents recorded per year.
4. Calculate, in row **22**, the average recorded accidents per year.
5. Insert a function in cell **B24** to calculate the number of member states.
6. Create in the same worksheet a line chart that represents the number of accidents recorded in Italy in the years considered.
7. Create a column chart that allows comparing the total number of accidents and those per year among the different countries.
8. Create a pie chart that displays the percentage values corresponding to the total number of accidents recorded in each country over the period.
9. Rename **Sheet1** with the name **Data**, **Sheet2** with the name **Percentages**, and **Sheet3** with the name **Rating**.
10. Copy the table headings (countries and years) from **Data** worksheet to **Percentages** worksheet.
11. Calculate, in the table of the **Percentages** worksheet, the percentage values corresponding to each country per year, of the total of each year, available in the **Data** worksheet. To carry out the calculation, write a single formula in the **Percentages** worksheet and copy it to all the other cells.
12. Copy the table headings again, from **Data** worksheet to **Ratings** worksheet.
13. Insert a function, in the table of the **Ratings** worksheet, which returns the result "Yes" if the number of accidents per country and per year is higher than the average for the year, otherwise "No". To carry out the calculation write a single formula in the **Ratings** worksheet and copy it to all the other cells.

Apply appropriate formatting and organize the data in a proper manner, to ensure maximum readability, and give a neat and professional appearance to the worksheets.

Save the changes and close the file.

EXERCISE 1.22 - Music sales

Open the file **Exercise 1.22 - Music sales.xlsx**. The file contains the sales figures of music for a two years period in some European countries. Values are expressed in euros.

You are asked to:

1. Calculate, in row **12** of **Sheet1**, the total number of units sold and revenues for each of the two years using the required function once and then copy the formula to the other cells.
2. Calculate, in columns **F** and **G**, the average of the units sold and revenues of the biennium for the different countries.
3. Delete row **1** of **Sheet1**. Then, rename **Sheet1** with the name **Sales**.
4. In the same worksheet, create a pie chart that represents the averages of units sold in the different countries. Show, next to each section, the label with the name of the nation and the corresponding percentage value. Do not show the legend.
5. In **Sheet2**, calculate the total value in cell **B14**.
6. In column **C**, add a function that calculates the percentage value, of the total, only for the values that exceed 100,000 euros, whereas as a result for the others returns the term "Irrelevant". Format the values thus obtained with percentage style and one decimal place.
7. Rename **Sheet2** with the name **Percentages**.
8. Sort the table in the **Percentages** worksheet based on the value in a descending order.
9. Create a column chart in the same worksheet, which allows comparing the value for the different types.
10. Set the orientation of the pages for printing of both the worksheets horizontally, center the content of the worksheets in horizontal and fit the print to 1 page wide by 1 long. Finally check the print preview.

Apply appropriate formatting and organize the data in a suitable manner, to ensure maximum readability, and give a neat and professional appearance to the worksheets. Save the changes and close the file.

EXERCISE 1.23 - Seven dwarfs

Open the file **Exercise 1.23 - Seven dwarfs.xlsx**. In the file, you find data regarding the seven dwarfs: height and weight before they met Snow White and weight after living with her for a year. It is said that Snow White is not a good cook, and that the health of the seven dwarfs suffered by living with her.

You are asked to:

1. Calculate, in column **E**, the weight variation for each of the seven dwarfs.
2. Calculate, in column **F**, the percentage variation in weight for each of the seven dwarfs.
3. Add in column **G** a function that returns as result for each dwarf "Thinner" if the weight variation is negative, otherwise "Fatter".
4. In column **H**, transform the percentage variations in their absolute values.
5. Calculate, in row **12**, the maximum heights and weights before and after Snow White, variation, and percentage variation.
6. Calculate, in row **13**, the corresponding minimum values and, in row **14**, the average values.
7. In cell **B16** use a function to calculate automatically how many the dwarfs are.
8. Create a scatter chart representing on the two axes the values of height and weight of the seven dwarfs post Snow White.

Apply appropriate formatting and organize the data in a suitable manner, to ensure maximum readability, and give a neat and professional appearance to the worksheets.

Save the changes and close the file.

EXERCISE 1.24 - Expenses

Open the file **Exercise 1.24 - Expenses.xlsx**. The file contains data relating to the expenditure of a household budget, in particular to the bills of electricity, gas, and telephone for the 12 months of a year (values in US dollars).

You are asked to:

1. Calculate, in cells **F5:I16**, the VAT due for each bill, knowing that it corresponds to 22% of the net value.
2. Calculate, in cells **J5:M16**, the total of each bill (including VAT).
3. Finally, in row **18**, enter the total of the corresponding figures, shown in each of the columns from **B** to **M**.
4. Calculate, in column **N**, the percentage value corresponding to each of the values in column **M** (total bills for the month, including VAT) with respect to the total value calculated in cell **M18**.
5. Create a pie chart that represents, as percentages with respect to the grand total of the bills, the three total values of electricity, gas, and telephone bills (in the cells **J18:L18**).
6. Create a column chart representing the total expenditure, including VAT, for each of the months considered.

Apply appropriate formatting and organize the data in a suitable manner, to ensure maximum readability, and give a neat and professional appearance to the worksheets.

Save the changes and close the file.

EXERCISE 1.25 - Three musketeers

Open the file **Exercise 1.25 - Three musketeers.xlsx**. The file contains data for the duels won by the Musketeers in four years from 1625 to 1628.

You are asked to:

1. Rename **Sheet1** with the name **Data**.
2. Calculate, in column **F**, the total number of duels in the four-year period, per musketeer.
3. Calculate, in row **9**, the total duels of the musketeers per year.
4. Calculate, respectively, in rows **10** and **11**, the maximum and minimum number of duels per year.
5. Calculate, in row **12**, the average duels per year with one decimal place.
6. In cells **B14:E14**, insert a function that allows assessing whether D'Artagnan was the best musketeer of the year, for each of the years considered. The function must return the result "Yes" if the number of duels won by D'Artagnan in the year corresponds to the maximum value already calculated in step 3, otherwise "No".
7. In cell B16, enter a function to calculate automatically how many musketeers were there.
8. Create a column chart, in the same worksheet, which allows comparing duels won by each musketeer in each of the four years considered.
9. Create a pie chart, in the same worksheet, which displays the percentage value corresponding to the number of duels won by each musketeer in the four years, compared with the total number of duels.
10. Rename **Sheet2** with the name **% per year**.
11. Copy into worksheet **% per year**, starting from cell **A1**, the headers of the table contained in **Data** worksheet (names of the musketeers and years). Referring to the numbers contained in the **Data** worksheet, calculate in cells **B2:E5** of the worksheet **% per year** the percentage value corresponding to the number of duels won per year, per musketeer, compared with the total number of duels of the four-year period calculated in column **F** of the **Data** worksheet. For the calculation use a single formula, written in cell **B2** and then copy it to all other cells in the table.

12. Also calculate the total percentage (which should correspond to 100%) in column **F** of the worksheet **% per year**.
13. Rename **Sheet3** with the name **% per musketeer**.
14. Copy into the worksheet **% per musketeer**, starting from cell **A1**, the headers of the table contained in **Data** worksheet (names of the musketeers and years). Referring to the numbers contained in the **Data** worksheet, calculate in cells **B2:E5** of the worksheet **% per musketeer** the percentage value corresponding to the number of duels won per year per musketeer, compared with the total number of duels during the four-year period calculated in row **9** of the **Data** worksheet. For the calculation use a single formula, write in cell **B2**, and then copy it to all other cells in the table.
15. Also calculate the total percentage (which should correspond to 100%) in row **7** of the worksheet **% per musketeer**.

Apply appropriate formatting and organize the data in a suitable manner, to ensure maximum readability, and give a neat and professional appearance to the worksheets.

Save the changes and close the file.

EXERCISE 1.26 - Murders

Open the file **Exercise 1.26 - Murders.xlsx**. The file contains data on the number of murders sentenced on appeal in the various Italian districts, between 2015 and 2020.

You are asked to:
1. Calculate, in rows **18:21**, the total, average, maximum, and minimum of the annual values available in the table above.
2. Calculate, in column **H**, the percentage variation between the value of 2015 and that of 2020, for each district and for the total.
3. Insert a function in cells **B23:G23** that allows comparing the values of the districts of Milan and Rome for each of the years considered. The function must return the result "Milan" if the value of the district of Milan is higher than that of Rome in the year indicated, otherwise it should return "Rome".
4. Insert a function in cell **B25** that returns as a result the number of districts considered.
5. Create a line chart that shows the trend in the total number of murders convicted in the six years considered.
6. Create a pie chart representing the percentage value corresponding to the number of murders convicted in 2020 for each district, of the total of the same year (without calculating the respective percentages in the worksheet).

Apply appropriate formatting and organize the data in a suitable manner, to ensure maximum readability, and give a neat and professional appearance to the worksheets.

Save the changes and close the file.

EXERCISE 1.27 - City council

Open the file **Exercise 1.27 - City council.xlsx**. This file contains the number of seats won in the municipal council of a small town by the parties who participated in the last four rounds of local elections.

You are asked to:

1. Calculate, in columns **J** and **K**, the maximum and minimum number of seats won by each party in the four elections considered.
2. Calculate, in row **20**, the total number of seats available in each of the four city council elections.
3. Insert a function in columns **C, E, G,** and **I** to calculate the percentage of each value out of the total number of seats available in the city council election. In case the value of seats is 0, the function should return a dash (-).
4. Create a pie chart that represents the composition of the city council in 2015, making sure that each section shows the corresponding number of seats.
5. Create a line chart that represents the comparison between the seats won by parties 9 and 11 in the four elections considered.
6. Create a column chart that allows comparing the maximum and minimum values of seats won by each party in elections considered.

Apply appropriate formatting and organize the data in a suitable manner, to ensure maximum readability, and give a neat and professional appearance to the worksheets.

Save the changes and close the file.

EXERCISE 1.28 - Parliamentary groups

Open the file **Exercise 1.28 - Parliamentary groups.xlsx**. This file contains data regarding the votes obtained by different parties in two rounds of parliamentary elections.

You are asked to:
1. Calculate, in row **16**, the total number of votes recorded in each of the two elections.
2. Calculate, in rows **17** and **18**, the maximum and minimum values of the votes obtained by the parties in each of the two elections.
3. Calculate, in columns **C** and **F**, the percentage value corresponding to the number of votes received by each party with respect to the total number of votes in each election.
4. In columns **D** and **G**, insert a function that returns the result "GROUP" in case the number of votes received by the party, in a single election, is at least equal to 200. Otherwise, the result must be a dash (-).
5. Calculate, in column **H**, the percentage variation between the votes of 2010 and those of 2015, for each party.
6. Use an Excel function in column **I** to eliminate negative signs from the newly calculated percentage variations, transforming all the values in positive numbers.
7. Create a column chart that allows comparing the votes obtained by each party in the two elections.

Apply appropriate formatting and organize the data in a suitable manner, to ensure maximum readability, and give a neat and professional appearance to the worksheets.

Save the changes and close the file.

EXERCISE 1.29 - Regional chief towns

Open the file **Exercise 1.29 - Regional chief towns.xlsx**. This file contains some data concerning the Italian regional chief towns regarding the environmental situation and the main structural features from Istat.

You are asked to:

1. Sort the table in **Sheet1** by geographical area and copy to **Sheet2** only the data regarding Center geographic area (including the column headings), then rename the sheet **Center of Italy**.
2. Graph the distribution of the number of cars per inhabitant in the regional chief towns of central Italy.
3. In **Sheet1**, calculate in row **28** the average for regional chief towns of all the numeric variables.
4. Again, in **Sheet1**, calculate, in column **L**, the population density (with one decimal) as the ratio between the resident population and municipal area.
5. In column **M**, enter a function that returns "High density" result when the population density is equal to or greater than 1,000 inhabitants per km^2. Otherwise, the result must be a dash (-).
6. Enter in cell **I29** the value of the total Italian population as on 01/01/2016 (60,665,551 inhabitants), and calculate in column **N**, the proportion of inhabitants represented by each municipality.
7. Calculate, in columns **O** and **P**, the total km^2 of urban green in the municipalities, respectively, as square meters per capita per the number of inhabitants (converted into km^2) and as percentage of green area per the total municipal area.
8. In column **Q**, calculate the absolute value of the difference between the two methods of calculating the total km^2 urban green; also, calculate the average of these values.
9. In column **R**, enter a function that returns "Acceptable approximation" when the difference in the **Q** column is below average, nothing in other cases.
10. In column **S**, enter a function that returns "Few overruns" if there were less than 30 days of slippage of particulate matter (PM$_{10}$), otherwise, it must display "Low air quality".

11. In column **T**, enter a function that allows understanding whether the municipality is mountainous: if the altitude exceeds 500 meters above the sea level there must appear the words "Mountain municipality," otherwise the cell must remain empty.
12. Represent with a horizontal bar chart with value labels (placed in a sheet of its own) the daily consumption of water for chief towns.
13. Rename the sheets suitably in accordance with the content and delete the unused ones.

Apply appropriate formatting and organize the data in a suitable manner, to ensure maximum readability, and give a neat and professional appearance to the worksheets.

Save the changes and close the file.

EXERCISE 1.30 - Population (summary exercise)

Revise the data related to the population of the EU on behalf of a market research company. The data to be revised are contained within the file **Exercise 1.30 - Population.xlsx**. The file contains three worksheets:
- The **EU Population** worksheet, with the total population registered between 2002 and 2013, of all the 28 EU countries
- The **Population 15-24** worksheet, with the percentage of population of those aged between 15 and 24, of all the 28 EU countries
- The **Forecasts** worksheet, with Eurostat projections on the growth of the European population in the next decades

You are asked to solve the following five problems:

1. In the **EU Population** worksheet, format the data in the table in such a way that all the values are provided in full, without decimal digits, and with a thousand separator.
   Therefore, add a new column, after the last year considered, with the heading "Variation". In this column, calculate for each country present in the table, the percentage variation of the population between the value of the first and that of the last of the years considered. Format the results so that they show two decimal places.

2. Again, in the **EU Population** worksheet, calculate the total European population for each year.
   Calculate, using the appropriate functions, the maximum and minimum values of the population for each year available in the table (i.e., the populations of the most and least populous countries).
   Also, calculate using appropriate counting function, the number of countries considered in the list.

3. Create a line chart that represents only the annual totals of the population. Make sure that the labels of the horizontal axis correspond to the table headers (the years 2002–2013). Then:
   - Move the chart into a new worksheet named **EU Population Chart**
   - Do not show the legend
   - Make sure that the chart is given a meaningful title

- Set the minimum value of the values axis to 475 million
- Set for the chart line an orange color and shading

4. In the **Population 15-24** worksheet, calculate the EU average of the values of each year.
   In the column after the year 2013 insert the new heading **Youngsters 2013**. Use a function in the new column to show, for every country, the text "Many youngsters" when the percentage of youngsters in the country in 2013 was greater than or equal to the average percentage just calculated for year 2013; otherwise the text "Few youngsters" should appear.

5. Calculate in two new columns in the **Forecasts** worksheet, the predicted percentage variation for the population of each country respectively, between 2020 and 2050 and between 2020 and 2070.
   Then, create in a new worksheet a column chart that displays the percentage variation just calculated, so that for each country the columns related to the two values are side by side. Format the chart so that the legend is positioned at the bottom, and then insert a meaningful title.

Apply appropriate formatting and organize the data in a suitable manner, to ensure maximum readability, and give a neat and professional appearance to the worksheets.

Save the changes and close the file.

Unit 2. From Simple Functions to Nested Functions

Topics of this unit:
Importing data, TRIM, AND, OR, COUNTBLANK functions, nested functions, conditional formatting, sorting on multiple levels, filter, Paste command options (Values).

EXERCISE 2.1 - Home loans

Create a new Excel file and save it with the name **Exercise 2.1 - Home loans.xlsx**. You have to analyze the data regarding the mortgages for home purchase distributed to households in the 2003-2014 period in some countries and in the whole euro area.

You are asked to:

1. Import the contents of the **Exercise 2.1 - ECB_home_loans.txt** file into the file you just saved. The file contains data provided by the European Central Bank (ECB) on the topic to be analyzed. Pay attention to the decimal separators (if necessary, change them during the import process); all values are in euros.
2. In a new column called % **Euro Area**, calculate the percentage variation between each value of the **Euro area** field and the previous value (i.e., between October and September 2014). Make sure that all possible calculation errors are replaced by the value "Not available".
3. Apply a formatting to the cells of the field % **Euro Area** so that positive variations are formatted with a fill of your choice, negative variations are formatted with a fill of your choice (different from the previous one), and cells with the value "Not available" are formatted with another fill of your choice (different from the previous ones). The formatting should change automatically when the contents of the cells change.
4. Create a line chart that shows the mortgages trend in Spain, Italy, and the Netherlands, and then move it in a new worksheet separated from the table with data.

5. Use a function, in a new column called **Direction**, that automatically shows as a result, for each period:
    a. "Both positive" if the percentage variations of France and Italy are both positive
    b. A blank cell for all other cases
   Make sure that any possible error in the calculation is replaced by the value "Not available".

Apply appropriate formatting and organize the data in a proper manner to ensure maximum readability, and give a neat and professional appearance to the worksheets.

Save the changes and close the file.

EXERCISE 2.2 - *Internet users*

Create a new file in Excel and save it as **Exercise 2.2 - Internet users.xlsx**.

You are asked to:

1. Import the data contained in the file **Exercise 2.2 - Internet and mobile phone users.txt**, paying attention to the decimal separators (if necessary, change them during the import process). The data you have just imported show the number of Internet users and the number of mobile phone users for each of the 212 countries considered.
2. Create two new columns called **% Internet** and **% phone users**, then calculate the percentages of Internet and mobile phone users for each country with respect to the total.
   Note: use a single formula to perform each calculation, without calculating separately the world total of Internet and mobile phones users.
3. Sort the data in the table with respect to the number of mobile phone users in a descending order and then create, in a new worksheet, a column chart that shows the number of mobile phone users of the first 15 countries. Make sure that the column representing the data for Italy is shown in a different color.
4. Apply a formatting in the worksheet with the imported data, so that the cells in the **Internet users** column with the 15 highest values are automatically formatted with a fill color of your choice. Note: The formatting should change automatically when the contents of the cells change. Repeat the same operation within the values of the **Mobile phone users** column, using a fill of your choice, different from the previous one.
5. Add a new column called **Ranking** to the table with the imported data. The cells in this column must contain a function that automatically shows as a result:
   - "Top ranking" for each country in the first 20 highest positions both as number of Internet and mobile phone users
   - Nothing for all the other countries

Apply appropriate formatting and organize the data in a suitable manner to ensure maximum readability, and give a neat and professional appearance to the worksheets.

Save the changes and close the file.

EXERCISE 2.3 - Top sellers

The **Exercise 2.3 - Sales data.txt** file contains data for some products sold and shipped from a supplier operating in Germany.

You are asked to:

1. Import into a new Excel worksheet the data contained in the **Exercise 2.3 - Sales data.txt** file. Pay attention to the decimal separator (if necessary, change it during the import process).
2. Save the file as **Exercise 2.3 - Top sellers.xlsx** and rename the worksheet with the imported data with the name **Sales data**. Delete the unnecessary rows (first 8), keeping only the dataset with column headings.
3. Sort the table by **PART NUMBER** and then by **Quantity** (both in a descending order).
4. Calculate the average price for the items on the list.
5. In a new column called **Sales**, use a formula so that next to the name of each product appears the result:
    - "Almost Top Seller" when the quantity is between 150 and 220 (including extremes)
    - "Top Seller" when the quantity is more than 220
    - Nothing (a blank cell) in other cases
6. Format the cells in the **Sales** column so that they are automatically formatted with a light green fill color and a dark green font color when containing the value "Top seller".
7. Count how many **AAID** are classified as Top Seller or Almost Top Seller and how many are not.
8. Filter the list showing only products that:
    - Have a price between 101 and 147 US dollars (including extremes)
    - Have a **PART NUMBER** that starts with the letters «AA»
    - Have a **Quantity** greater than or equal to 100
9. Copy in a new worksheet (called **Large quantities**) the filtered list keeping the formatting, but not the formulas.
10. In the **Large quantities** worksheet plot in the same chart **Quantity** and **Unit Price (Euro)** using the **Serial Number** on the horizontal axis and using customized y-axes. Display **Unit Price (Euro)** labels on the chart.

11. Again, in **Large quantities** worksheet, format the cells in **Unit Price (Euro)** column so that the two cells with the highest value are automatically formatted with a fill color of your choice.

Apply appropriate formatting and organize the data in a suitable manner to ensure maximum readability, and give a neat and professional appearance to the worksheets.

Save the changes and close the file.

EXERCISE 2.4 - Alphabet Inc.

1. Search the international version of **Yahoo! Finance** website for the daily historical prices for the period from September 29, 2014 to December 6, 2014 of **Alphabet Inc.** shares **(symbol GOOGL)**.
2. Import the data into a new Excel file, using the Copy and Paste commands.
3. Rename the worksheet used as **Alphabet Inc.** and save the file as **Exercise 2.4 - Alphabet Inc.xlsx**.
4. Format the date of the stock quotes in the format mm/dd/yyyy and all the values of the stock quotes (NOT the ones related to volumes) with two decimal digits.
5. Sort the list by **Date** in an ascending order.
6. Calculate, for each field of the list, the maximum and minimum values.
7. In a new column called **Performance**, use a function that will show the expression "Higher than average performance" when the **Adjusted Close** value of the title (Adj Close) is greater than the average value, otherwise the cell should be empty.
8. In a new column called **Stress**, use a function that will show the expression "Crucial Day" when the daily minimum is less than 530 or when the maximum is higher than 580. In all the other cases, the expression "Normal Day" should be shown.
9. Format the cells of the **Stress** column so that they are automatically formatted with a bold white font and a dark colored background of your choice if they contain the value "Crucial Day".
10. In a new worksheet called **Alphabet chart** create a chart that represents the trend of the **Alphabet** stock trading volumes.
11. Insert in the chart the title "Daily stock trading volumes 9/29/2014-12/6/2014"; set the display unit of the values in thousands.
12. Filter the table by highlighting only the days in which the **Close** was not more than 570 and the **Volume** between 1,300,000 and 1,800,000 (both inclusive); copy the filtered table in a new worksheet called **Filtered table** (without copying the formulas but retaining formatting) and leave the filter in the active worksheet **Alphabet Inc.**, but delete the selection.
13. In the **Filtered table** worksheet, remove the conditional formatting from the column **Stress**.

14. Again, in the **Filtered table** worksheet, use a formula to calculate how many days had a performance equal to or below average.

Apply appropriate formatting and organize the data in a suitable manner to ensure maximum readability, and give a neat and professional appearance to the worksheets.

Save the changes and close the file.

EXERCISE 2.5 - Show

Open the file **Exercise 2.5 - Show.xlsx**. The file contains information about the ticket price in euros for a theatrical performance and the reductions provided for young and elderly theatregoers. You need to create a simple tool to help the cashier of the theater, so that by entering in the "Calculations" table the category of seat and the age of the customer, Excel automatically returns the corresponding final price. To do this, you are asked to:

1. Insert a function in cell **B16** to calculate the price of the seat that corresponds to the category entered in cell **B13**. If the code inserted is not among those admitted, the result should be 0.
2. Insert a function in cell **B17** to calculate the reduction according to the customer's age entered in cell **B14** (pay attention to the different types of reduction related to the age).
3. Insert a formula in cell **B18** that calculates the final price depending on the values resulting from steps 2 and 3.
4. Apply conditional formatting using icons (e.g., arrows) on the seat prices that allows understanding easily which the most and the least expensive tickets are.
5. Enter in cell **D14** a message reminding the cashier to ask the age if cell **B14** is left blank, by displaying in the cell the text "Ask the age!".
6. Insert a conditional formatting on cell **D14**, so that the fill color becomes yellow with dark yellow font color if the cell contains the text "Ask the age!".
7. Enter in cell **D18** a message reminding the cashier that children under 14 should be accompanied by an adult (e.g., the phrase "Attention! Children must be accompanied by an adult"). The same phrase should appear, but in upper case, if the ticket is for the stalls; if the age is greater than or equal to 14 years, the cell should be blank.

Apply appropriate formatting and organize the data in a suitable manner to ensure maximum readability, and give a neat and professional appearance to the worksheets.

Save the changes and close the file.

EXERCISE 2.6 - Productivity

The management of 5M Engineering, a company operating in the mechanical engineering market with several offices in Europe, has decided to encourage the productivity of its more qualified staff through some production bonuses. The file **Exercise 2.6 - Productivity.xlsx** contains the list of the workers of all the 5M Engineering offices, with additional information such as the gender, the days of absence from work, the hours worked during the last month and a coefficient measuring the average wear of the machinery used, and the units produced last month.

You are asked to:

1. Calculate which employees will be assigned to each of the four production bonuses provided by the 5M Engineering management. Considering that there is no limit to the number of bonuses to be assigned and that each worker may also receive more than one bonus, create five new columns in which different functions must be inserted, showing as a result Bonus A, Bonus B, Bonus C, Bonus D, and Bonus E for each worker who is entitled (nothing must be shown in all other cases), under the following conditions:
    - Bonus A: units produced equal to or greater than 3,000
    - Bonus B: days of absence from work less than 3 and units produced equal to or greater than 2,800
    - Bonus C: average wear of machinery coefficient equal to or less than 0.20 or hours worked equal to or greater than 235
    - Bonus D: average wear of machinery coefficient equal to or less than 0.3 and days of absence from work less than 5 or units produced equal to or greater than 2.800 and hours worked equal to or greater than 200
    - Bonus E: female gender (F) and average wear of machinery coefficient equal to or less than 0.20 or female gender (F) and units produced equal to or greater than 3,000
2. Apply a formatting to the values of each of the five columns just created so that the cells containing Bonus A, Bonus B, Bonus C, Bonus D, and Bonus E area are formatted automatically with a fill color of your choice

(different for the values of each column). The formatting should change automatically when the contents of the cells change.
3. At the end of the table, calculate in percentage with respect to the total number of workers and for each bonus category, how many workers are not eligible for a bonus.

Apply appropriate formatting and organize the data in a suitable manner to ensure maximum readability, and give a neat and professional appearance to the worksheets.

Save the changes and close the file.

EXERCISE 2.7 - Customer care

The manager of the customer care services of a toy seller's website wants to analyze the data regarding assistance requests made by customers during the purchase transactions. Open a new Excel file and save it as **Exercise 2.7 - Customer care.xlsx**.

In order to help the manager of the customer care services you are asked to:

1. Import the data contained in the file **Exercise 2.7 - Customers.txt**, paying attention to the decimal separators (if necessary, modify them during the import process). Purchase values are expressed in US dollars.
2. The website has three customer care services offices, in Tokyo, Rome, and London. Each assistance request must be forwarded to the relevant office based on the origin country of the customer. In a new column with the heading **Helpdesk** use a function showing as a result:
    - "Tokyo Helpdesk" when the country of origin of the customer is Japan or China
    - "Rome Helpdesk" when the country of origin of the customer is Italy, France, or Germany
    - "London Helpdesk" in all other cases
3. In a new column with the heading **Priority** use a function showing as a result:
    - "Urgent" for the assistance requests with reason "Broken product" and purchase value greater than the average
    - Nothing in all other cases
4. Sort the table based on the country (in ascending order), then based on the reason of the assistance request (in an ascending order) and on the purchased value (in a descending order).
5. Apply a data bar conditional formatting to the cells of the **Purchase value** column.

Apply appropriate formatting and organize the data in a proper manner to ensure maximum readability, and give a neat and professional appearance to the worksheets.

Save the changes and close the file.

EXERCISE 2.8 - Istat

You are working with a company, which was commissioned an analysis of the Italian population.

To help the company you are asked to:

1. Create a new Excel file and save it with the name **Exercise 2.8 - Istat.xlsx**.
2. Import in a blank worksheet, starting from cell **A1**, the file **Exercise 2.8 - Population2014.csv**, which contains an extraction of data on the Italian population made from the Istat website. Pay particular attention to the type of delimiter used in the file, and rename the worksheet with the name **Population2014**.
3. Delete row **106**.
4. Highlight the following data using a format that is automatically updated as data changes:
    - With a yellow fill color, the cell containing the age that corresponds to the highest number of married women
    - With a red font color and bold, the cell containing the age that corresponds to the largest number of widowed men
5. Using an Excel feature, replace in the table all the cells that contain the value "0" with empty cells. Be careful to replace only the zeros that represent the entire content of the cell, without deleting those that are part of other figures.
6. Calculate, for each type of "marital status" and for all totals, how many years do not have any observation (have empty cells).
7. Import in a blank worksheet, starting from cell **A1**, the file **Exercise 2.8 - HistoricalPopulationCensuses.csv**, which contains an extraction of data made from the data warehouse Istat Population Census, 2011. Rename the worksheet with the name **Historical Censuses**.
8. Filter the table for Territory = Italia and copy it to a new worksheet called **Trend analysis**.
9. In column **H**, starting from row **3**, calculate the percentage growth rate of the Italian population compared with the value recorded in the previous census, shown in column **Population**. In cell **H3**, you must therefore calculate the variation between the data of 1971 and the one of

1981, and so on in the following cells. If you write the correct formula once in cell **H3**, you can then copy it into the cells below.
10. Enter a formula in column **I** that shows as a result the text "Maximum growth rate" when the percentage increase in the corresponding cell in column **H** is the maximum observed, "Minimum growth rate" if it is the least, a dash (-) in other cases.
11. Filter the table in **Historical Censuses** applying the following criteria:
    - Code begins with IT
    - Census year is 2011
    - Territory is equal to these values: Northwest, North East, Center, South, and Islands

    Then copy the filtered table, and paste it from cell **A1** in a new worksheet called **Territorial areas**.
12. In the **Territorial areas** worksheet, calculate the total resident population in 2011. Insert in column **Population** a conditional formatting with data bars.
13. Clear the filter from **Historical Censuses** worksheet, then sort the table based on the following criteria:
    - **Census Year** descending
    - **Code** ascending
14. Filter the table in **Historical Censuses** worksheet to display only the rows for which the Code begins with "IT".

Apply appropriate formatting and organize the data in a suitable manner to ensure maximum readability, and give a neat and professional appearance to the worksheets.

Save the changes and close the file.

EXERCISE 2.9 - Planets (summary exercise)

Marco loves astronomy, and one Sunday afternoon he decides to delve into a study on the planets of the solar system. To satisfy his curiosity, he decides to perform an online search to see if he can find a table that compares the planets. He manages to download, from a specialized website, two text files containing all the data he needs (**Exercise 2.9 - Solar System.txt** and **Exercise 2.9 - Planets.txt**). Marco, who is not very good with computers, asks your help to process the data he has found.

You are asked to solve the following five problems:

1. Import the data contained in the **Exercise 2.9 - Solar System.txt** file into a new Excel file. Save the file with the name **Exercise 2.9 - Planets.xlsx**. Rename the worksheet as **Solar system**.
   Proceed with the following data cleaning operations:
   - Remove all the degrees Centigrade symbols "°C" shown in the last column (specify that data are in degrees Centigrade in the column heading)
   - Remove all the question marks "(?)" shown in the table
   - Remove the days symbol "d" shown in the **Planets orbital period** column (pay attention to blanks), then change the column heading so that it contains the unit of data (days)
   - Delete the **Planets Inclination of axis** column
   - Use the Replace command to remove the word "Planet" from all the planets' names
   - Use the Replace command to remove the word "Planets" from all the column headings (except "Planets and Sun")

   Sort the table in an ascending order with respect to the mean distance from the Sun.
   Then calculate, using appropriate functions, the average, maximum, and minimum values of the mean distance from the Sun.

2. Use conditional formatting on the original values of the mean distance from the Sun (i.e., not on the average, maximum, and minimum values just calculated) and on the values of the equatorial diameter, so that the

two biggest and two smallest values of each of the two columns are shown using different fill colors.

Insert then the heading **Details** in the first empty column beside the table. Insert a function in the column **Details**, so that:
   a) The text "Largest diameter" is shown beside the planet with the largest diameter.
   b) The text "Lowest orbital velocity" is shown beside the planet with the lowest orbital velocity.
   c) Nothing is shown in all other cases.

Please note: the possibility that the same planet has both the largest diameter and lowest orbital velocity is excluded.

3. Copy in a new worksheet the names of the planets and the data of their mass, excluding the Sun (using the filter). Sort the new table in a descending order with respect to the value of the mass.
Then calculate in percentage terms how much the mass of each planet is with respect to the total.
Create at this point a chart representing the percentage values just calculated, choosing the type of chart that is most suitable for the data.

4. Import the data contained in the **Exercise 2.9 - Planets.txt** file in a new worksheet called **Planets**. Sort the data in the table by the year in which the planet was discovered (**Discovery** field, from the oldest to latest), then by orbit size in a descending order, and finally by the date in which the data were updated (**Update** field, from the latest to oldest).
Calculate how many planets do not have the inclination value and how many planets do not have the orbit size.

5. In a new column of the **Planets** worksheet with the heading **Revolution**, use a function that returns as a result:
   - The text "Value above the average" for planets with a revolution period (**Period** column) greater than the average of the revolution periods of all the planets
   - A blank cell for all the other planets

In a new column with the heading **Comparison**, use a function that returns as a result:
- "Similar to Earth" for the planets with a revolution period between 300 and 450 and a mass between 0.01 and 1 (**Mass** column)
- A blank cell for all the other planets

Apply appropriate formatting and organize the data in a suitable manner to ensure maximum readability, and give a neat and professional appearance to the worksheets.

Save the changes and close the file.

EXERCISE 2.10 - Home Sweet Home (summary exercise)

At the end of each semester **Home Sweet Home**, a small real-estate agency located in Milan, needs to verify its sales situation. The file **Exercise 2.10 - Home Sweet Home.xlsx** contains the **Sales** worksheet, with a list of apartments sold in the last semester in different areas of the city (each one identified by a code). The agency's owners are also considering opening a new agency in the nearby town of Opera, and want to begin studying the recent trends in sales prices of that area. The file **Exercise 2.10 - Opera quotations.txt** contains data and quotations (in euros) of the last semester available, related to the town of Opera. You are asked to solve the following five problems:

1. Import the content of the file **Opera quotations.txt** in a new worksheet in the file **Home Sweet Home.xlsx**, called **Opera**, starting from cell A1.
   Sort the imported data by **Type** (in ascending order), then by **Value Max (€/m²)** (in a descending order).

2. In the **Sales** worksheet add a new column to the existing table, with the heading **Price per m²**. Then calculate, with a single formula, the price per m² of each apartment, taking into account that for the apartments with single or double garage the expression "Price of the garage to be estimated" should appear.
   Below the list, calculate using a function how many of the apartments do NOT have a garage.

3. Add a new worksheet named **Area C12 No garage**; filter the table in the **Sales** worksheet to show only the data related to the apartments in the area **C12** without a garage. Copy the filtered table into a new worksheet, excepting the row with the number of apartments without a garage. Sort the table you have just copied in the worksheet **Area C12 No garage** by number or rooms, then (when the number of rooms is the same), by price, both in a descending order. Turn off the filters in the **Sales** worksheet.
   Then, calculate in the **Area C12 No garage worksheet** the total sales price of the area. Add a new column to the table to calculate what percentage of the total is the price of each apartment.

4. Add two new columns to the table in the **Area C12 No garage** worksheet, with the heading **Size** and **Bis Sales**.

In the Size column, insert a formula that will result either in the expression "Small size" if the apartment has a single room and its size is equal to or less than 30 m² or in an empty cell in any other case. Use therefore appropriate formatting so that the cells containing the expression "Small size" are automatically highlighted with a fill color of your choice.

Using only one formula, make sure that in the **Price rating** column "OK" is shown when the price of the apartment is higher than the average price of the apartments sold in the area; in all other cases the result should be an empty cell.

In the same worksheet, create a chart that shows the price per m² of the apartments sold in the area. Use the addresses of the apartments as labels of the category axis. Show data labels with the value of each apartment.

5. Add a new column with the heading **Commission** to the table in the **Area C12 No garage** worksheet and calculate the expected commission for each apartment's salesman, knowing that Home Sweet Home calculates the commissions of its sales representatives in the following way:
   - If the sale price of the apartment is the highest on the list, the commission corresponds to **3%** of the sale price
   - If the sale price per m² of the apartment is the highest on the list, the commission corresponds to **2.5%** of the sale price
   - In all other cases the commission corresponds to **1.5%**

   Use a Data Bars formatting within the cells of the **Commission** column.

Apply appropriate formatting and organize the data in a suitable manner to ensure maximum readability, and give a neat and professional appearance to the worksheets.

Save the changes and close the file.

Unit 3. Math Functions and Advanced Charts

Topics of this unit:
SUMPRODUCT, COUNTIF, AVERAGEIF, SUMIF functions, conditional formatting with formulas, Subtotal, Remove Duplicates command, linking cells, creating charts with a trend line, charting mixed charts and with two axes.

EXERCISE 3.1 - Drugstores

Open the file **Exercise 3.1 - Drugstores.xlsx**. The file contains one single worksheet named **List**, in which you can find revenues data (in euros) of some drugstores located in different districts of northern Italy.

You are asked to:

1. Create a new worksheet named **Functions**, in which to calculate in a column with the heading **N. Drugstores**, the number of drugstores located in each district, using appropriate Excel functions (not subtotals).
2. Calculate, in a new column of the **Functions** worksheet with the heading **Total turnover**, the total turnover for each district.
3. Calculate then, in a new column of the **Functions** worksheet with the heading **Average turnover**, the average turnover of the drugstores for each district.
4. In the same worksheet insert a chart to show, without performing new calculations, the revenues percentage of each district turnover compared with the total turnover.
5. Insert another chart, mixed and with two axes, to show together the number of drugstores and the average turnover for each district.
6. Create a new worksheet named **Totals**, in which to copy all the data available in the **List** worksheet. In the new worksheet, calculate using the subtotals tool the total revenue for each district and the grand total.
7. Calculate, in the **List** worksheet, the total turnover for the listed drugstores. Then, calculate the percentage of the turnover for each store, compared with the total.

Apply appropriate formatting and organize the data in a suitable manner to ensure maximum readability, and give a neat and professional appearance to the worksheets.

Save the changes and close the file.

EXERCISE 3.2 - Men at work

The construction company of the three associates John, Mike, and David is dealing with the construction of a small building. At the end of the first quarter from the start of the work, the accounting manager needs to assess the costs incurred for the purchase of materials from the supplier.

In the file **Exercise 3.2 - Men at work.xlsx** you can find the **Purchases** worksheet containing quantities of materials purchased by the three associates, and the **Price list** worksheet, which lists the unit prices in euros applied to each type of material purchased.

You are asked to:

1. Show above the table of the **Purchases** worksheet, the data related to the price list applied by the supplier. These data are available in the **Price list** worksheet. Following the specific request of the accounting manager, the values should be shown in the **Purchases** worksheet so that any change made to the **Price list** worksheet is immediately visible.
2. Calculate, in a new column of the **Purchases** worksheet with the heading **Total expenditure**, the total expenditure for each of the 12 purchases made during the quarter.
3. Ensure that in the table showing the purchases, the cells containing the names of the associates are automatically highlighted with a bold font and a yellow fill color when the corresponding total expenditure exceeds the credit limit of € 300 set by the supplier for each purchase.
4. Create a new worksheet named **Quantity** in which to calculate the amounts of different types of material used each month.
5. Calculate, in the same worksheet created in the previous step, the number of purchases made in the quarter by each of the three associates.

Apply appropriate formatting and organize the data in a suitable manner to ensure maximum readability, and give a neat and professional appearance to the worksheets.

Save the changes and close the file.

EXERCISE 3.3 - Car Insurances

Using the data collected by the National Association of Insurance Companies, our insurance company intends to perform some elaborations to evaluate its future strategies.
In the file **Exercise 3.3 - Car Insurances.xlsx**, you can find the **Statistics** worksheet containing data collected at a national level. The information available are related to the cars circulating in major Italian cities during the period taken into account, accidents occurred during the same period, and related costs (in euros) incurred by insurance companies.

You are asked to:

1. Calculate, in two new columns of the **Statistics** worksheet, the percentage of accidents referred to the number of cars circulating, and the average cost per accident for each city.
2. Create a new worksheet named **Totals**, in which to copy all the data available in the **Statistics** worksheet. In the new worksheet, use the subtotals tool to show the average values of circulating cars, accidents, and costs for each region.
3. Calculate in a new row of the **Statistics** worksheet the total numbers of circulating cars, accidents, and total cost.
4. Using the values computed in step 3, calculate the percentage of accidents compared with the total number of circulating cars, and the average cost considering the total number of accidents.
5. Highlight using a single formula in a new column of the **Statistics** worksheet:
   - The cities where the accident rate on circulating cars is higher than the overall percentage of accidents, with the symbol *
   - The cities where the average cost per accident is higher than the overall average, with the symbol €
   - If both conditions are met, both symbols (* and €) should be shown
   - In all other cases, a blank cell should be shown.
6. Make sure that in the **Statistics** worksheet the name of the city with the highest average cost per accident is automatically formatted with a bold, white font, and with a red fill color.

7. Create a chart, mixed and with two axes, which compares the average cost per accident with the number of circulating cars for each city. The chart should be inserted in a new worksheet named **Chart**.

Apply appropriate formatting and organize the data in a suitable manner to ensure maximum readability, and give a neat and professional appearance to the worksheets.

Save the changes and close the file.

EXERCISE 3.4 - Exam

The secretary's office of the university has just sent you the results of the 2nd exam of the students who passed the 1st exam. These data are provided in the worksheet **Scores** of the file **Exercise 3.4 - Exam.xlsx**, whereas in the worksheet **Historical values 2nd exam**, you can find the average scores of the 2nd exam for a 6-years period.

You are asked to:

1. Calculate, in a new column of the worksheet **Scores**, with the heading **Difference (abs)**, the difference in absolute terms, between the scores of the 2nd and 1st exams, for each student.
2. In another new column of the worksheet **Scores**, with the heading **Difference% (abs)** calculate, the percentage change between the scores of the 2nd and 1st exams, again in absolute terms and for each student.
3. Ensure that, in the table of the worksheet **Scores**, the cells containing the badge numbers of the students are automatically formatted with a fill color of your choice when the corresponding percentage change in absolute terms between the scores of the 2nd and 1st exams is greater than 30%.
4. In a new column of the worksheet **Scores**, with the heading **Final Result**, use a function to display the expression "Failed" when the score of the 2nd exam is lesser than 18; in all other cases display the averages between the scores of the 2nd and 1st exams.
5. Ensure that, in the table of the worksheet **Scores**, the cell containing the surname of the student who scored the highest is automatically formatted with a fill color of your choice.
6. Calculate, in cells **E58** and **F58**, the average of the scores of the 1st and 2nd exams, respectively. Show the average of the scores of the 2nd exam, just calculated in cell **F58**, in cell **B8** of the worksheet **Historical values 2nd exam**, ensuring that the value of cell **B8** changes with the variation of the value of cell **F58** of the worksheet **Scores**.
7. Create a chart, in the worksheet **Historical values 2nd exam**, to represent the historical trend of the average scores of the 2nd exam in the last few years, making sure that the trend is explicitly shown.

Apply appropriate formatting and organize the data in a suitable manner to ensure maximum readability, and give a neat and professional appearance to the worksheets.

Save the changes and close the file.

EXERCISE 3.5 - *Clothing Store*

The owner of a clothing store has asked your help to make some analysis of the sales of the last month. Data are provided in the **Sales** worksheet of the file **Exercise 3.5 - Clothing store.xlsx**. Please note that prices are expressed in US dollars.

You are asked to:

1. Create a new worksheet named **Analysis** in which to calculate, in a new column with the heading **N. Products**, the number of products sold by each sales representative, using the appropriate Excel function (not subtotals).
2. Calculate, in a new column of the **Analysis** worksheet with the heading **Turnover**, the turnover for each sales representative (equal to the sum of the prices of each product sold).
3. In the same worksheet insert a chart, mixed and with two axes, which displays together the number of products sold by and the turnover for each sales representative.
4. Ensure that in the table of the worksheet **Sales**, the cells containing the ID of the products are automatically formatted with a fill color of your choice when the corresponding price is greater than 500 US dollars.
5. Filter the table of the worksheet **Sales** to show only the sales of the men's collection. Copy the filtered table in a new worksheet called **Man** and remove the filter from the table of the worksheet **Sales**.
6. Delete conditional formatting rules from the **Man** worksheet and calculate, using the subtotals tool, the turnover for each sales representative. Then, add a second level of the subtotals to calculate the number of products sold by each sales representative. Make sure that the third level of grouping of the results is shown.

Apply appropriate formatting and organize the data in a suitable manner to ensure maximum readability, and give a neat and professional appearance to the worksheets.

Save the changes and close the file.

EXERCISE 3.6 - Beauty Business

The marketing director of the Italian branch of a company in the cosmetics industry needs to provide a report to the headquarters, highlighting the performance of its brand (BIOLIFE) compared with its main competitors. In your role as an assistant to the marketing director, you are asked to provide support in the preparation and presentation of the data in Excel.
Open the file **Exercise 3.6 - Beauty Business.xlsx**, which contains retail data of BIOLIFE brand and its competitors, collected nationwide in all the cosmetics stores. Please note that prices are expressed in euros.

You are asked to:

1. Make sure to automatically highlight with a bold text and a green fill color, the cells of the periods in which the units sold were higher than the average of units sold over the entire year.
2. In the same way, highlight with a blue, bold, and italic text, the names of the products with a price higher than 70 euros. In a new worksheet named **Trend**, calculate within a new column with the heading **Total Unit per Period** and using the appropriate Excel functions, the total number of units sold in the market for each period.
3. In the same worksheet, create a second column with the heading **Average Price per Period**, in which to calculate the average price per period registered in the market.
4. Calculate, with a single Excel function and using the data available in the **Trend** worksheet, the total sales in euros registered on the market over the entire year.
5. In the same worksheet, create a chart to represent the historical trend of units sold, making sure that the trend is explicitly shown.
6. Copy all the data available in the **Analysis** worksheet into a new worksheet called **Competitors**. Delete conditional formatting rules from the **Competitors** worksheet and then calculate, using subtotals tool, the total units sold for each brand. Then, add a second level to the subtotals to calculate the average price for each brand.
Make sure that the third level of grouping of the results is shown.

Apply appropriate formatting and organize the data in a suitable manner to ensure maximum readability, and give a neat and professional appearance to the worksheets.

Save the changes and close the file.

EXERCISE 3.7 - Cosmetics Shop

The sales director of a company operating in the cosmetics industry needs to finalize a report on the performances of both the sales force and the Italian network of authorized retailers. In your role as assistant to the sales director, you are asked to provide support in the preparation and presentation of the data in Excel, using the file **Exercise 3.7 - Cosmetics Shop.xlsx**. Please note that sales data are expressed in euros.

You are asked to:

1. Calculate, in a new column of the **Registry** worksheet with the heading **% difference**, the growth rate of sales in the current year compared with that of the previous year.
   Then, apply a formatting to the values in **% difference** column, so that they are automatically formatted with a dark red font color and a light red fill color when the growth is negative. Similarly, highlight with a dark green font color and a light green fill color the positive values.
   Highlight also, in an automatic manner, the **Customer code** of those stores that have registered a growth rate above 20%, with a bold font and a yellow fill color. Formatting should automatically update as the data changes.
2. Calculate, in the **Registry** worksheet, the total sales registered in the entire network of authorized retailers in the previous and current years.
   Create a new worksheet named **Statistics**, writing in cells **A1** and **B1** the headings **Total sales previous year** and **Total sales current year**, respectively. Then, make sure that in cells **A2** and **B2** the two totals calculated in the **Registry** worksheet are shown so that the content of these cells is updated for any change in the original data.
3. Create a table in the **Statistics** worksheet in which to calculate, for each agent, the number of retailers he is responsible for. Also, calculate the total sales achieved in the current year by all the retailers each agent is responsible for. Then, calculate in a new column the percentage rate of the sales just calculated, compared with the total available in cell **B2**.
4. Create a second table, in the same worksheet, in which to calculate the number of authorized retailers for each type of **License**.

Apply appropriate formatting and organize the data in a suitable manner to ensure maximum readability, and give a neat and professional appearance to the worksheets.

Save the changes and close the file.

EXERCISE 3.8 - *International Education*

International Education Ltd. is specialized in language training and in the organization of study tours. In your role as an assistant in organizing tours in the European countries for university students, you have to support the planning of study-abroad programs for next year. The information concerning each student have been provided in the Excel file **Exercise 3.8 - International Education.xlsx**, which contains a single worksheet named **Database**.

You are asked to:

1. Apply a formatting to the values of **ID** column, so that they are automatically highlighted with a bold red font if the student is less than 21 years of age.
   Similarly, highlight with a bold font and a light blue fill color those cities (**Destination**) chosen by the students for study programs of 12 months duration.
2. Create a new worksheet named **Statistics**, in which to calculate the total number of students and their average age for each possible duration of the programs.
   In a different table on the same worksheet, calculate the number of students for each level of first language and the corresponding percentage on the total number of students.
3. Calculate, in a new table in **Statistics** worksheet, the total number of students and the average duration of the programs for each **Destination**. Then, make sure that the names of those destinations that have an average duration of more than 6 months are automatically highlighted with a fill color of your choice.
4. Create, in the same worksheet, a mixed chart with two axes using as title "European Destinations - Statistics". The chart should simultaneously show the number of students and the average duration of the programs per destination.
5. Copy the data of the **Database** worksheet into a new worksheet named **2nd Foreign Language**. Delete conditional formatting rules from the new worksheet. Then calculate, using subtotals tool, the number of students who speak each of the languages listed in the column **2nd Foreign Language**. Display the intermediate level of the subtotals.

Apply appropriate formatting and organize the data in a suitable manner to ensure maximum readability, and give a neat and professional appearance to the worksheets.

Save the changes and close the file.

EXERCISE 3.9 - Dinner with classmates (summary exercise)

As it happens every year, George's former classmates spend a pleasant evening of memories together. This year George has prepared a nice game to play at the end of the dinner, based on the data about the employment situation of his old classmates. After creating the Excel file **Exercise 3.9 - Dinner with classmates.xlsx**, George summarized the data in the **Initial data** worksheet, asking for some help with the final elaborations. Please note that income data are expressed in euros.

More specifically, you are asked to:

1. Calculate in a new column in the **Initial data** worksheet, the total hours of commitment for each of George's former classmates, as the sum of "hours dedicated to work" and "hours dedicated to home/family".
   To highlight the results, use then a green fill color for the cells referring to the **names** of his most active friends (>3000 total hours of commitment) and a red fill color for the names of the laziest ones (<2000 total hours of commitment).
   At this point, rename the **Initial data** worksheet in **Calculations**.

2. Create, in the same worksheet, a summary referring to the categories Male and Female, using the appropriate functions to calculate:
   a. The total amount of hours dedicated to work
   b. The total amount of hours dedicated to home/family
   c. The total hours of commitment (work + home/family)
   d. The average hours of commitment per person (work + home/family)

3. Create a second summary, in the same worksheet, to calculate using the appropriate functions:
   a. The total income from work for males and females
   b. The number of males and females of George's class
   c. The average per capita income for males and females
   To emphasize the differences between males and females create a mixed chart on two axes, which shows the number of classmates and the total income from work for males and females.

4. In order to help George understand the relation between incomes and towns where the old classmates work, create a new worksheet named **Towns** in which to insert the list of all the towns, and then calculate, with a function, the average income for each town, without distinction between males and females.
   At this point, copy the main table available in the **Calculations** worksheet, pasting it in the **Towns** worksheet starting from cell **A12**. After having deleted the conditional formatting from all the cells, use the Subtotals tool to calculate the average number of hours dedicated to work and the average number of hours dedicated to home/family for each town. Once accomplished the task, show only the level 2 of the table.

5. Calculate, in a new column of the **Calculations** worksheet, the hourly wage for each former classmate of George based on the income from work and on the hours dedicated to work.
   At this point, find out how much the total income of his old classmates would have been if all the invested hours had been paid (not just those dedicated to work, but also those dedicated to home/family). To do this, use a single function to calculate the hypothetical overall income of the entire class, by using the hourly wage just calculated and the total number of hours of commitment.

Apply appropriate formatting and organize the data in a suitable manner to ensure maximum readability, and give a neat and professional appearance to the worksheets.

Save the changes and close the file.

EXERCISE 3.10 - Wages (summary exercise)

The management of a manufacturing company has asked for your help to review its organizational structure and, in particular, the earnings situation. The worksheet **Employees** of the **Exercise 3.10 - Wages.xlsx file** contains, for each of the 50 employees of the company, data on the job titles, previous year's wages, and an estimated wage (in US dollars) for the current year, which will end in a few days.

You are asked to solve the following five questions:

1. Calculate in a new column of the worksheet **Employees** the difference in absolute terms, between the wages of the current and previous year for each employee. In another new column calculate in absolute terms and for each employee, the percentage change between the wages of the current and previous year.
Use an appropriate formatting on the values of the last column you just created to automatically highlight with a fill color of your choice the five cells with the higher percentage change in absolute terms.

2. In a new worksheet called **Analysis** create a summary table in which to calculate using the appropriate functions and for every job title:
   a. The number of employees
   b. The average wage of the current year
   c. The total wage of the current year

3. In addition, in the spreadsheet **Analysis**, calculate the number of employees with an annual current wage greater than 45,000 US dollars.
Use appropriate formatting on values of the **Badge number** column of the worksheet **Employees** to automatically highlight, with a fill color of your choice, the badge number of those employees with an annual current greater than 45,000 US dollars.

4. Copy the data of the worksheet **Employees** in a new worksheet called **Wage comparison**, and eliminate all conditional formatting rules from the new worksheet. Then, calculate using the subtotal tool the total wages for each job title both in the current and previous year. Make sure that the second level of grouping of the results is shown.

5. After ordering the average wage data in the table of the **Analysis** worksheet in a descending order, create a chart, mixed and with two axes, which compares the number of employees and their average wage for each job title. The chart should appear in a new worksheet called **Graph**.

Apply appropriate formatting and organize the data in a suitable manner to ensure maximum readability, and give a neat and professional appearance to the worksheets.

Save the changes and close the file.

Unit 4. Financial Functions and What-If Analysis

Topics of this unit:

Financial functions: PMT, FV, naming cell or ranges, Paste command options (Transpose), Scenarios, and Goal Seek.

EXERCISE 4.1 - Emerald

Open the file **Exercise 4.1 - Emerald.xlsx**. The worksheet **Mortgages** contains the mortgage terms offered by four banks regarding a request for a 10 years funding of 500,000 euros in favor of the Emerald Inc. company necessary to purchase a new machine.

You are asked to:
1. Calculate the quarterly installment to be paid at the end of each period and the total cash outlay resulting from the proposal of each bank.
2. Using the specific Excel functionality, format with a green fill color and a white font color the bank whose proposal provides the lowest total payment. The format should automatically update according to the possible variations of the terms offered by the banks.
3. Once you have identified the bank that offers the best conditions, copy and transpose the data related to that bank (including headers) in a new worksheet called **Installment goal**. Then, remove from the worksheet **Installment goal** the formatting rules that are defined in step 2.
4. The management of Emerald Inc. acknowledges that even the installment of the best proposal results in excessive costs and evaluates the possibility of reducing the amount of funding requested, with the aim of paying a quarterly installment of 15,000 euros: calculate the necessary amount of funding to achieve the required installment.
5. The Research and Development division of Emerald Inc. considering the success of a product placed on the market and recently patented, asks the management to reserve a small part of the monthly revenue generated by that product with the aim of accruing resources to finance new field studies in the future before the patent's expiry date. In a new worksheet called **Patent**, calculate the future value of a monthly payment of 10,000 euros to be paid at the end of each period for five years at an annual interest rate of 3%.

Apply appropriate formatting and organize the data in a suitable manner to ensure maximum readability, and give a neat and professional appearance to the worksheets.

Save the changes and close the file.

EXERCISE 4.2 - Smart Courses

Smart Courses Inc. is a small company specialized in the organization of business computer courses. The file **Exercise 4.2 - Smart Courses.xlsx** contains, in the worksheet **Courses**, data on Excel courses at different levels (basic, intermediate, and advanced) and duration.

You are asked to:

1. Change the name of the cell **B4** from "Part" to "Participants".
2. In a new column called **Teacher rate**, using a function, calculate for each type of course the overall rate based on the type of teacher (junior or senior) and the expected duration.
3. In a new column called **Classroom rent**, calculate the total rent of the classroom based on the number of days expected for each type of course.
4. In a new column called **Total Cost**, calculate the total cost for each course; then, calculate in a new column called **Cost per participant** (using in the formula the name of the cell **B4**), the rate for each participant.
5. Create a new scenario called "Decreased rates", where a daily rate of 350 euros for junior and 530 euros for senior teachers is assumed.
6. As the cost per participant is rather high, the management considers organizing courses with a greater number of participants. However, for such courses, a bigger and more expensive classroom needs to be rented. Create then a new scenario called "More participants" in which 40 participants and a daily rent of the classroom of 200 euros are assumed.
7. In a new worksheet called **Scenario Summary** show, using the Excel specific tool, the change of the total cost and the cost per participant for the different courses in the different scenarios created. Remember to make the summary as readable as possible, naming the changing cells and result cells, making sure that in the scenario summary they are automatically represented by the name assigned, and not by their cell references.

Apply appropriate formatting and organize the data in a suitable manner to ensure maximum readability, and give a neat and professional appearance to the worksheets. Save the changes and close the file.

EXERCISE 4.3 - Credits and debts

In order to keep up with the technological progress, a manufacturing company needs to renew its machinery. In a series of meetings with the sales departments of the manufacturers, it has been possible to reach an agreement about the cost for the whole production plant renovation, including testing, on-site support, and staff training. The total agreed price is 6.5 million euros, to be paid in the following way: 3 million euros on signing the contract and 3.5 million euros in exactly 5 years. To fulfil the due payments, the company's financial department has decided to finance 3 million euros asking for a mortgage. To pay the 3.5-million-euros balance, the financial department has decided to save and invest periodically a portion of the cash flow generated by the company with the goal to have in 5 years the exact amount needed to settle the balance.

In the file **Exercise 4.3 - Credits and debts.xlsx** you can find:
- The mortgage conditions offered by some banks surveyed by the financial department (**Mortgages** worksheet)
- The conditions offered by the same banks for investment plans, where a periodical investment of the amounts saved over a period of 5 years (**Investment** worksheet) is expected

You are asked to:

1. Calculate, for each type of loan in the **Mortgages** worksheet:
   a) The installment amount (using a single formula) considering that it may be monthly, quarterly, or six-monthly
   b) The total cash outlay for each loan, by considering what should be paid at each deadline and the number of installments
2. Calculate in the **Investment** worksheet, using a function, the future value of each investment plan; the payment will always occur at the end of each period.
3. In the **Investment** worksheet, sort the table by decreasing the future value (the investment plan returning the greatest future value should be found in a higher position).
4. Find the periodical payment of the most convenient investment plan (the one that offers the greatest value) to obtain a final value equal to the

value necessary for the balance of the second part of the contract (3.5 million euros).
5. In the **Investment** worksheet, create a chart that allows you to compare the final value of the different investment plans.

Apply appropriate formatting and organize the data in a suitable manner to ensure maximum readability, and give a neat and professional appearance to the worksheets.

Save the changes and close the file.

EXERCISE 4.4 - Cloth Paradise

The owner of a tailor shop at the request of many of his loyal customers is evaluating the possibility of turning his passion, the realization of tablecloths and accessories, in a real structured activity. She is thus preparing a simple business plan, whose initial data are collected in the **Data** worksheet of the file **Exercise 4.4 - Cloth Paradise.xlsx**. To help her, you are asked to:

1. Calculate, for each product, in a new column called **Cloth cost**, the cost of the cloth required for its realization, based on the cloth price and square meters necessary.
2. Then, calculate in a new column called **Labor cost**, the cost of labor for each product on the basis of the daily cost of labor and the number of pieces that can be produced in a day (assume that, to optimize the process only one type of product is produced in a given day).
3. Calculate, in a new column called **Variable cost**, the sum of the costs related to the cloth and labor.
4. Given that the owner is not able to calculate the exact share of overhead costs attributable to the individual product, in a new column called **Total Cost** you are requested to estimate the total cost by increasing by 20% the variable cost previously calculated.
5. Calculate, in a new column called **Margin**, the unit margin of each product, meaning the difference between the sale price and total cost.
6. Create a column chart, in the same worksheet, which allows comparing the unit margin calculated for different products.
7. In cell **B11** calculate, based on the sales forecasts and using a single function, the overall margin from the sale of products, using the unit margin calculated in step 5.
8. Not satisfied with the return on investment, the owner imagines the possibility of optimizing costs; first, by negotiating a lower price with the cloth supplier by submitting a single and very large order, and, second, by reducing the cloth that gets wasted in the production of round tablecloths by producing napkins as well. Thus, you are required to create:
    - A "Decreasing cloth price" scenario with the assumption of a cloth price per square meter of 4.5 euros.
    - A "Waste optimization" scenario with the assumption of only 6 m^2 of cloth needed for the production of the round tablecloth.

- A "Max Optimization" scenario with both of the above assumptions.
9. In a new worksheet, create a scenario summary showing the performance of the margin of each product and the overall margin; remember to make the summary as readable as possible, conveniently naming the changing and result cells, making sure that in the scenario summary they are automatically represented by the name assigned, and not by their cell references.
10. To focus the analysis on the product Small tablecloth, copy the data (including the headers) and paste them as values, transpose, starting from cell **A1** of a new worksheet called **Small tablecloth**.
11. In a new worksheet called **Sewing Machine**, calculate the amount of the monthly installment (to be paid at the end of each period) for the purchase of a new sewing machine under the following conditions:
    - Amount: 4,999 euros
    - Term: 3 years
    - Annual interest rate: 7%
    - Final payment: 700 euros

Apply appropriate formatting and organize the data in a suitable manner to ensure maximum readability, and give a neat and professional appearance to the worksheets.

Save the changes and close the file.

EXERCISE 4.5 - Discount on rates

Open the file **Exercise 4.5 - Discount on rates.xlsx**. The **Mortgages** worksheet contains the mortgage requests made by APG Bank clients. Before giving its clients its best conditions, the bank wants to consider some changes to the interest rates to apply to the mortgages. All data are in US dollars.

You are asked to:

1. Calculate, in two new columns named **Standard Installment** and **Total cash outlay**, the monthly installment to be paid at the end of each month and the total cash outlay for each APG Bank client. **Note**: standard annual interest rate applied to APG Bank mortgages can be found in cell **B1**.
2. APG Bank wants to consider a discount on the interest rate applied to mortgages based on the profession of its clients. In particular:
   a) If the client is a government employee, the interest rate applied to the mortgage should be decreased by 0.75%
   b) If the client is a journalist, the interest rate applied to the mortgage should be decreased by 0.65%
   c) To all the other clients the standard interest rate should be applied
   Based on these conditions, calculate, in a new column named **Discount 1 installment**, the monthly installment to be paid at the end of each month by each APG Bank client.
3. APG Bank now wants to consider different interest rates based on the mortgage term. In particular:
   a) For mortgages with the term greater than 20 years, standard interest rate should be increased by 0.50%
   b) For mortgages with the term lower than 20 years, standard interest rate should be decreased by 0.8%
   c) For mortgages with the term equal to 20 years, the standard interest rate should be applied
   Based on these conditions, calculate, in a new column named **Discount 2 installment**, the monthly installment to be paid at the end of each month by each APG Bank client.
4. APG Bank wants to consider different interest rates based on the mortgage requested principal. In particular:

a) For mortgages with requested principal equal or greater than 175,000 US dollars, the applied interest rate is equal to 2.75%
   b) For mortgages with requested principal less than 175,000 US dollars, the applied interest rate is equal to 1.65%

   Based on these conditions, calculate, in a new column named **Discount 3 installment**, the monthly installment to be paid at the end of each month by each APG Bank client.
5. Apply a format to the cells of the **Discount 3 installment** field with a fill color of your choice when the value of the discounted installment is less than the value of the standard installment (the format should automatically change following any changes in the conditions offered by the bank).

Apply appropriate formatting and organize the data in a suitable manner to ensure maximum readability, and give a neat and professional appearance to the worksheets.

Save the changes and close the file.

EXERCISE 4.6 - Smart Investments Bank

Open the file **Exercise 4.6 - Smart Investments Bank.xlsx**. The **Investments** worksheet contains the contractual conditions of the 30 main investment plans offered by Smart Investments Bank to companies. All the investment plans have a 10-year long period, a periodic payment, and sometimes even a single payment made at the beginning of the investment plan. All data are in US dollars.

You are asked to:

1. Calculate, in a new column named **Future value**, the future value of each investment, considering that all the investment plans have periodic payments at the beginning of each period. **Note**: the standard interest rate applied by Smart Investments Bank to all the investment plans can be found in cell **B1**.
2. The management of Smart Investments Bank is thinking of increasing the interest rate applied to investment plans by 0.45% when the periodic payment is equal or greater than 35,000 US dollars. Based on these conditions calculate in a new column named **Future value 1**, the future value of each investment plan.
3. The management of Smart Investments Bank now wants to try to apply the following conditions to the interest rate applied to all investment plans:
   a) When the periodic payment is equal to or greater than 35,000 US dollars, the interest rate applied to the investment plan increases by 0.25%
   b) When the periodic payment is equal to or less than 25,000 US dollars, the interest rate applied to the investment plan decreases by 0.35%
   c) When the periodic payment is between 25,000 and 35,000 US dollars, the interest rate applied to the investment plan does not change

   Based on these conditions calculate in a new column named **Future value 2**, the future value of each investment plan.

4. The management of Smart Investments Bank now wants to try to apply the following conditions to the interest rate applied to all investment plans:
   a) When there is a payment at the beginning of the investment and the periodic payment is equal to or less than 20,000 US dollars, the interest rate applied to the investment plan increases by 0.37%
   b) When the periodic payment is equal or greater than 35,000 US dollars, the interest rate applied to the investment plan increases by 0.25%

   Based on these conditions, calculate in a new column named **Future value 3**, the future value of each investment plan.

Apply appropriate formatting and organize the data in a suitable manner to ensure maximum readability, and give a neat and professional appearance to the worksheets.

Save the changes and close the file.

EXERCISE 4.7 - Garden Center (summary exercise)

Garden Center is a Tuscan operator in the gardening sector, specialized in evergreen trees sales. It owns three subsidiaries in the provinces of Florence, Arezzo, and Lucca for the selling and distribution of its cultivation. Garden Center owns several garden centers of its property, where it cultivates evergreen trees. At the end of the year, Garden Center has to deal with several administrative activities. To help the management you have available a file called **Exercise 4.7 - Garden Center.xlsx** containing:

- The retail price list and the amount of sales per dealer for the current year (**Sales** worksheet)
- The terms of contract proposed by the banks for financing the purchase of new land (**Banks** worksheet)
- Some information about a particular shrub called Posillipo (**Posillipo** worksheet)

To make its managing decisions, the Garden Center management team asks you to:

1. Copy the entire table of the **Sales** worksheet in a new worksheet called **Totals**, then use subtotals to calculate the total amount sold for each Item (regardless of the size), for each center. Show the intermediate level of detail.
   Returning to the worksheet **Sales**, format with a green fill color and a white font color the items with a selling price higher than the average price (formatting should automatically update with any changes in prices).

2. Using Excel functions calculate, in a new worksheet called **Turnover**, the total turnover for each type of tree (regardless of the size), for each center.
   Still within the **Turnover** worksheet, in a new column called **Center**, add a function that returns the name of the center that, achieved the highest turnover for each type of tree.

3. Among all the trees that Garden Center is selling, "Posillipo" has become fashionable and it performs outstanding results in sales. The management team is now figuring out the best way for enhancing the value of this product. In order to analyze the different strategies available, we have at our disposal (in the **Posillipo** worksheet) the sales forecasts for this tree referring to the 2018 to 2020 period, and the related turnover. You are asked to assume two different cases of pricing (considering sales estimates already available in the table) to compute the sales turnover in each hypothesis:
   a. Small increase (price = 1,250.00 euros for all the three years)
   b. Significant increase (price = 1,250.00 euros for 2018; 1,300.00 euros for 2019; and 1.350,00 euros for 2020)

   Create then a **Scenario Summary** in a new worksheet, showing the turnover for the three years in the two different cases. Remember to make the summary as readable as possible, conveniently naming the changing cells and result cells, making sure that in the scenario summary they are automatically represented by the name assigned and not by their cell references.

4. In the **Banks** worksheet, assign to the cell **B6** the name "Principal"; calculate, for each proposal received from the Credit Institutions and using in the function the name just assigned, the amount of the quarterly installment to be paid at the beginning of each period.
   Then, calculate the total cash outlay for each proposal.

5. Still within the **Banks** worksheet, sort the table to have in the first place the proposal with the lowest quarterly installment; calculate the amount of funding to make the quarterly installment equal to 2,500 euros.
   Then, copy the data for this proposal (including the headers) and paste them transposed into a new worksheet called **Installment OK**.

Apply appropriate formatting and organize the data in a suitable manner to ensure maximum readability, and give a neat and professional appearance to the worksheets. Save the changes and close the file.

EXERCISE 4.8 - GreenBio (summary exercise)

GreenBio is a company that buys and sells wholesale organic foods. At the end of each year, the management of GreenBio must analyze the data regarding its clients asking to fund their purchases through a loan (granted by the subsidiary GreenBio Financial), and must decide how to invest its profits. To help the management you have available a file called **Exercise 4.8 - GreenBio.xlsx** containing:

- The clients who have purchased GreenBio products during the last month and have requested a loan (**Clients** worksheet)
- The investment plans offered by the bank to invest the monthly cash flow generated by GreenBio (**Investments** worksheet)
- A table to evaluate different investments to increase in the future all the activities for family members of employees (**Variations** worksheet)

To help GreenBio management decide, you are asked to solve the following five problems:

1. In the **Clients** worksheet, calculate the installment each GreenBio client should pay at the end of each period, using the annual interest rate applied to all the loans by GreenBio (cell **B1**), and considering the different payment frequency of each loan.
    In a new worksheet named **Principal**, calculate the total amount GreenBio lends its clients, for each product category.

2. Copy all the **Clients** worksheet data to a new worksheet named **Analysis**, then use subtotals to show at the same time, for each product category, the number of clients who have requested a loan and the average amount (principal) of the requested loans. Show an intermediate level of detail, so that only the averages, counts, and overall average and count are visible.

3. In the **Investments** worksheet, calculate the future value of each of the seven investment plans offered to GreenBio, considering payments to be made at the beginning of each period.
    Then, copy all the data regarding the investment plan with the highest future value and paste them, transposed, in a new worksheet named **Best**

choice. Then, find for which value of the periodic payment the future value of the investment is equal to 160,000 US dollars.

4. In the **Investments** worksheet, create two new scenarios assuming the following interest rate values for each of the seven investment plans:

Investment Plans	"Outlook1" scenario	"Outlook2" scenario
Investment 1	2.10%	1.75%
Investment 2	2.15%	2.45%
Investment 3	2.60%	2.85%
Investment 4	1.95%	2.05%
Investment 5	3.85%	3.55%
Investment 6	3.75%	4.10%
Investment 7	3.75%	4.65%

In a new worksheet named **Scenario summary**, create a summary using the Excel specific tool, showing the future value of each investment, in the different scenarios created. To make the summary as readable as possible, name the changing cells and result cells, making sure that in the scenario summary they are automatically represented by the name assigned, and not by their cell references.

5. GreenBio management is considering investing part of its profits to increase in the future all the activities for family members of employees in an investment plan with a 15,000 US dollar payment initially and 2,000 US dollar payments quarterly. GreenBio management wants to understand which future value to expect based on different lengths and different interest rates, so a table with all the possible lengths and interest rate values has been prepared in the **Variations** worksheet.
Complete the table of the **Variations** worksheet, using in cell **C6** a formula (to be copied in the other cells of the table without editing it) calculating the future value of the investment plan considering:

a) The payment to be made at the beginning of the investment (cell **B2**)
b) The periodic payments (cell **B1**)
c) The length of the investment plan
d) The interest rate applied to the investment plan
e) All the payments occur at the beginning of each period

Apply appropriate formatting and organize the data in a suitable manner to ensure maximum readability, and give a neat and professional appearance to the worksheets.

Save the changes and close the file.

EXERCISE 4.9 - PhotoMagic (summary exercise)

The photo gear shop PhotoMagic proposes its customers a series of offers to increase the sales of digital cameras. Apart from the competitive prices on novelties and top models of different brands, the sales department wants to insert some less-recent products in the monthly leaflet, with the double aim of reducing stock in the warehouse and sell out the stock of discontinued products.

Every month less-recent products in the warehouse are analyzed and some are chosen to be included in the leaflet of the upcoming month. In the **Warehouse** worksheet, within the **Exercise 4.9 - PhotoMagic.xlsx** file, you have the list of the less-recent products found in the warehouse at the moment, each with the following information: brand and model, number of megapixels, dimensions of the LCD screen, optical zoom and weight, list price, cost incurred to buy the product from the supplier, and quantity available in the warehouse.

To help the management, you are asked to solve the following five problems:

1. List – in the first column of a new worksheet named **Statistics** – the name of all the manufacturers present in the **Brand** column of the **Warehouse** worksheet, keeping only the unique values and eliminating any duplicates. In a new column with the heading **Number of model (Brand)** calculate, using the appropriate function, the number of models available in the warehouse for each brand in the list.
Still within the **Statistics** worksheet, copy and keep the unique values of the **LCD Screen** column of the **Warehouse** worksheet. Then, calculate using a function in a new column with the heading **Number of models (LCD)**, the number of models available in the warehouse for each dimension of the LCD screen available in the list.

2. Using just one formula calculate, in cell **H53** of the **Warehouse** worksheet, the **total cost** sustained by PhotoMagic to acquire all the models present in the list (considering the unitary cost and the quantity available in the warehouse).

Format the cells of the **Model** column so that a red font color is applied automatically to the names of the models for which more than 6,500 euros was spent (consider the total cost for each model, given by the acquisition cost multiplied by the quantity available).

3. Calculate, in a new column of the **Warehouse** worksheet, with the heading **Margin %**, the revenue margin in percentage for each product available in the list (i.e., the difference between the list price and the acquisition cost in percentage terms). Note: the margin is calculated with respect to the list price and not the acquisition cost (e.g., if the price is 100 and the cost 80, the margin percentage will be 20%).
Insert therefore, in a new column with the header **Discount %**, a function that returns as a result - for each product - the percentage of discount that PhotoMagic intends to apply on the list price, calculated as follows:
    - **8%** discount, if the margin % just calculated is less than or equal to 10%
    - **15%**, if the margin % is between 10% and 20% (extremes excluded)
    - **25%**, if the margin % is greater than or equal to 20%

4. The sales department now wants to classify the promotional products to be put on the leaflet in three categories. In a new column in the **Warehouse** worksheet with the heading **Offers**, insert a function that returns as a result:
    - "Until stocks last" when the discounted price of the product (applying to the list price the percentage of discount just calculated) is greater than the acquisition cost, and the quantity available in the warehouse is less than 25
    - "Super Offer" when the discounted price of the product is greater than the acquisition cost and the quantity present in the warehouse is greater than or equal to 25
    - "Underpriced" when the discounted price of the product is less than or equal to the acquisition cost

5. Calculate in the **Statistics** worksheet, for each brand, the average quantity of the product in the warehouse and the average discount %.

Sort this table in a descending order according to the number of models; if the number of models is equal, sort in a decreasing order according to the average quantity. Then, in the same worksheet create a chart that represents at the same time the average quantity (column chart on the main axis) and the average discount (line chart on the secondary axis).

Finally, copy the whole table of the **Warehouse** worksheet into a new worksheet named **Totals** and count, using subtotals, how many models are included in each of the three categories of the offer and the total number of models.

Apply appropriate formatting and organize the data in a suitable manner to ensure maximum readability, and give a neat and professional appearance to the worksheets.

Save the changes and close the file.

EXERCISE 4.10 - Bright Sun (summary exercise)

Bright Sun Corp. is a sunglasses manufacturer that is considering the purchase of a new innovative machinery to expand its production. The worksheet **Proposals** in the file **Exercise 4.10 - Bright Sun.xlsx** contains the conditions proposed by four different banks regarding a request for funding of 100,000 euros to be repaid in 15 years.

You are asked to solve the following five problems:

1. Assign the name "Euribor_3M" to cell **B1** and use this name to calculate, in a new column the **Total interest rate** and using a function, the interest rate relative to each proposal. The total interest rate will be equal to:
   - The rate in the case of a fixed interest rate financing
   - The sum of the rate and the Euribor 3 months in case of a variable interest rate financing

   Use a function to calculate, in cells **B14** and **B15**, the average of the total interest rate for the two types of rates (fixed and variable).

2. In a new column **Monthly installment**, calculate for each proposal, the monthly installment to be paid at the end of each period, which in the case of fixed-rate loans will be constant throughout the period of the loan, while for variable rate loans will be the current installment that varies as the reference rate changes.

   In a new column **Total cash outlay**, calculate the total cash outlay relative to each proposal. Sort the table so that the most convenient proposal (the one with the lowest total cash outlay) is at the top, and the least convenient is at the bottom.

   Using the Excel formatting tools and making sure that the formatting will automatically update as the terms offered by the banks vary, format:
   - With a green fill color and a white font color, the name of the bank with the lowest total cash outlay
   - With a red fill color and a white font color, the name of the bank with the greatest total cash outlay

3. As the variable rate proposals are currently cheaper than those with fixed rates are, create two new scenarios "Small increase" and "Significant increase" in which you should assume that the three-month Euribor reaches, respectively, 1% and 2%.
In a new worksheet **Scenario Summary**, show, using the Excel tools, the trend of monthly installments according to the scenarios created earlier; remember to make the summary as readable as possible, naming the changing cells and result cells, making sure that in the scenario summary they are automatically represented by the name assigned, and not by their cell references.

4. Once detected the convenience of variable rate proposals, copy the data (including the headers) of the cheapest proposal, previously identified using conditional formatting, and transpose it into a new worksheet called **Max installment**. Then, remove from the worksheet **Max installment** any existing conditional formatting rule.
Because of some temporary financial difficulties, Bright Sun Corp. would consider the possibility of buying a less-expensive machinery, to be able to lower the amount of the monthly installment. Calculate the amount of funding required to lower the current amount of the monthly installment to 600 euros.

5. As part of a social responsibility program, a sample of 20 employees with different qualifications was selected and asked to estimate the monthly amount that they would be willing to donate to a project of social solidarity, coordinated and primarily funded by the company. The results of the survey are contained in the worksheet **Focus Group**. In a new worksheet called **Analysis**, calculate the monthly average amount and represent the results obtained by creating an appropriate chart for each qualification.
In addition, as part of the social responsibility program, Bright Sun Corp. is considering promoting a campaign in support of children of the employees; the campaign would allow the creation of a fund generated by a voluntary payment of 30 euros per month by mothers-to-be, to which the company would add 30 euros. The total amount would be paid on a monthly basis (at the end of the month) for 18 years. In a new worksheet called **Investment**, compute what would be, after 18 years, the

value of the investment calculated based on an annual interest rate of 3%.

Apply appropriate formatting and organize the data in a suitable manner to ensure maximum readability, and give a neat and professional appearance to the worksheets.

Save the changes and close the file.

Unit 5. Text Functions and Pivot Tables

Topics of this unit:

Text functions: RIGHT, LEFT, MID, CONCATENATE, UPPER, LOWER, PROPER, LENGTH, SEARCH, statistical functions: COUNTIFS, SUMIFS, AVERAGEIFS, pivot table, pivot chart, data validation.

EXERCISE 5.1 - IBAN codes

Open the **Exercise 5.1 - IBAN codes.xlsx**, containing some bank accounts identification codes.
The International Bank Account Number (IBAN) is an internationally defined code that uniquely identifies a bank account throughout the world. It consists of 27 digits:
- Two letters for the Nation (IT for Italy)
- Two check digits
- The BBAN national code, which in turn consists of:
  - One digit for the CIN code
  - Five digits for the ABI code
  - Five digits for the CAB code
  - Twelve digits for the bank account number

You are asked to:

1. Extract from each code, in column **B**, the digit related to the CIN code.
2. Extract from each code, in column **C**, the digits related to the ABI code.
3. Extract from each code, in column **D**, the digits related to the CAB code.
4. Extract from each code, in column **E**, the digits related to the bank account number.

Apply appropriate formatting and organize the data in a proper manner to ensure maximum readability, and give a neat and professional appearance to the worksheets.

Save the changes and close the file.

EXERCISE 5.2 - Names

Open the file **Exercise 5.2 - Names.xlsx**, containing a list of names. Each name is made up of a first and a last name, in lowercase.

You are asked to:

1. In column **B**, enter a function to extract only the first name of each person, with the first letter in uppercase. For example, for the name george lawrence the result will be George.
2. In column **C**, enter a function to extract only the last name of each person, with the first letter in uppercase. For example, for the name george lawrence the result will be Lawrence.
3. In a new column called "Gender" it should be possible to select from a drop down menu "M" for males and "F" for females. The validation list for the drop down menu must be in a new worksheet called **Validation list**.

Apply appropriate formatting and organize the data in a suitable manner to ensure maximum readability, and give a neat and professional appearance to the worksheets.

Save the changes and close the file.

EXERCISE 5.3 - *Superstore*

Open the file **Exercise 5.3 - Superstore.xlsx**, containing information related to the more than 8,000 orders received in 2020 by a large Canadian wholesaler of office products. All values are expressed in US dollars.

You are asked to:

1. Create a new worksheet called **Products** and calculate, for each product sub-category, the number of orders with value greater than 500 dollars and shipping cost less than 10 dollars.
2. Create a new worksheet called **Customers** and calculate – using the available Excel functions – the value of orders received from each region and for each customer segment.
3. Create a new worksheet called **Delivery** and calculate the average value of orders shipped during the first half of 2020, for each shipping mode.

Apply appropriate formatting and organize the data in a suitable manner to ensure maximum readability, and give a neat and professional appearance to the worksheets.

Save the changes and close the file.

EXERCISE 5.4 - Beauty

Open the file **Exercise 5.4 - Beauty.xlsx**, which contains data related to last year's sales of an important store of beauty products. The table available in the **Sales** worksheet contains sales details for each product, in each month of the year considered.

You are asked to:

1. Create, in a new worksheet named **Pivot**, a pivot table to show the total quantity of the **Units sold**, by **Product** and by **Period**.
2. Group the list of products by **Brand**, so that only the detail of brand level is visible, except for STARFACE (for which besides the details of the brand level details with the name of each product should also be visible.)
3. Group the text labels of the months (**Period** field) in quarters, using the customized labels **First quarter**, **Second quarter**, **Third quarter**, and **Fourth quarter**.
4. Use filters in the table so that all the data available can be filtered by **Category**; then, show only values for the Skincare category.
5. Customize rows and columns labels to show, respectively, **Brand/Product** and **Quarters**.

Apply appropriate formatting and organize the data in a suitable manner to ensure maximum readability, and give a neat and professional appearance to the worksheets.

Save the changes and close the file.

EXERCISE 5.5 - Europe sales

Open the file **Exercise 5.4 - Europe sales.xlsx**. The file contains sales data for a three-year period, concerning a company that has several subsidiaries located in four areas of Europe (North, South, East, and West). All values are expressed in euros.

You are asked to:

1. Create in a new worksheet named **Totals** a pivot table that displays the sum of sales by area of Europe and by year (grouping the data if necessary).
2. Replace the groups just created, grouping dates by quarters (Qtr1, Qtr2, etc.).
3. Finally, group the areas of Europe by the two macro-areas North-East and South-West, and display the data showing only the macro-area level.
4. Create a Pivot Chart from the Pivot Table. The chart, titled "Sales per region", has to be created in a new worksheet called **CHT_Totals** and it should show the values of each quarter, comparing the two regions.
5. Hide all the Pivot Chart buttons.

Apply appropriate formatting and organize the data in a suitable manner to ensure maximum readability, and give a neat and professional appearance to the worksheets.

Save the changes and close the file.

EXERCISE 5.6 - Erasmus

Open the file **Exercise 5.5 - Erasmus.xlsx**. The worksheet **Applicants** shows a list of submissions sent by student applicants to the International Relations Office of an Italian University for the Erasmus Exchange Program.

You are asked to:

1. Add a new column after column **A** of the **Applicants** worksheet. In cell **B1** insert the heading **Student ID**. In the other cells of column **B**, extract the ID number of each student that is, the first 7-digit code that you find in column **A** (e.g., "0577609" for the first student).
2. In the same worksheet, add a new column with the header **Name**, after **Student ID**. In this column, for each student, extract the first name and last name that you find after the initial alphanumeric code, with the initial capital letters (e.g., "Andres Quiceno Candamil Adrian" for the first student).

In the worksheet **Ranking Form**, the office has created a form that will be used to publish the final ranking of applications.

You are asked to improve the form as follows:

3. The cells in column **Ranking (A2:A21)** must include only integer values from 1 to 20; in case the user inserts a wrong value, Excel has to show the Warning message with title "Attention!" and text "The ranking must be a number included between 1 and 20".
4. The cells in column **Student ID (B2:B21)** must accept only strings composed of seven digits; in case of wrong input, Excel has to show the Stop message with title "Attention!" and text "The student ID must be a seven-digit string".
5. The cells in column **Score (C2:C21)** must accept only integer values included between 0 and 100; in case of wrong input Excel has to show a Stop message (with title and text of your choice).
6. The cells in column **Name (D2:D21)** must prevent wrong entries by showing a drop down menu presenting the names available in the **Applicants** worksheet.

7. The cells in the column **Date of birth (E2:E21)** must accept only dates included between the minimum and the maximum of the dates of birth available in the **Applicants** worksheet (column **D**). In case of wrong input Excel has to show the Stop message with title "Warning!" and text "The date you entered is incorrect".
8. The cells in column **School (F2:F21)** must show a drop down menu with the list of schools available in the **Lists** worksheet.
9. The cells in column **Destination (G2:G21)** must show a drop down menu with the list of destinations available in the **Lists** worksheet.
10. The cells in column **Grant (H2:H21)** must accept only decimal values included between 50% and 80%. In case of wrong input, Excel has to show a Stop message with title "Attention!" and text "The grant must be included between 50% and 80%".

Once you have completed the form, hide the **Lists** worksheet.

Apply the appropriate formatting and organize the data in a suitable manner to ensure maximum readability, and give a neat and professional appearance to the worksheets.

Save the changes and close the file.

EXERCISE 5.7 - Vitanic

Open the file **Exercise 5.7 - Vitanic.xlsx**. The **Passengers** worksheet reports information about the 1309 passengers of the transatlantic liner Vitanic, which had a shipwreck in the early 20th century. The Excel dataset shows the class to which each passenger was assigned (1, 2, and 3), their fate after the accident (Safe, Missing), their name, gender (M, F), age (if available), ticket id, the fare they paid (in US dollars), and the cabin number.

You are asked to create a new worksheet called **Analysis**, where you are asked to:

1. Insert a function to calculate the **average age** of passengers per **class** and **fate**.
2. Verify your results with a pivot table (created in the same worksheet, next to the previous calculation) and represent the result of the pivot table with a pivot chart on a separate worksheet.
3. Insert a function to calculate the **number of passengers** divided by **gender**, **age range** (<11 years and >=11 years), and **fate**.
4. Calculate the **average cost** of fares per **class** and **fate** and check your results with a pivot table (created in the same worksheet, next to the previous calculation).

Apply appropriate formatting and organize the data in a proper manner to ensure maximum readability, and give a neat and professional appearance to the worksheets.

Save the changes and close the file.

EXERCISE 5.8 - Office Line

Open the file **Exercise 5.8 - Office Line.xlsx**. The Products worksheet contains a list of new articles that should be included in the catalogue of products marketed by our company. In order to import these items into our database, we first need to run some elaborations on the data available in the table of the Product worksheet.

You are therefore asked to:

1. Create a new column with the heading **Category** to show the category of belonging for each item, as the first word of the **Description** in column **A**.
2. In the cells of another column, with the heading **New product ID**, create an internal code composed as follows:
    - The first letter of the first name of the Vendor
    - The first letter of the second name of the Vendor (note that each vendor has a name with two words, separated by an underscore "_")
    - A dash ("-")
    - The original code available in the Vendor ID column

    For instance, the item with vendor "Brame_LM" and with vendor ID "480-0680-327", will have "BL-480-0680-327" as a New product ID.
3. Create one last column with the heading **Markup** to insert the percentage of markup to be applied to each product. Although we should let the sales department insert any percentage they want, we want to give them some support so to avoid uncommon values of markup. Apply therefore a data validation to allow percentages between 5% and 45%, setting an **Input** message with text "It is advisable to apply a markup between 5% and 45%", and an **Information** message with text "Are you sure you want to apply this markup?".

Apply appropriate formatting and organize the data in a suitable manner to ensure maximum readability, and give a neat and professional appearance to the worksheets.

Save the changes and close the file.

EXERCISE 5.9 - Greenwich Village (summary exercise)

You have been hired as a data analyst at **NY Fashion llc.**, one of the most dynamic companies in the US fashion industry. Considering your excellent background of studies, the retail manager asks for your support on some elaborations that he has to run on the performances related to a specific store that is experiencing some issues. Data about last year have been collected in an Excel file named **Greenwich Village.xlsx** (all prices are in US dollars).

Open the file **Exercise 5.9 - Greenwich Village.xlsx**. In order to support the retail manager, you are asked to solve the following five problems:

1. In the **Sales** worksheet create a new column with the heading **Pieces to reorder** in which it should be possible to enter, per model, the number of pieces needed to integrate the stock. Make sure that only integer numbers between 1 and 100 (inclusive) can be entered. In case of invalid entries, a Warning message with title "Attention!" and text "The value you entered is not valid. It is possible to reorder a maximum of 100 pieces" should be shown.

2. Create a new worksheet, to be named **Calculations**, in which to list all the categories available in the table of **Sales** worksheet. Each single category should be listed just once. Use therefore the list just created to edit a table with two columns, one with the heading **Category** and one with the heading **Total Pieces "Made in USA" Sold**, and calculate the total amount of pieces "Made in USA" sold per each category.

3. Create in a new worksheet named **Pivot**, a pivot table based on the data available in **Sales** worksheet, to show the total sales of the year per category and per area of production. Customize the labels used in the table, so as to read **Production** instead of Column Labels, and **Category** instead of Row Labels. Insert then a pivot chart to show the situation in the most effective way.

4. In the **Sales** worksheet create a new column with the heading **Model ID** to show a text string created as follows:
   - The first two characters of the Model name (uppercase)
   - The last character of the Model name (uppercase)
   - A slash ("/")
   - The first three characters of the Category (uppercase)
   - A dash ("-")
   - The first two letters of the country of production, not considering the string "Made in" (uppercase)
   - An underscore ("_")
   - The word "low" in case the retail price is lower than 25 US dollars; "mid" in case the price is between 25 and 40 US dollars (inclusive); "high" in case the price is higher than 40 US dollars (the word should be lowercase)

   For instance, the Organizer Briefcase, belonging to the category SPORT BAGS & TOTES, Made in China, with a retail price of 42.99 US dollars, will have as Model ID: "ORE/SPO-CH_high".

5. The IT department of NY Fashion llc. has a concern regarding the length of certain names in the **Model** field (column **A** of the **Sales** worksheet), which might be truncated by the new software in use to manage the stores. You are therefore asked to highlight with a light blue background color those names that contain more than 25 characters.

Apply appropriate formatting and organize the data in a suitable manner to ensure maximum readability, and give a neat and professional appearance to the worksheets.

Save the changes and close the file.

EXERCISE 5.10 - Black-yellow supporters (summary exercise)

The "Dragons Football Club (DFC)" football team, whose colors are black and yellow, is concluding one of the best seasons of its centenary history, with a good chance of winning both the league and the European Cup in which it takes part. In the last few months, there has been an increase in both the number of supporters who subscribed for the next season from all over the world, and in the online purchases made on the official web store of the team. The management of the club has therefore decided to reward some of the supporters with discount coupons, and to analyze carefully the data of purchases made, to see if the launch of a new promotional campaign could further increase the revenue of the Club.

In the file **Exercise 5.10 - Black-yellow supporters.xlsx**, you find three worksheets. The **Supporters** worksheet contains data of those fans who have subscribed to the next season the day after the last victory of the team. The **Online store** worksheet contains data relating to purchases made on the official web store of the team in the past 48 hours. The **Gifts** worksheet contains the list of some types of products that the management of the Club has decided to give to some of the supporters.

You are therefore asked to solve the following five problems:

1. In a new column of the **Supporters** worksheet with the heading **Supporter code**, create a new code to uniquely identify each supporter, as follows:
    - the first two letters of the surname (all uppercase)
    - the last four digits of the ID
    - the gender (lowercase)
    - the first three letters of the Country (all uppercase)
    - a dash (-)
    - one of the following abbreviations:
        - YNG for supporters of less than 26 years of age
        - STD for supporters of an age between 26 and 60 years (inclusive)
        - SEN for supporters above 60 years of age

    For instance, the supporter Magalotti Edoardo, male, 48 years old, with ID 708343 and from Italy, should be identified with the code "MA8343mITA-STD".

2. The management of the Club has decided to give a discount coupon to each supporter listed in the **Supporters** worksheet. It is therefore necessary to send a message to each supporter to invite him or her to visit the Club website where all information on how to use the coupon is available. The message should be customized with the name of the supporter and with the web address corresponding to his home country.
In particular, supporters from Italy should be addressed to the Italian website (www.black-yellow.com/it), whereas all the other supporters should be addressed to the English website (www.black-yellow.com/en). For each supporter, the message must be placed in a new column of the **Supporters** worksheet, with the heading **Message**.
Considering, for instance, the supporter Magalotti Edoardo from Italy, the message to be created using a single nested function should be "Dear Edoardo, you have gained a discount voucher to spend on purchases on our website! For more information, please visit our web page at www.black-yellow.com/it".

3. To best analyze the top selling types of subscription, the management of DFC wants to run an analysis about the age and gender of the supporters who have purchased a subscription on the day following the last victory of the team. In a new worksheet named **Pivot**, create a pivot table to compute, using the data available in the **Supporters** worksheet, the number of supporters that have made a purchase based on the type of subscription and on the age. Then:
    - Make sure that the age of the supporters is grouped into clusters of 20 years, starting from the age 30 (so that those supporters aged less than 30 will all be in the same cluster "<30")
    - Make sure that for every value of the **Subscription type** field, the gender of the supporters (M or F) is shown, setting first M and then F
    - Use the **Country** field as a filter for the table
    - Change the default rows and columns labels, respectively, in "Type of subscription by gender" and "Age clusters"
    - Set the name "Number of supporters" for the field used in the Values pane.

Then, create, in a new worksheet, a pivot chart that represents the data available in the table.

4. The management of the DFC now wants to analyze purchases made in the past 48 hours on the official online store of the Club. In a new worksheet named **Purchases**, use a function to calculate, for each product, the total receipts from customers that have made at least one other purchase, based on the data available in the **Online store** worksheet.
Then, calculate, using a function, the average receipts for each product purchased by Italian customers alone.
In the **Purchases** worksheet calculate now the number of supporters, for each country of origin, which have made purchases with quantities greater than one and at least one other purchase, referring again to the data available in the **Online store** worksheet. Sort the results based on the number that you have just calculated, from the largest to smallest.

5. In a new column of the **Online store** worksheet, with the heading **Gift**, make sure that for each supporter it is possible to enter the gift offered by DFC, selecting values from a drop-down list available in the cell. As the list of products, use the data already available in the **Gifts** worksheet, without making any copy of the data in other worksheets. Then, hide the **Gifts** worksheet.
In a new column, with the heading **Discount**, make sure that it is possible to insert a value that indicates the percentage of discount that each customer will benefit for the next purchase on the online official store. Entries should be limited to percentage values between 5% and 35%. Also, make sure that any incorrect entry is prevented and an error message is shown, with title "Attention!" and text "The discount must be between 5% and 35%".

Apply appropriate formatting and organize the data in a suitable manner to ensure maximum readability, and give a neat and professional appearance to the worksheets.

Save the changes and close the file.

Unit 6. Managing Dates and Times

Topics of this unit:

Formulas with dates and times, normalization of time units, date and time functions: DAY, MONTH, YEAR, HOUR, MINUTE, SECOND, WEEKDAY, DAYS, TODAY, NOW, DATE, DATEDIF, IFERROR function.

EXERCISE 6.1 - Two hours

The worksheet **Training sessions** of file **Exercise 6.1 - Two hours.xlsx** reports data regarding sports training designed to reach a level of physical preparation that will allow enduring two hours of continuous running, starting from a fairly good physical shape. More in detail:
- Column **A** indicates the sequence number of the training session
- Column **B** indicates the training date
- Column **C** indicates the training start time
- Column **D** indicates the training end time

You are asked to solve the following problem:
1. In column **E**, with the heading **Duration HH:MM:SS**, calculate the duration of the training so that it is displayed in the following format: hh:mm:ss, i.e., hours, minutes, and seconds.
2. In column **F**, with the heading **Duration in minutes**, calculate the duration of the training in minutes (seconds should be represented as decimal numbers).
3. In column **G**, with the heading **Duration in hours**, calculate the duration of the training in hours (in this case decimal numbers should represent minutes and seconds).
4. Insert in cell **I1** the heading **Difference between the best and worst training**. In cell **I2**, calculate the difference, in the hh:mm:ss format, between the longest and shortest training period in terms of duration.
5. In cell **J2**, with the heading **Total duration of training**, calculate the total period of all trainings expressed in hours, so that minutes and seconds are represented by decimal numbers.
6. In cell **K2**, with the heading **Elapsed days**, calculate how many days of training were carried out, as the difference between the last and first dates.

Apply appropriate formatting and organize the data in a suitable manner to ensure maximum readability, and give a neat and professional appearance to the worksheets.

Save the changes and close the file.

EXERCISE 6.2 - Timesheet

The **Hours worked** worksheet of the file **Exercise 6.2 - Timesheet.xlsx** includes data concerning the hours of work carried out by an employee for his own consulting firm in 2020.
More in detail:
- Column **A** includes all days of the year 2020
- Column **B** includes the hours of work
- Column **C** includes the minutes of work (in addition to the hours already indicated in the column B)
- In columns **B** and **C**, empty cells correspond to Saturdays and Sundays, "Public Holiday" indicates a national holiday, whereas "Vacation" means the days of vacation taken by the employee.

You are asked to perform the following tasks:

1. In column **D**, with the heading **Day**, calculate by means of a function, the day of the week corresponding to the dates of column **A**. The day is to be displayed in full (e.g., Monday).
2. In column **E**, with the heading **Hours Worked**, calculate the hours worked each day. Minutes should be expressed as decimal numbers. If the corresponding day is a Saturday, Sunday, public holiday, or vacation, the message "None" should appear.
3. In the **Analysis** worksheet, ensure that in cells **A2:A6** appear the days of the week from Monday to Friday; then, in the same worksheet perform the tasks as indicated below.
4. In column **B**, calculate how many times the employee (throughout the year 2020) worked for more than 8.5 hours in day of the week, indicated in the corresponding cell in column **A**.
5. In column **C**, calculate for each day of the week the average number of hours worked by the employee as overtime (i.e., daily hours exceeding 8.5).
6. In column **D**, calculate the total cost charged by the consulting company to the client for the overtime hours carried out by the employee, taking into account the hourly cost reported in cell **B8**.
7. In cell **B9**, calculate with a single formula and using the data available in the **Hours Worked** worksheet, the percentage of working days carried

out by the employee in the months from June to September (including both).

Apply appropriate formatting and organize the data in a suitable manner to ensure maximum readability, and give a neat and professional appearance to the worksheets.

Save the changes and close the file.

EXERCISE 6.3 - Date check

Open the file **Exercise 6.3 - Date check.xlsx**. The purpose of the exercise is to create a tool that allows verifying the consistency of the components of a given date, by inserting references in cells **B2:B4** of the **Date** worksheet. In detail, the tool must meet the following requirements:

1. In cell **B2** of the **Date** worksheet, it should be possible to insert only an integer between 1 and 31, to represent the days of a month.
2. In cell **B3**, it should be possible to choose one of the months of the year, indicated by the number 1 to 12, using a drop down list in the cell. Insert the list in a new worksheet called **Lists**, hiding it once the task is completed.
3. In cell **B4**, it should be possible to insert the year, indicated by an integer between 1900 and 9999.
4. The day of the week in full should appear automatically in cell **B5** based on the values entered in cells **B2**, **B3** and **B4**. Should the day refer to a non-existent date (e.g., February 31), the formula should return the message "Non-calculable day".
5. In cell **C2**, insert a formula that returns the message "Warning, the day of the month entered is incorrect" should the day of the month entered not exist (e.g. February 31).
6. In cell **C4**, you are asked to insert a formula so that, by inserting a given year in cell **B4** (e.g., 2020), it returns as a result the text "(Leap)" if the year is a leap year, otherwise an empty cell.

The final result, in the **Date** worksheet, should be similar to that shown in the following figure.

	A	B	C
1			
2	Day	31	Warning, the day of the month entered is incorrect
3	Month	11	
4	Year	2020	(Leap)
5	Day of the week	Non-calculable day	

Apply appropriate formatting and organize the data in a suitable manner to ensure maximum readability, and give a neat and professional appearance to the worksheets.

Save the changes and close the file.

EXERCISE 6.4 - Linguistic certifications

You are doing an internship at a language training center. The head of the test center, who issues internationally recognized certifications, is asking you for a help with elaboration of the data of an exam session that took place on February 22, 2020.

You are provided with an Excel file, **Exercise 6.4 - Linguistic certifications.xlsx** that contains two worksheets. The first one, **Exam Results**, reports the collected data, whereas the second one, **Elaborations**, includes a table designed for elaborations of data.

You are requested to perform the following tasks:

1. In the **Exam Results** worksheet, in a new column, with the heading **Age**, calculate the age of all the students on the day of the exam. The age should be represented as the number (integer) of years actually reached (i.e., already celebrated).
2. In the same worksheet, in a new column, with the heading **Duration**, calculate the duration of each exam expressed in minutes. The fractions of minutes should be displayed as decimal digits.
3. In the **Elaborations worksheet**, in cell **C2**, calculate the total number of exams passed during the exam session considered, knowing that the exam score is expressed in hundredths and that to pass the exam you need to get at least 75 points out of 100.
4. In cell **C5** of the same worksheet, calculate the number of exams passed in less than 45 minutes by students aged from 19 to 24 years. In cell **D5**, show the percentage rate of this value against the value of the total exams passed.

Apply appropriate formatting and organize the data in a suitable manner to ensure maximum readability, and give a neat and professional appearance to the worksheets.

Save the changes and close the file.

EXERCISE 6.5 - Techno Building

You are the project manager of Techno Building Inc., a construction company specializing in commercial complexes and tourist villages. Given the recent events, in which some of your customers have demanded compensations for delayed delivery of projects, you decide to develop a tool to monitor the deadlines and the costs necessary to complete the work you are supervising.
For this reason, you have prepared in Excel the file **Exercise 6.5 - Techno Building.xlsx**, in which there is only one worksheet called Times and costs.

Given that today you have some available time to dedicate to this matter, you decide to complete this task by performing the following steps:

1. Ensure that cell **D8** always displays the current date (i.e., on any day the file is opened).
2. Make sure that in cell **D12**, one can insert only a date subsequent to the current date (i.e., successive to the date in cell **D8**). If the date inserted does not comply with this condition, an error message should appear with the title "Attention!" and message "The date of delivery must be subsequent to the current date."
3. In cell **D14**, a message should appear that alternates between two variations, depending on whether the delivery date is prior to or subsequent to the agreed date.
   In particular, if the delivery is dated in advance regarding the agreed date, the cell should report the following:
   - The word "Dear"
   - The client company name present in cell **D6**
   - The text: ", we would like to inform you that the project will be delivered"
   - The difference in months (in number) between the two delivery dates, without counting eventual fractions of months
   - The text: "months in advance."

   In case the delivery date was delayed with respect to the agreed one, the message should be as follows:
   - The word "Dear"
   - The client company name present in cell **D6**

- The text: ", we would like to inform you about the expected delay of"
- The difference in months (in number) between the two delivery dates, without counting eventual fractions of months
- The text: "months in delivery of the project."

E.g.: for CineDreams Ltd., a hypothetical client company of yours, if the agreed delivery date was 09/15/2021 and the expected delivery was 07/01/2021, we would read "Dear CineDreams Ltd., we would like to inform you that the project will be delivered 2 months in advance.". In case the agreed delivery date was 09/15/2021 and the expected delivery date was 12/01/2021, we would read: "Dear CineDreams, Ltd., we would like to inform you about the expected delay of 2 months in delivery of the project."

4. Finally, ensure that cell **D18** shows the costs necessary to complete the work in relation to the expected delivery date and to the average daily cost of the construction site (available in cell **D16**). Furthermore, make sure that cell **D18** remains empty, should there be no expected delivery date inserted or should the formula return an error.

Apply appropriate formatting and organize the data in a suitable manner to ensure maximum readability, and give a neat and professional appearance to the worksheets.

Save the changes and close the file.

EXERCISE 6.6 - Hotel Booking

You are the manager of a new hotel that recently opened its doors in a highly touristic resort. You want to provide the colleagues working at the reception with a tool to calculate quickly the price of an eventual stay at the hotel. Currently, you are in the phase of prototype development (to improve it and to release the final version, you will need Excel functionalities that are part of the successive units of this workbook). The current rates provide different prices for adults and under 15s and a series of additional charges and discounts based on the characteristics of the stay.

Starting with the worksheet **Form** of the **Exercise 6.6 - Hotel Booking.xlsx** file, you decide to proceed according to the following instructions:

1. In the **Form** worksheet, make sure that in cells **B2** and **B3** only dates equal or later than 1/1/2021 can be entered. In case of an incorrect entry, a message "Pay attention!", "Please enter a date equal or later than 1/1/2021" should appear.
2. Enter in cells **C2** and **C3** a formula that returns the day of the week corresponding to the date of check-in and check-out. The day should be shown with its own name, in full (i.e. Monday). The cell should remain blank when the corresponding cell containing the check-in or check-out date is empty.
3. Insert a formula in cell **A5** that returns "Pay attention! The check-out date should be later than the check-in date" if the check-out date is prior to the check-in date, otherwise "Dates entered correctly".
4. Make sure that cell **A5** is automatically formatted with any fill when the check-out date is before the check-in date.
5. Allow for insertion in cell **B8** of integer values between 1 and 8 (providing the error message: "Pay attention!", "Please enter a value between 1 and 8").
6. Due to space problems in the rooms, it is possible to add a maximum of two beds for a person under 15 years old for each adult. Then allow the insertion in cell **C8** of integer values between 0 and double the number entered in cell **B8** (expecting the error message "Pay attention!", "Enter a value between 0 and twice as many adults").

7. Enter a formula in cell **G8** that calculates the year of the Check-in date. The cell must show a blank cell if the cell with the check-in date is empty (cell **B2**).
8. Insert in cell **G9** a formula that shows the number of days included between the check-in and check-out dates. When the check-in date is after the check-out date the cell must show 0 (zero). The cell should remain blank when even just one of the cells containing the check-in and check-out dates is empty (cells **B2** or **B3**).
9. Enter a formula in cell **G10** that writes "Yes" in if the check-in takes place on Friday or Saturday, otherwise writes "No".
10. In the **Calculations** worksheet, enter in cell **B8** a formula that returns the total cost of the stay (i.e., Price per night per person, times the Total number of nights, times the Total number of people), without considering eventual additional charges or discounts. Should the formula return an error because of the occurrence of any type of problems with the data present in the sheet, cells **G13** and **H13** should remain empty.
11. Calculate in cells **C14:H16** the amount of additional charges for adults and under 15s, considering that for both:
    - The additional charge for short stays, equal to the percentages in cells **G3** and **H3**, applies to the amount without additional charges or discounts when the stay is less than 4 days.
    - The additional charge for the month of August, equal to the percentages in cells **G4** and **H4**, applies to the amount without additional charges or discounts when the check-in date is between August 6th and 18th (both included) of the year considered
    - If Check-in takes place on Friday or Saturday, an additional charge equal to the percentages in cells **G5** and **H5** is applied to the amount without additional charges or discounts

    In case an additional charge should not be applied, in the corresponding cells of the range **G14: H16**, the amount must be equal to 0 (zero)
12. In cell **B11** calculate the total cost of stay as follows:
    - sum the amount without additional charges and the values calculated in the previous point for adults and under 15s

- apply an overall discount equal to the percentage in cell **G6** when the stay is equal to or greater than 7 days

Apply appropriate formatting and organize the data in a suitable manner to ensure maximum readability, and give a neat and professional appearance to the worksheets.

Save the changes and close the file.

EXERCISE 6.7 - My Friends

The **Friends list** worksheet of the file **Exercise 6.7 - My Friends.xlsx** includes the names and birth dates of some of your friends living abroad. To avoid forgetting their birthday, you want to prepare an Excel file such that it automatically highlights the names of those who have birthdays the same day you are consulting the file. Take into account the fact that – for reasons independent from your will – all the names in column **B** (Name) have been inserted in the table with an incorrect spacing between the words. At the same time, all the surnames in column **A** have been inserted with all the characters uppercase.

To proceed with the file development, you need to do the following:

1. Insert a new column, with the heading **Age**, in which the age of each friend is shown. The age should represent the (integer) number of years actually completed.
2. In a new column, with the heading **Message**, make sure that when the month of the birth date and of the current date are the same a message is written in the cells. The message should be as follows:
   - The name of the person with no extra spaces
   - The surname of the person with only the first character in capital letter
   - The phrase "is having his/her birthday this month!"

   When the month of the birth date is different from the month of the current date, an empty cell must be shown. For example, if the person identified as WHITE John was having his birthday in the same month as the current date, the message: "John White is having his/her birthday this month!".
3. In a new column with heading Birthday date, use a function to calculate the birthday of each friend in the current year. For example, if we are in 2021, John White's birthday will be 02/20/2021.
4. In a new column with heading Days, calculate how many days are missing or have passed since each friend's birthday in the current year. Note: in the case of a birthday that has already passed, the number of days must be positive, otherwise negative.

5. Make sure that the day on which your friends celebrate their birthday, the cells that contain their surname, name, and the date of birth are all automatically highlighted with a fill color of your choice.
6. Make sure that when one of your friends is over 35 and the month of his/her birthday is the same as the current month, the cells containing the last name, first name and birth date are automatically highlighted with a fill color of your choice (different from that of point 5)

Apply appropriate formatting and organize the data in a suitable manner to ensure maximum readability, and give a neat and professional appearance to the worksheets.

Save the changes and close the file.

EXERCISE 6.8 - Temporary workers

You are the manager of a department in a shoe manufacturing company. In your department, there are some resources from temporary employment agencies. Because of your numerous work commitments, you cannot be present in your department all day and therefore you cannot check the actual working hours of the employees. Actually, the entry and exit of employees are recorded on a paper-format register, but no one has ever checked it because it did not seem that there were cases of non-compliance with working hours. However, because of some complaints from colleagues in the department, you decide to check if all workers really behave appropriately. More specifically, you choose to check the history of Marco B., who has collaborated with the company from April 10, 2020 to February 6, 2021, and whose contract provided for a working time of 7 hours and 30 minutes a day. One of your collaborators has set up an Excel file that includes all the entry and exit information about Marco B.

On opening the file **Exercise 6.8 - Temporary workers.xlsx**, you can find the date and time of entry in column A of the **Entry and exit** worksheet, and the date and time of exit in column **B**.

You are suggested to proceed according to the following steps:

1. In cell **B4**, use a formula to convert the working time of 7 hours and 30 minutes, present in cells **B3** and **C3**, into a single figure expressed in the decimal number format.
2. In column **C**, with the heading **Actual working hours**, calculate the hours worked, expressing minutes as decimal numbers.
3. In column **D**, with the heading **Compliance**, indicate the word "Compliant" if the actual working time is the same as agreed (7 hours and 30 minutes), with a tolerance of minus six minutes, otherwise indicate "Non-compliant".
4. In column **E**, with the heading **Hours**, calculate the value corresponding to the number of hours actually worked. For example, if one cell of column **C** reports 5.78 hours, the corresponding cell in column **E** should indicate 5.
5. In column **F**, with the heading **Minutes**, calculate the value corresponding to the minutes actually worked. For example, if one cell

of column **C** reports 5.5 hours, the corresponding cell in column **F** must indicate 30.
6. In column **G**, with the heading **Deviation minutes**, calculate the difference in minutes compared with the agreed working time (7 hours and 30 minutes) only in case of non-compliance. The result should be an integer. In case of compliance, the cell should indicate the value 0.
7. Finally, in column **H**, indicate the following message only in case of non-compliance: "We inform you that on mm/dd/yyyy you worked *n* hours and *n* minutes. There is therefore a deviation of *n* minutes compared with the contract. Kind regards." For example, if on April 10, 2020 Marco worked 7 hours and 16 minutes, the message would be: "We inform you that on 4/10/2020 you worked 7 hours and 16 minutes. There is therefore a deviation of 14 minutes compared with the contract. Kind regards."

Apply appropriate formatting and organize the data in a suitable manner to ensure maximum readability, and give a neat and professional appearance to the worksheets.

Save the changes and close the file.

EXERCISE 6.9 - Payments (summary exercise)

A small company, which sells gadgets through its website, has offered the possibility of having discounted purchases during a certain period of the year.

In the **Purchases** worksheet of the **Exercise 6.9 - Payments.xlsx** file, you can find data regarding customers who made discounted purchases. In particular, the first and last names of each customer are available with the relative date and time of purchase, as well as the possible amount they still have to pay.

The management of the company wishes to have a clear table to summarize the situation; therefore, they ask you to prepare a worksheet for the next phase of analysis, performing the following tasks:

1. Insert a new column in the worksheet, after the **Name** column, with the heading **Clean name**. Use the functions provided by Excel to have as a result, in the new column, the names of the customers without the possible initials of the second name. Where the second name is not present, the result should be the same name already shown in the **Name** column.

2. The discount campaign provides the possibility to pay the amount with a deferred payment. The payment deferment depends on the period in which the purchase was made:
   - For purchases made until 3/15/2020 (included), the provided deferment is 90 days
   - For purchases made after 3/15/2020 the provided deferment is 120 days

   Create a new column with the heading **Deadline** in which you are asked to calculate, using the functions provided by Excel, the payment deadline for each customer (do not forget the payment deferment calculated above). Also, pay attention to the fact that some customers have already paid: in these cases, in the **Deadline** column the text "Already paid!" should appear.

3. In a new column with the heading **Day**, calculate the day of the week corresponding to the payment deadline for each customer (values of the **Deadline** column). When the deadline is not available, the corresponding cell in the **Day** column should not show any value.

Make sure that the cells of the **Day** column show the full name of the weekday (Monday, Tuesday etc.) and that Saturdays and Sundays are automatically formatted in bold, with a dark-blue font and a light blue fill color. Formatting should be automatically updated as data change.

4. To celebrate its first five years, the management has decided to reward all customers who already benefitted from the discount, by granting them further discount according to the following scheme:
   - To all customers whose purchase was done after 11:10 PM of each day, a discount of 15% will be applied on the amount to be paid
   - To all other customers (who made their purchase at a different time from that noted in the point above), a discount of 5% will be applied on the amount to be paid
   - To customers who have already paid, the company will send a voucher to be used for future purchases

   Following this scheme, insert a new column with the heading **New Discounted Amount** in which you are asked to calculate, using the most appropriate functions, the new amount to be paid by each customer. For the customers who have already paid, the result should be "Send Voucher".

5. In order to prepare the notification to be sent to the customer, who will receive the voucher, create a new column with the heading **Message**, in which you will indicate a following message (only for the customers receiving the voucher):
   - The opening courtesy form "Dear"
   - The Cleaned name and the Last Name, all uppercase
   - The text "you can spend this voucher of $20 by"
   - The deadline for utilizing the voucher, calculated considering validity of 1 year from the purchase date

   For example, a customer, whose first name is "Amit H" and the last name "Assaf", and who made his purchase on 02/13/2020, will receive the following message: "Dear AMIT ASSAF, you can spend this voucher of $20 by 02/13/2021."

Apply appropriate formatting and organize the data in a suitable manner, to ensure maximum readability, and give a neat and professional appearance to the worksheets.

Save the changes and close the file.

EXERCISE 6.10 - Stationery (summary exercise)

The company that you work for (a small distributor of office stationery) entrusts you with the creation of a report system showing the turnover performance for its products.
In the **Exercise 6.10 - Stationery.xlsx** file you will find:
- In the **Catalogue** worksheet, the products list (Product ID, description, price etc.)
- In the **March sales** worksheet, the details of orders for March 2020
- In the **Online sales** worksheet, the list of sales made through the e-commerce website in the first week of April
- a worksheet already prepared to enter the suppliers discount rates (**Discounts** worksheet)

You are asked to solve the following five problems:

1. Create a new product ID in a new column of the **Catalogue** worksheet (after the **Supplier** column) composed as follows (all capital letters):
   - The old product ID
   - A slash ("/")
   - The first and last characters of the type of item
   - A slash ("/")
   - The first character of the second word of the item name

   For example, the item "Micro Ballpoint pen" of the "Pen" type with the old product ID PM01 will have a new product ID PM01/PN/B.
   Insert a new column in the **Online sales** worksheet, after the Shipment date and time, with the heading **Day**. In the new column calculate, using a function, the day of the week related to each sale date. Make sure that each day is shown with its full name (Sunday, Monday, Tuesday etc.).

2. In a new worksheet named **Pivot**, insert a pivot table based on the **Online sales** worksheet, so that it will be possible to compare the quantity sold online both by Item and by Sale date and time. Then, perform the following operations:
   - Group sale times by hour
   - Set the Day field as filter

- Show only those products whose name ends with "Blocknotes"

Create now a pivot chart to show, in the most efficient way, the values just calculated.

3. In the **Discounts** worksheet, you can find a small table prepared to insert the discount rates that will be communicated later on by each supplier. You have to prepare all the cells in column **B** of the table (excluding the header) so that next to each supplier it is possible to enter the discount percentage that will be communicated as a decimal value between 0 and 1. The insertion of other values must be prevented and in case of an inconsistent entry, an error message with the title "Warning!" and text "The value must be between 0% and 100% must be shown."

4. The company asks you to perform specific analysis on product sales in March. In a new column of the **March sales** worksheet, with the heading **Turnover**, calculate the turnover for each order issued. Then, use an Excel function to calculate, in the same worksheet, the total revenue for each type of product, considering only the sales carried out in the first 10 days of the month (from 1 to 10, inclusive).

   In a new worksheet called **Analysis** insert, in column **A**, the list of items sold by the company in the month of March (the list is available in the **March sales** worksheet), removing any duplicate. Then, calculate for each product:
   - In column **B**: the number of orders issued with a quantity greater than or equal to 100 units
   - In column **C**: the total turnover for orders greater than or equal to 100 units
   - In column **D**: the average turnover for orders issued before 03/11/2020

5. In the **Online sales** worksheet calculate, in a new column with the heading "Time of delivery", the time (expressed as the number of hours) elapsed between the date and time of the sale and that of shipping (e.g., if it took 2 days and 2 hours the result will be 50).

   Also calculate, in a table to be created in the same worksheet, the number of single products sold (not the sum of the quantities) for each day, whose shipping time was less than 100 hours, and the number of those whose shipping time was equal to or greater than 100 hours.

Apply appropriate formatting and organize the data in a proper manner to ensure maximum readability, and give a neat and professional appearance to the worksheets.

Save the changes and close the file.

Unit 7. Lookup & Reference Functions, Data Protection

Topics of this unit:
Lookup & Reference functions: VLOOKUP, MATCH, INDEX, statistical function RANK.EQ, worksheet protection, workbook protection, file protection and encryption.

EXERCISE 7.1 - Rocky Sports

Open the **Exercise 7.1 - Rocky Sports.xlsx** file. In the file, you can find data on the turnover of a sportswear brand sold in a variety of stores located in the main European cities.

You are asked to solve the following problems:

1. Use a function to show in column **D** of the **Stores** worksheet, next to each store, the name of the area agent, as indicated in the table available in the **Agents** worksheet.
2. Rocky Sports pays to its agents a percentage commission based on the turnover achieved in each store of the agent's assigned area. Using the commission rates in the **Commission rates** worksheet calculate, in a new column of the **Stores** worksheet with the heading Commission, the commission to be paid by Rocky Sports to the agent assigned to the area of each store.
3. In a new worksheet called **Average**, insert the heading **Country** in cell **A1**. Then, make sure that in cell **A2** it is only possible to insert the name of the country using a drop-down list in the cell (Note: Refer to the list of countries directly from the **Agents** worksheet).
4. Insert the heading **Average turnover** in cell **B1**. In cell **B2**, use a function to calculate, depending on the country selected in cell **A2**, the average commission to be paid by Rocky Sports, when the store turnover is greater than 500,000 euros. Make sure that if it is not possible to calculate the average commission, the function does not show an error as a result but a dash.

Apply appropriate formatting and organize the data in a suitable manner to ensure maximum readability, and give a neat and professional appearance to the worksheets.

Save the changes and close the file.

EXERCISE 7.2 - Property Evaluation

The real estate agency SweetHome wants to create an Excel tool to quickly evaluate properties values. After a careful analysis of the factors that affect the value of a property, the agency decides to use the following procedure:
- An initial estimate is made considering the delivery date of the building (once the construction is completed) and the surface. To this end, in the **Property age** worksheet of the **Exercise 7.2 - Property evaluation.xlsx** file, there is a table showing the value per square meter, depending on the age of the property. Then, the value of the initial estimate is calculated by multiplying the number of square meters by the value per square meter.
- Then, according to the corrective parameters given in the Location, Noisiness, Heating, and Public transport facilities tables available in the **Parameters** worksheet, some improving or worsening rates are applied to the initial estimated value, to obtain the final property estimated value.

You are asked to:

1. Use the most suitable features of the spreadsheet to ensure that, by entering the values of a property in cells **B2:B3** and **B9:B12** of the **Evaluation** worksheet, the following values will be automatically calculated:
   a) The exact age in years of the property (to the current date, so that the result is automatically updated) in cell **B4**
   b) The value per square meter in cell **B5**
   c) The initial estimate of the property in cell **B6**
   d) The improving or worsening rates, in percentage terms, in cells **C9:C12**
   e) The improving or worsening rates, in euros, in cells **D9:D12**
   f) The final estimated value of the property in cell **D13**
   Ensure that cells containing formulas or functions will not show possible error messages: in these cases, cells should remain blank.
2. Protect the **Evaluation** worksheet (without using any password), making sure that the data can only be inserted in cells **B2:B3** and **B9:B12**,

whereas in any other cells it should not be possible to select or modify the content
3. Hide the **Property age** and **Parameters** worksheets.
4. Protect the workbook (without using any password), making sure that the hidden worksheet cannot be shown.

Apply appropriate formatting and organize the data in a suitable manner to ensure maximum readability, and give a neat and professional appearance to the worksheets.

Save the changes and close the file.

EXERCISE 7.3 - Copy shop

Mr. Reds, owner of the copy shop "CtrlC-CtrlV", wants to create with Excel a tool aimed to produce quotations of simple photocopying jobs, to be promptly communicated to his customers. For this kind of jobs, Mr. Reds will apply discounts for regular customers based on the quantity.

After opening the **Exercise 7.3 - Copy shop.xlsx** file, the price list with the cost per page (depending on the number of copies) and a draft of how he would like the tool to appear, Mr. Reds asks for your help to complete the task.

You are asked to:

1. Make sure that in cell **B1**, the type of client can be selected from a drop-down list containing the following three types: New, Occasional, and Regular. Insert the source values of the list in another worksheet named **Lists**.
2. Make sure that the amount to be entered in cell **B2** can only be non-negative integers. In case an invalid value is entered, the message "Attention: Check the amount inserted" should be shown.
3. Make sure that in cell **B4**, the cost per page for the number of copies required is shown, considering the price list available in the **Price List** worksheet. In case the function returns an error, cell **B4** should be blank.
4. Calculate, in cell **B5**, the total cost to be communicated to the customer, considering that a discount of 10% is applied if the following two conditions are satisfied:
   - Regular customer
   - Quantity greater than 200 copies

   In case even one of the two input cells (**B1** and **B2**) is empty, cell **B5** should be blank.
5. Make sure that in the **Quotation** worksheet only the input cells (**B1** and **B2**) can be selected and modified. Do not use any password.
6. Hide the **Price list** and **Lists** worksheets; then, protect the workbook (without using any password) so that the hidden worksheets cannot be shown.

Apply appropriate formatting and organize the data in a suitable manner to ensure maximum readability, and give a neat and professional appearance to the worksheets.

Save the changes and close the file.

EXERCISE 7.4 - *Paper and related*

Open the file **Exercise 7.4 - Paper and related.xlsx**. The file contains data for some products sold by a stationer.

You are asked to:

1. In the worksheet **Price list** enter, in a new column headed **Premium/top**, a function that returns the following result:
    a. "Premium product" for the five most expensive products of the list
    b. "Top product" for products from the sixth to tenth most expensive
    c. Nothing (an empty cell) for all other products
2. Ensure that the cells of the column **Product ID** are automatically formatted with a fill color of your choice for Premium products, and another fill color of your choice (but different) for Top products.
3. Ensure that in the cells of column **B** (excluding the header present in **B1**) it will be possible to enter only the values available in the **Lists** worksheet, under the heading **Categories**, selecting them in a drop-down list. In the event that you attempt to insert an item not listed you will receive the message "Warning! Item not available in the list".
4. Hide the worksheet **Lists**; then, protect the workbook with the password "Pap3r" so that it cannot be shown.

Apply appropriate formatting and organize the data in a suitable manner, to ensure maximum readability, and give a neat and professional appearance to the worksheets.

Save the changes and close the file.

EXERCISE 7.5 - Purchasing Department

As the assistant to the director of a fashion company purchasing department, you have been asked to analyze, at the end of the accounting period, the costs and other information concerning the suppliers of your company. All the data you need are available in the **Accounting** worksheet of the **Exercise 7.5 - Purchasing Department.xlsx** file.

You are asked to:

1. Create a new column in the **Accounting** worksheet with the heading **Alert** in which you have to make sure that one of the following messages is shown (by using a single function):
   a. "Warning! Costs are increasing" when the costs registered in the current year have increased over the previous year
   b. "Excessive increase in costs!!" when the cost increase over the previous year was more than 100,000 euros
   c. Nothing should be shown in all the other cases
2. Make sure that the text "Excessive increase in costs!!" is automatically shown in red and bold.
3. Show, in a new column of the **New Conditions** worksheet with the heading **Department to inform**, the name of the department that should be informed about the contractual amendments requested by the suppliers, listed in the same worksheet.
4. Highlight in an automatic manner, in the table of the **Accounting** worksheet, the cells in the column **Supplier code**, for those suppliers to which are attributed costs exceeding 180,000 euros in the current year, using a red fill color.
5. Calculate, in a new worksheet named **Costs**, the total costs incurred by each department in the previous year. In the same way, in a second column, calculate the total costs incurred in the current year.
6. Create, in the **Costs** worksheet, a mixed chart with title "Costs trend". The chart should simultaneously show the trend of costs in the previous year and in the current one, for each department.

Apply appropriate formatting and organize the data in a suitable manner to ensure maximum readability, and give a neat and professional appearance to the worksheets.

Save the changes and close the file.

EXERCISE 7.6 - DoReMi

The file **Exercise 7.6 - DoReMi.xlsx** contains, in the worksheet **Final balance**, data related to turnovers and costs of all products sold in the year just ended by the company DoReMi, specialized in the marketing of musical instruments and electronic equipment for sound reproduction.

You are asked to solve the following problems:

1. In a new column of the worksheet **Final balance**, calculate the turnover excluding VAT, assuming a VAT of 22%.
2. In a new column, calculate the cost of sales and distribution, assuming that they have an average incidence of 5.5% turnover excluding the VAT.
3. In a new column, calculate the net margin, defined as the difference between revenues excluding VAT and the total cost (of goods sold, selling, and distribution).
4. In a new column, calculate the percentage margin, defined as the ratio between net margin and turnover excluding the VAT.
5. In a new column with the heading **Type of margin** show, for each product and using a function, the type of margin (Minimum, Low, Medium, and High) based on the values contained in the worksheet **Margin**.
6. In a new column of the spreadsheet **Final balance**, estimate for each product the turnover excluding VAT for the coming year based on the expected increases in the worksheet **Increases**.
7. Create a chart that shows simultaneously, for each product, net turnover of VAT (column chart on the main axis) and the net margin % (line chart on the secondary axis); place the chart in a new worksheet called **Chart**.
8. Hide the worksheets **Margin** and **Increases** and then protect the workbook so that the two worksheets are not visible unless by typing the password "Marg1n".

Apply appropriate formatting and organize the data in a suitable manner to ensure maximum readability, and give a neat and professional appearance to the worksheets.

Save the changes and close the file.

EXERCISE 7.7 - Thinkstore

The PC seller Thinkstore needs to create a configurator tool to present its offers. The application, starting from the different components needed to build a custom PC, must show the description linked to each component, calculate the total cost of selected components, find the right discount rate based on the total cost, calculate the offer total discounted cost, and apply the 22% VAT rate to present to the customer the final price.

The file **Exercise 7.7 - Thinkstore.xlsx** contains the worksheet **Configurator** where you can find the structure of the application. The **Components** worksheet shows the list of components that could be part of the custom PC, with data about the Component ID, Description, and Price (in US dollars and VAT excluded). The worksheet **Discount** shows the discount rates that should be applied according to the total cost of selected components. Discount rates are thus divided by cost range (from 0 to 499 US dollars, from 500 to 1000 US dollars, from 1001 to 1500 US dollars, from 1501 and above).

In the **Configurator** worksheet, you are asked to:

1. Work on the cell range **C5:C14** to allow the user to select from a drop-down menu one of the codes of components shown in the worksheet **Components**.
2. Based on the code selected in column **C**, show in column **D** the description associated to that code, and in column **E** the cost associated to the component. When cells in column **C** are empty, cells in columns **D** and **E** must be empty too.
3. Calculate in cell **E15**, the total cost of the components selected.
4. Show in cell **E16** the discount rate that should be applied to the total cost of components according to the ranges shown in the **Discount** worksheet. If no component is selected, cell **E16** does not have to show an error message.
5. Calculate in cell **E17**, the total cost of selected components after discount. If any component is selected, cell **E17** does not have to show an error message.
6. Calculate in cell **E18**, the value of the VAT (22% of the total, net of discount), and in cell **E19** the final price of the configuration. If no

component is selected, both cells **E18** and **E19** do not have to show an error message.
7. Protect the **Configurator** worksheet leaving the possibility for users to work only on the cell range **C5:C14**; all other cells must be locked and hidden (use the password "config").
8. Hide the worksheets **Components** and **Discounts** and protect the workbook (use the password "config").

Apply appropriate formatting and organize the data in a suitable manner to ensure maximum readability, and give a neat and professional appearance to the worksheets.

Save the changes and close the file.

EXERCISE 7.8 - Print Service

Print Service is a wholesaler focused on the distribution of printers. Wholesaler's customers are small resellers who serve their local markets. Print Service needs to create a tool to automate its billing process. After the entry of quick input data, such as the customer and product ID, the tool must automatically recall some basic information (for a customer, Customer Name, Address, City, VAT number, Discount rate; for a product, its Description and Unit Price), and calculate the total value of the invoice, discount, shipping costs (based on the discounted total), VAT and, eventually, final value of the invoice.

The file **Exercise 7.8 - Print Service.xlsx** contains the **Invoice** worksheet where you can find the structure of the tool. The **Customers** worksheet contains the customer master data, with data about Customer ID, Customer Name, Address, City, VAT Number, Discount rate. The **Products** worksheet contains the product master data, with information such as Product ID, Description, and Unit Price. The **Shipping** worksheet shows the costs that must be applied according to the discounted total. All prices are in euros.

In order to create the invoicing tool, in the worksheet **Invoice** you are asked to complete the following requests:
1. Insert a function in the cell **F3** to have an automatic update of the date.
2. Create a drop-down menu in the cell **B6** from which it must be possible to select only customer IDs included in the **Customers** worksheet.
3. Based on the customer ID selected in **B6**, row cells from **C6** to **F6** must automatically recall the related information about the customer; if **B6** is empty, all other cells will be empty too.
4. Validate the cell range **B9:B18** to create a drop-down menu with the product IDs shown in the **Products** worksheet.
5. Based on the product IDs selected, the tool must automatically recall the product description (**C9:C18**) and its unit price (**E9:E18**) taken from the **Products** worksheet; if no product ID is selected in cells **B9:B18**, all other cells must be empty too (**C9:C18**; **E9:E18**).
6. In the cell range **F9:F18**, calculate the total of each row. The total is based on the quantity (manual input) and the unit price; if no product in cells **B9:B18** is selected, cells **F9:F18** must be empty too.
7. Calculate the total value in **F19**.

8. Based on the customer ID selected in **B6**, cell **F20** should automatically recall the related discount rate applied to the customer; if **B6** is empty, **F20** must be equal to 0.
9. Calculate the discounted total (Total – Discount) in **F21**.
10. Automatically indicate in cell **F22**, the shipping cost that has to be applied based on the discounted total (**F21**) and the cost ranges reported in the **Shipping** worksheet; this value should be 0 when **F21** is 0.
11. Calculate in cell **F23**, the value of VAT (22% of the sum of total net discount and shipping cost); VAT value should be 0, if **F21** is 0.
12. Calculate the total of the invoice in **F24**.
13. Hide the **Customers**, **Products**, and **Shipping** worksheet and protect the workbook with the password "print".
14. Protect the **Invoice** worksheet, so that only cells **B6**, **B9:B18**, and **D9:D18** can be edited. All the Excel formulas must be hidden. Use again the password "print".

Apply appropriate formatting and organize the data in a suitable manner to ensure maximum readability, and give a neat and professional appearance to the worksheets.

Save the changes and close the file.

EXERCISE 7.9 - European University

The administrative director of the European University wants to perform some analyses on repeating students.
The file **Exercise 7.9 - European University.xlsx** contains the **Sample** worksheet with a sample of repeating students selected by the statistics office.

To help the administrative director of the European University you are asked to:

1. Calculate the age of each student in the list of the **Sample** worksheet.
2. In two new columns of the **Sample** worksheet, use a function to show the admission year and the bachelor's full name, for each student, using the data in the **Careers** worksheet. Given the complexity of the Careers worksheet, do not use the number of columns but the field heading.
3. Create, in a new worksheet, a pivot table that shows the average age and the number of students for each admission year and for the bachelor full name; then:
    a. Group the admission year by 10-year intervals (1990-1999, 2000-2010)
    b. Make sure that for every value of the Bachelor full name field, the gender of the students is shown (M or F), setting first M and then F
    c. Use the **Country** field as filter of the pivot table, and show only the data for Italy
    d. Format the values of the age field as number with one decimal place
    e. Modify the default labels of the field in the Values area as "Average age" and "Students"
4. Create a new column in the **Sample** worksheet and show, for each student, one of the following values: annual fee, status, second year average, or total average. The choice of the field has to be done by selecting it from a drop-down menu in the heading of the new column. Save the list of fields to be selected in a new worksheet named **List**.
5. Hide **Careers** and **List** worksheets, then protect the workbook (without using any password), so that the hidden worksheets cannot be shown.

Apply appropriate formatting and organize the data in a suitable manner to ensure maximum readability, and give a neat and professional appearance to the worksheets.

Save the changes and close the file.

EXERCISE 7.10 - Consulteam

Consulteam is a management consulting firm. The company needs a new tool to plan the project budget and develop more accurate proposals for its corporate clients.

The file **Exercise 7.10 - Consulteam.xlsx** contains the **Budget** worksheet, where you can find the structure of the new planning tool. The **Fees** worksheet records useful data related to the different professionals that can be assigned to a project. The **Markups** worksheet shows the different markup rates that are linked to each professional. All prices are in euros.

In order to create the new budget application, you are asked to work on the **Budget** worksheet and to follow these steps:

1. Cells in the range **B3:B9** should accept only professional profiles included in the **Fees** worksheet, which can be selected from a drop down menu.
2. Cells in the range **C3:C9** should accept only the lengths included in the **Fees** worksheet, which can be selected from a drop down menu.
3. Create, in cells **D3:D9**, a single ID for any possible combination of professional and length, with:
    a. The text string from the profile
    b. Underscore (_)
    c. The text string from the length

   For example, when **B3** is on "Partner" and **C3** is on "Full," the code in **D3** has to be "Partner_Full"; when **C3** is empty, any code will be displayed.
4. For each single ID created in cells **D3:E9**, indicate in cells **E3:E9** the fee associated with the same ID in the **Fees** worksheet; if cells in **D3:E3** are empty, cells **E3:E9** will be empty too.
5. Calculate in cells **G3:G9**, the baseline cost of the service as a result of unit fee multiplied by the quantity (manual input); if there is no quantity indicated in cells **F3:F9**, the baseline cost should be empty.
6. Calculate in the cells **H3:H9** the cost for customer of each professional, as a result of the baseline cost multiplied by the markup rate reported in the **Markups** worksheet; if there is no quantity indicated in cells **F3:F9**, the cost for customer should be empty.

7. Calculate in cell **H12**, the total amount for the customer.
8. Cell **C13** must accept only the values "New" or "Old" and cell **E13** must accept only one of the values "Ok" or "Ko," choosing from a drop-down list.
9. Enter a formula in cell **H13** that shows the possible extra markup applied to the customer, calculated as follows:
   a. If the customer is "New", a 10% extra-margin is applied
   b. If the customer is "Old", a 15% extra-margin is applied if the last bill is paid ("Ok"), or a 20% extra-margin if the last bill is unpaid ("Ko")
   c. If the customer is "consolidated" and **E13** is empty, **H13** will appear empty
   d. If both cells **C13** and **E13** are empty, **H13** will appear empty too
10. Calculate the final budget in cell **H14** (Total cost + Extra markup); if in **H13** there is no extra markup, the cell must appear blank.
11. Hide the worksheets **Fees** and **Markups** and protect the workbook (using the password "consult").
12. Protect the **Budget** worksheet. Users must be able to work only on cell ranges **B3:B9**, **C3:C9**, **F3:F9** and on cells **C13** and **E13**. All the other cells must be locked and all the Excel formulas must be hidden (use again the password "consult").

Apply appropriate formatting and organize the data in a suitable manner to ensure maximum readability, and give a neat and professional appearance to the worksheets.

Save the changes and close the file.

EXERCISE 7.11 - *Candidates selection*

You work at a management training company, which provides training courses aimed at people working in companies and willing to improve their management skills.

In recent years, the company has received several inquiries about the possibility to attend courses free of charge, because of difficult business or personal conditions. Of course, it would be impossible to provide free courses to every participant, but to support some deserving people it was decided to admit a free participant for each course delivered. To select participants who are eligible to participate for free, an evaluation system has been developed.

The **Candidates** worksheet of the **Exercise 7.11 - Candidates.xlsx** file includes a list of people who have applied for free participation in the course. The following data are reported for each person:

- The numerical code (ID) assigned to each candidate
- Name and surname
- Date of birth
- Gross annual average income of the last 3 years
- Employment status (employed, unemployed)
- If unemployed, since when (in months)
- Curriculum Vitae (CV) assessment, that is, the score assigned by a commission to the CV on a scale of 1-10
- Interview assessment, namely the score assigned on a scale of 1-10 by the head of the course as a result of a telephonic interview

To help the company in the selection of candidates you are asked to complete the following five tasks:

1. In cell **B1**, insert a function that returns the current date, so that it automatically updates itself. To select the winner, it is necessary to calculate an overall score based on all the variables listed above. To this end, the following data on the basis of the data included in the **Scores** worksheet, must be entered in the **Candidates** worksheet:
    - In column **J**, with the heading **Age Score**, the score concerning the age

- In column **K**, with the heading **Income Score**, the score concerning the gross annual average income
- In column **L**, with the heading **Job Position Score**, the score concerning the current job position
- In column **M**, with the heading **Employment Status Score**, the score concerning the unemployment period (if not applicable, the cell must be blank)

2. In column **N**, calculate the total score as average of all the above scores obtained and those concerning the CV and interview assessments. Then, in cell **N14**, calculate the overall average of all candidates. The **Historical data** worksheet includes the number of candidates, best score, and average score of the last 20 editions of the course, wherein the twentieth is the one being analyzed. In cell **B22**, calculate the number of candidates in the current edition, in cell **C22** the best score of the current edition and in cell **D22** the average score of the current edition, with reference to the data contained in the **Candidates** worksheet.
3. In a new worksheet called **Statistics**, calculate:
   a. The number of editions with the maximum score greater than 8 and with average score higher than 7.5
   b. The average score of editions with at least 10 participants
   c. The number of persons that took part in editions with an average score higher than 7 and with maximum score greater than 8
4. Create a mixed chart with two axes showing together the trend in the number of candidates and in the score of the 20 editions. Move the chart in a new worksheet called **Historical chart**.
5. Hide the **Scores** worksheet. Protect the workbook, without any password, so that it is not possible to show the hidden worksheets. Protect the **Candidates** worksheet so that no formula is visible and no content can be modified. Also, in this case do not insert any password.

Apply appropriate formatting and organize the data in a suitable manner to ensure maximum readability, and give a neat and professional appearance to the worksheets.

Save the changes and close the file.

EXERCISE 7.12 - MagicWood

The furniture factory MagicWood is facing an economic crisis and the management is thinking about changes in production and sales strategies to improve profitability without losing its customers.

The **Exercise 7.12 - MagicWood.xlsx** file contains data regarding the products listed in MagicWood catalogue. The **Products** worksheet shows, beside the specifications for each product (Code, Description, Category, and Price), the resources used for the production process in terms of:

- Raw material (type of wood and quantity in Kg)
- Processing (machinery used and producing time expressed in hours and minutes)
- Labor (expressed in hours and minutes)

In the **Unit costs** worksheet, you can find production costs in terms of costs incurred for raw material, processing, and labor. All prices are in euros.

You are therefore asked to:

1. Calculate for each product, in two new columns of the **Products** worksheet:
   a. The Raw material cost, considering unit cost per type of wood and quantity used, paying attention to the unit
   b. The Processing cost, considering machinery used and time needed, paying attention to results normalization (consider that time is expressed in Time format)
2. In two new columns of the **Products** worksheet, calculate the Labor Cost considering time and hourly cost (again, pay attention to results normalization), and the total production cost for each product.
3. Calculate, in three new columns of the **Products** worksheet, the percentage of each of the three costs on the total cost, for each product. To do this, write a single formula using the correct relative/absolute references, and then copy it all over the cells of the three columns that need to be calculated.
4. In a new column of the **Products** worksheet with the heading **% Profit**, calculate in percentage of the price charged to retailers, the profit that MagicWood obtains from each product (that is the percentage of price

remaining to the company, excluding the production cost). In a new column of the **Products** worksheet with the heading **Rank**, calculate the rank of the percentage of profit that MagicWood obtains from each product found in the previous point (the highest profit must correspond to rank 1).

5. Then, apply a format to the cells of the **Description** field so that the cells corresponding to the first five ranks are highlighted with a fill color of your choice (the format should automatically change following any changes in the ranks).
6. In a new worksheet named **Pivot**, calculate the average percentage profit that MagicWood obtains by price of the product and the type of wood used. Then, group the price for ranges of 500 euros from 0 to 10,000 euros (0-499, 500-999 etc.) and set the **Category** field as a filter of the pivot table.
7. In a new worksheet called **Average** calculate, for each product category, the average price of the products with processing time lower than 1 hour (1:00:00). Make sure that where the function does not find values to calculate the average, it returns a dash (-).

Apply appropriate formatting and organize the data in a suitable manner to ensure maximum readability, and give a neat and professional appearance to the worksheets.

Save the changes and close the file.

EXERCISE 7.13 - Phone calls (summary exercise)

You work for a car with driver Rental Company called Luxury Car Rental. The file **Exercise 7.13 - Phone calls.xlsx** contains all the data of the call center of the company.

In particular, in the file you will find three worksheets:
- **Calls**, which contains data about all the phone calls made by the company Luxury Car Rental for the period May 2020 to April 2021
- **Destinations**, which contains data that associate each phone number called to its corresponding operator or destination
- **Discount**, which contains a table with discounts on the cost of calls charged by the telephone company, based on the length

The Luxury Car Rental call center works 24/7, therefore it generates a significant phone call traffic. The agency's management would like to analyze the calls made to find out the dynamics of the costs to decide if it is worth changing their telephone operator and the call rates now applied.

You are asked to solve the following problems:

1. Show in the **Calls** worksheet, using a new column headed **Destination/Operator**, the destination or operator corresponding to each phone call.
   Then, show in a new column of the same worksheet headed **Landline/Mobile**, the labels "Landline" and "Mobile" to identify whether the calls were made to a landline or a mobile number (consider that landline numbers start with 0 and mobile numbers start with 3, excluding the country code 39, which is common to both).

2. Calculate, in a new column of the **Calls** worksheet headed **Call Duration**, the duration (length) of each call expressed in hours, minutes, and seconds.
   The current call rates applied to Luxury Car Rental distinguish between calls made to landline and mobile phones, and, only for the calls made to mobile phones, different call rates based on the day of the week on which the phone call is made, according to the following scheme.

Calls to landline phones	$0.15 per phone call
Calls to mobile phones: • made on Sunday, Monday, and Tuesday • made from Wednesday to Saturday	$0.0015 per second $0.0020 per second

Calculate with the most appropriate function, in a new column of the **Calls** worksheet with the heading **Cost of Call**, the cost of each phone call.

3. Knowing that the phone company applies a discount on the cost of calls (both to landline and mobile phones), according to the table available in the **Discount** worksheet, calculate in a new column of the **Calls** worksheet with the heading **Discounted cost** the discounted cost of each call, depending on the end time of the call.

   Then, in a new worksheet named **Pivot**, create a pivot table in which to calculate the total cost of all the calls based on the type of call (to Landline/to Mobile) and the starting time of the call.

   Then, group the starting time of the call by hour, and add the field **Destination/Operator**, together with Landline/mobile, in such a way that it will be possible to see the details of all the calls made to each destination/operator.

   Customize the headings of the row and column labels with "Destination/Operator" and "Time".

4. In a new worksheet named **Control**, insert in cell **A1** the heading **Phone call ID** and in cell **B1** the heading **Discounted cost**. Make sure that in cell **A2** it is possible to select from a drop down list the identification code of each phone call, using the list available in the **Phone call ID** column of the **Calls** worksheet. Based on the code selected, cell **B2** should automatically show the discounted cost of the call (obtained by using a function): given the complexity of the **Calls** worksheet, do not use the number of columns but the field heading. If no code is selected, the function should show a dash (-) and not an error.

   Protect the worksheet with the password "control" in such a way that the only cell that can be modified is the one with the code of the phone call (**A2**). Make sure that the function used to calculate the cost cannot be seen when cell **B2** is selected.

5. In a new worksheet named **Cost Jan 2021**, show in column **A** the list of the destinations and operators using the list available in the **Destinations** worksheet, removing any duplicate.
   Use therefore a function to calculate, in the cells of column **B**, the average cost of calls sustained by Luxury Car Rental in January 2021 for each destination/operator (taking into account the discounted cost). Make sure that, when there are no calls made toward a specific destination/operator, the function does not return an error and shows a dash (-).
   Finally, hide the **Discount** worksheet and protect the workbook, without adding any password.

Apply appropriate formatting and organize the data in a suitable manner to ensure maximum readability, and give a neat and professional appearance to the worksheets.

Save the changes and close the file.

EXERCISE 7.14 - Box Office Star (summary exercise)

You work for Box Office Star, a company operating in the movie market analyses sector. The workbook **Exercise 7.14 - Box Office Star.xlsx** contains data regarding the most popular movies in the United States in 2016. The CEO of Box Office Star wants you to analyze these data. In particular, in the file there are two worksheets:
- **Boxoffice**, with data regarding movies seen in theaters in the United States in 2016: Movie title, Studio, Gross amount ($), Theaters, Opening date, Director, Genre, and Country
- **Lists**, containing a table with the extended name of the most important studios

You are asked to solve the following problems:

1. In the **Boxoffice** worksheet, create a new first column with the heading **Movie ID**. Then, create an ID for each movie to be formed using a single nested function as follows:
   a) Four characters of the movie title: when the title begins with the letters "The", use the characters from fifth to eighth, whereas in all other cases use the first four characters
   b) the last two digits of the year of the movie's opening date
   c) the first two characters of the studio
   d) a dash (-)
   e) the text "NEW" when the opening date of the movie is equal to or later than 6/1/2016, the text "OLD" in all the other cases
   E.g., the movie Central Intelligence, produced by WB studio and with the opening date 6/17/2016, will have "Cent16WB-NEW" as ID.

2. In a new column of the **Boxoffice** worksheet with the heading **Studio description**, use a function to show the studio description of each movie, using the data available in the **Lists** worksheet.
   In a new column of the **Boxoffice** worksheet with the heading **Months**, use a function to calculate, for each movie, the number of months passed between the opening date and the current date. The result should change automatically when the present date changes.

Apply a format to the cells of the **Movie title** field, so that the cells corresponding to a movie with gross amount between 50 and 100 millions of US dollars are highlighted with a fill color of your choice. The format should automatically change following any changes in the gross amount values.

3. Create a new worksheet named **Movie**. In cell **A1** of the same worksheet, create the heading **Movie ID** and make sure in cell **A2** it is possible to select a film ID from a drop-down menu (use the list of film IDs created in point 1).
   Then, in cells **B1** and **C1** of the **Movie** worksheet, create two drop-down menus from which it will be possible to select one of the field headings of the **Boxoffice** worksheet (if needed, create a new list in the **Lists** worksheet).
   Now, in cell **B2**, use a function that based on the movie ID and on the selected heading from the drop-down menu in cell **B1**, shows the desired value. Repeat the same operation in cell **C2**, making sure that when cell **A2** is empty, cells **B2** and **C2** do not have to show an error message.
   Note: the values of cells **B2** and **C2** should automatically update when another heading is selected in cells **B1** or **C1**.

4. Using Excel functions, in a new worksheet named **Genres** calculate, for each genre, the total gross amount of movies with an opening date later than 3/30/2016 and the number of movies played at least in 1,500 theaters.
   Copy all the data in the **Boxoffice** worksheet into a new worksheet named **Studio**; delete all existing formatting rules; then, use subtotals to show at the same time, for each studio, the total gross amount and the average number of theaters. Show an intermediate level of details, so that only totals and grand totals are visible.

5. In a new column of the **Boxoffice** worksheet with the heading **Rank**, use a function to calculate the rank of the total gross of each movie (the lowest total gross must correspond to rank 1).

Protect the **Movie** worksheet so that the only cells that can be selected (and edited) are those containing the drop-down lists created (**A2**, **B1**, and **C1**). Use the password "Movie".

Apply appropriate formatting and organize the data in a suitable manner to ensure maximum readability, and give a neat and professional appearance to the worksheets.

Save the changes and close the file.

EXERCISE 7.15 - Sunshine Events (summary exercise)

Sunshine Events is a company active in the field of theatrical, cultural, and musical events organization. The management of the company has decided to perform some elaborations on the data regarding the events planned for the June-August 2021 quarter. For this reason, the file **Exercise 7.15 - Sunshine Events.xlsx** has been set.

Within the file, the following three worksheets are available:
- The **Events** worksheet, which contains a list of the events organized by Sunshine Events in the June-August quarter, including details with regard to the city, date and genre of each event as well as information on the category of the tickets, the number of available tickets, and the number of tickets that have been sold so far
- The **Descriptions** worksheet contains a list of the ticket categories sold and a description of each
- The **Margins** worksheet contains a summary for the calculation of the percentage turnover margin for Sunshine Events connected to the price of tickets sold

All prices are in euros.

You are asked to solve the following five problems:

1. In a new column of the **Events** worksheet titled **Description**, show by means of a function, the description corresponding to each ticket category using the data available in the **Descriptions** worksheet.
   As the pre-sale of tickets always ends the day before each event and the majority of tickets are sold during working days (weekdays from Monday to Friday), the management of Sunshine Events would like to know the exact number of working days left until each event. In a new column of the **Events** worksheet titled **Days** calculate, using a function, how many days are there between the present day and the day before each event (extremes included). The result should change automatically when the present date changes.

2. Create, in a new worksheet named **Pivot**, a pivot table that allows calculating the total number of tickets sold for each ticket category and event date.

Unit 7. Lookup & Reference functions, data protection

Group the dates of the event by months and insert for each date the genre of the event (Ballet, Classical etc.); then, insert the field **City** as a filter of the pivot table.

3. In a new column in the **Events** worksheet titled **Margin**, show the percentage turnover margin (available in the **Margins** worksheet) corresponding to each range of the ticket price. In case the ticket price is not available, the text "N.A." should be shown.

   Considering the number of tickets actually sold, calculate in a new column titled **Margin (euros)**, the turnover margin (in euros) that Sunshine Events earns for each ticket category of each event. In case the ticket price is not available, the text "N.A." should be shown.

   Finally, create a new column titled **Percentage of sales** and calculate, for each ticket code, the percentage of tickets that Sunshine Events managed to sell, using the data available in the **Tickets Available** and **Tickets Sold** columns.

4. In the **Events** worksheet, insert as the first column of the table a new column with the heading **Ticket Code**. Then, create using a single formula, a code which identifies in a unique way each ticket, all upper case, to be formed as follows:
   a. The last two digits of the year of the date of the event
   b. A dash (-)
   c. The ticket category
   d. The first three letters of the name of the event
   e. A dash (-)
   f. The first three letters of the city where the event will take place
   g. The number of the day of the month (from 1 to 31) on which the event will take place
   h. A forward slash (/)
   i. The number of the month in which the event will take place

   For example, the code for the ticket with category SC1 for the event Aida taking place in Vienna on 06/10/2021, will be: 17-SC1AID-VIE10/6.

   Insert a new column in the **Events** worksheet titled **Rating**, making sure that, for each event listed in the spreadsheet, it is possible to insert a number between 1 and 10 (including decimals). If a wrong number is inserted, the error alert "Warning! You can only enter a number between 1 and 10" should appear.

5. In a new worksheet named **Calculations**, for each genre of event (Ballet, Classical, etc.) calculate using the appropriate function:
    a. The Total margin (in euros) for the events organized in the month of July (for the calculation use the data in the **Margin (euros)** column computed in point 3)
    b. The average percentage of sales for the events organized in the month of July (for the calculation use the data in the **Percentage of sales** column computed in point 3)

Apply a format to the cells of the Ticket code field so that the cells corresponding to events with at least 500 tickets available and event date equal to or later than 7/21/2021 are highlighted with a fill color of your choice. The format should automatically change following any changes in the ranks.

Apply appropriate formatting and organize the data in a suitable manner to ensure maximum readability, and give a neat and professional appearance to the worksheets.

Save the changes and close the file.

Unit 8. Macros and Elements of VBA

Topics of this unit:

Recording a macro in Excel, assigning a macro to a shape or a button, simple VBA editing, elements of VBA coding.

EXERCISE 8.1 - Students

Open the file **Exercise 8.1 - Students.xlsx**. The file contains the personal data of 200 former university students. You are asked to:

1. Save the file in the correct format to contain Macros, renaming it **Exercise 8.1 - Students macro.xlsm**
2. In the current workbook, create a macro, named **Format_and_sort**, which performs the following operations in the **Students** worksheet:
   a) Apply bold font to the table's headings (cells **A1:H1**)
   b) Sort the list by **Name** (ascending order)
   c) Select cell **A1**

Save the changes and close the file.

EXERCISE 8.2 - Tickets

Open the file **Exercise 8.2 - Tickets.xlsx**. You are asked to:

1. Save the file in the appropriate format to contain macros, renaming it **Exercise 8.2 - Tickets macro.xlsm**
2. Create in the current workbook a macro named **Format** that performs the following operations in the **Events** worksheet:
    a) Apply a color of your choice to the font of the values in the column **Ticket Code** (headings excluded)
    b) Apply a fill color of your choice to the column headings
    c) Sort the list by **City**, then - with the same city - by **Description**
    d) Select cell **A1**
3. Assign the macro to a shape (e.g., a rectangle) on the worksheet and enter a description text (e.g., the name of the macro).

Save the changes and close the file.

EXERCISE 8.3 - Product list

Open the file **Exercise 8.3 - Product list.xlsx**. You are asked to:

1. Save the file in the correct format to contain macros, renaming it **Exercise 8.3 - Product list macro.xlsm**
2. Add a new worksheet called **Macro**, then create a macro (saving it in the current workbook with the name **Sort**), which performs the following tasks:
   a) Copy the entire table of the **Products** worksheet in the **Macro** worksheet, starting from cell **A1**
   b) Still in the **Macro** worksheet, perform the following operations:
      - Delete row **1**
      - Italicize and underline the field headings (Code, Description, Category etc.)
      - Adapt columns width to their content
      - Sort the table by **Price** in a descending order
      - Select cell **A1** in the **Macro** worksheet
3. Assign the macro to a Button (Form Controls) on the **Products** worksheet, with the following text: **Copy and sort**.
4. Delete the current **Macro** worksheet and create a new one, also called **Macro**, to test the correct functioning of the newly created macro.

Save the changes and close the file.

EXERCISE 8.4 - *Stores*

Open the file **Exercise 8.4 - Stores.xlsx**. The file contains data related to the turnover of several stores of a multinational company, located in different European countries. You are asked to:

1. Save the file in the correct format to contain macros, renaming it **Exercise 8.4 - Stores macro.xlsm**
2. Create in the current workbook a macro named **Format** that performs the following tasks in sequence, in the **Stores** worksheet:
   a. Format the table headings (cells **A1:C1**) with a fill color of your choice and a thick lower border
   b. Format cells related to the Turnover, from **B2** to the last cell containing a value, with currency format and the Dollar symbol
   c. Select cell **A1**
3. *(optional)* Clean the macro code deleting useless rows, in particular those related to the properties about the borders that are not applied.
4. Create a second macro in the workbook, named **Delete_formats**, which deletes all formats in the entire worksheet **Stores** and then selects cell **A1**.
5. Assign the macros to two buttons of the Form Controls type, named **Format** and **Delete formats**, respectively.

Test the two macros using the buttons. Finally, save all changes and close the file.

EXERCISE 8.5 - *Household linens*

Open the file **Exercise 8.5 - Household linens.xlsx**. The file contains data relating to last year's production of a tailor's shop specializing in the production of tablecloths. After converting the file to xlsm format, create the following macros that apply specific conditional formatting to the data in the table, using the recorder:

1. **Costs_above_average**:
   Red fill and white font in the Variable cost cells
2. **Maximum_values**:
   Light blue fill with dark blue and bold font at Max Revenue and Max Margin
3. **Best_seller**:
   Bold, italic and purple font to the product (column **A**) with most sold pieces
4. **Graph**:
   Gradient Fill Data Bars on the Selling price column

Also, record a macro that removes all conditional formatting from the sheet. At the end of each macro, **C1** must be the active / selected cell.

Match each macro to a button, using explanatory descriptive texts.

Test all macros. Finally, save all changes and close the file.

EXERCISE 8.6 - Arithmetic

You want to entertain your little cousin, who has just started elementary school, with a nice calculator in Excel. In the file **Exercise 8.6 - Arithmetic.xlsm** you will find the calculator structure already set, you just have to create the macros to match the five shapes present in the sheet using the recorder.

The macro that does the **Addition** must:

1. Hide the texts in cells **A2** and **A7**, making the font white.
2. Show the text in cell **A10**, making the font black.
3. Select cell **D10** and write the formula for the sum of cells **C4** and **E4**.
4. Select cell **A1** (and stop recording).

Match it to the correct shape.

Macros related to other arithmetic operations must work in a similar way.

The macro that brings the calculator back to the initial condition must:

1. Show the texts in cells **A2** and **A7**, using the black font.
2. Hide the writing in cell **A10** with the white font.
3. Select cells **C4**, **E4** and **D10** and delete their contents.
4. Select cell **A1** (and stop recording).

Match it with the shape "Clean up the cells".

Test the macros. Finally, save the changes and close the file.

EXERCISE 8.7 - Airbnb

Your manager wants to analyze the data that Airbnb makes available for free on the real estate market of many cities around the world. The file **Exercise 8.7 - Airbnb.xlsm** is already set up to read London 2019 data from an external file. To prepare the data files (available in tab-delimited text format) for subsequent analyzes, he asks you to record the **Update** macro that reads the dataset for London 2019 and performs the following operations:

1. Update the connection to the **Exercise 8.7 - Airbnb_2019.txt** file in the **Airbnb - London** sheet.
2. Delete the **host_name** column.
3. Format the column headings centered horizontally, with a dark bold font and light fill.
4. Apply British pound currency formatting - i.e., £ English (United Kingdom) - to the **price** column, excluding the header.
5. Sort the table by **last_review** descending.

To check the macro, delete the formatting of the worksheet and set all column widths to 6. Try running the macro by reading the file **Exercise 8.7 - Airbnb_2020.txt**.

Note: when recording the macro keep in mind that the 2020 file has more lines than the 2019 file (11,000), so check that the pound formatting goes all the way!

Save the changes and close the file.

EXERCISE 8.8 - Filtered data

The **Exercise 8.8 - Filtered data.xlsm** file contains data that you need to analyze often using only the data relating to the Lombardy "Skincare" license each time. To simplify your future work, you are asked to assign the following macro, created using the recorder, to the shape present in the **MyMacros** sheet:

1. The **Filter** macro must copy the table in the **Registry** sheet, after filtering it by Lombardy region and "Skincare" license, into a new worksheet named **Data**.
2. At the end of the execution, the selected cell in each worksheet must be **A1**.
3. The filter must not be present in the **Registry** worksheet.
4. The macro must return to the **MyMacros** worksheet.

Note: to test the correct functioning of the macro, you must delete the created **Data** sheet each time, close the file (saving it) and reopen it.

Save the changes and close the file.

EXERCISE 8.9 - Deliveries

The **Exercise 8.9 - Deliveries.xlsm** file contains, in the **Summary** worksheet, the analysis of the value of orders processed in 2015 by customer segment and delivery methods (Ship mode).

You are asked to record a macro that starts from the existing pivot table to:

1. Create a stacked bar pivot chart, with the legend at the top, located on the **Summary** worksheet below the pivot table.
2. Change the value axis to display them in Million unit without decimals.

Record a second macro to delete the chart.
Associate each macro with a button (Form Controls), located to the right of the pivot table.

Note: the macro that creates the chart works correctly only the first time it is run; to try it several times you must delete the chart created, close the file (saving it) and reopen it.

Test the two macros using the respective buttons. Finally, save the changes and close the file.

EXERCISE 8.10 - Subtotals

Open the file **Exercise 8.10 - Subtotals.xlsx**. You are asked to:

1. Save the file in the correct format to contain macros, renaming it as **Exercise 8.10 - Subtotals macro.xlsm**
2. Create a macro named **Compute_totals** that inserts subtotals in the list, computes the sum of the selling prices for each seller, adapts the width of columns to their content, displays level 2 of the subtotals and selects the cell containing the value of the grand total as the active cell.
3. Create a new macro, named **Delete_totals** that deletes the subtotals from the list and sorts the table by **Price**, in a descending order, and then selects cell **A1**.
4. Assign the macros to two buttons located in a new worksheet, with the appropriate descriptive texts.

Note: before calculating the subtotals, the list must be properly sorted by the macro!

Test the two macros using the buttons. Finally, save all changes and close the file.

EXERCISE 8.11 - Table

To optimize formatting operations of the Excel files employed by a company, you are asked to perform the following tasks:

1. Record a macro, named **Format**, to format the table in the **Table** worksheet of the **Exercise 8.11 - Table.xlsm** file, accordingly to the following criteria:
   - Field headings (exactly the range of cells **A1:C1**) in bold font and with a fill color of your choice, centered horizontally and vertically, with wrapped text
   - Thin borders to all cells in the table (exactly the range **A1:C6**)
   - Percentage format without decimals on market shares (**C2:C6**)
   - Column width **B** equal to 9
2. Delete from the recorded macro any unnecessary/duplicated code generated by applying the alignments in the table headers and borders.
3. Create a second macro, named **Delete_formats**, that deletes all formatting from the entire **Table** worksheet, returns the width of column **B** to 6, and then selects cell **A1**.
4. Assign the macros to two buttons on the worksheet.
5. Test the two macros.
6. Modify the **Format** macro so that it works even if the table in the **Table** sheet is modified to any dimension in terms of rows and columns. Verify that the button is properly paired with this modified macro.
7. Test the two macros by adding or removing manually rows or columns from the table and verifying if the formats are applied correctly to the entire table, regardless of its dimensions.

Note: be careful when deleting rows from the table not to delete the two buttons too!

Save the changes and close the file.

EXERCISE 8.12 - *Worksheet protection*

Open the file **Exercise 8.12 - Worksheet Protection.xlsm**. A mathematical and statistical analysis company wants to protect its Excel worksheets from curious people. The type of protection applied is common to all worksheets, and to make the operation quicker, the company has decided to record a macro.

Therefore, you are required to:

1. Record a macro that, in addition to not showing formulas and preventing changes to cell contents, protects the worksheet (regardless of how is called) while still allowing:
    - The selection of locked and unlocked cells
    - Changes to formats / formatting (third, fourth and fifth options in the list of allowed operations)
    - The use of filters (AutoFilter) and the editing of objects

   Set the password **test**.
2. Modify the macro so that the user is asked which password must be used for protection (the parameter Password of the *Protect* method must be used).
3. Assign the macro to a button in the **SecretFormulas** worksheet.

Test the macro. Finally, save the changes and close the file.

EXERCISE 8.13 - Chart axis

The analysts of the Stats Research company are often required to create charts to share their data analysis with the company's top management. To improve the aspects of those charts, they set manually the maximum value of the vertical axis. An example of the data analyzed is in the **Curves** worksheet in the **Exercise 8.13 - Chart axis.xlsm** file.

In order to facilitate their job, you are asked to:

1. Record a macro for the creation of a scatter chart using the data in the **Curves** worksheet, setting the maximum value of the vertical axis to 180.
2. Modify the macro so that the maximum value of the axis matches exactly the maximum value in the series (Y), obtained through the formula in cell **C3**.
3. Assign the macro to a button.

Delete manually the chart and test the macro.

Note: the macro recorder performs some operations that should be deleted. After the creation of the chart, which is carried out by writing the following two lines of code:

ActiveSheet.Shapes.AddChart2(240, xlXYScatterSmooth).Select
ActiveChart.SetSourceData Source:=Range("Curves!$B$5:$C$26")

it is necessary to delete from the recorded macro the lines containing the instructions *ActiveSheet.Shapes ...*, that the recorder may have added.

Save the changes and close the file.

EXERCISE 8.14 - Table template

When data are inserted in the Excel files of the EuroSales company, the same formatting scheme is always applied. You are asked to automate the formatting operation, as follows:

1. Create a new Excel file, naming it **Exercise 8.14 - Table Template.xlsm**
2. Create a macro that is able to create a table template for data inputting, i.e. a table consisting of 5 columns and 20 rows with thin borders.
3. In the first row of the table, set the font to bold and a light fill color of your choice.
4. Modify the macro just created so that, once defined the table template, its activation allows to apply the formatting simultaneously to all worksheets of the active Excel file.

To test the macro, create two or three xlsx files containing different amounts of sheets on which to apply the modified macro.

Save the changes and close the file.

EXERCISE 8.15 - *Alternate rows*

Create a new Excel file, saving it as **Exercise 8.15 - Alternate rows.xlsm**. You are asked to:

1. Record a macro that formats a row in the active worksheet as follows:
   - Bold font
   - Light yellow filling (described as "Gold, Accent 4, Lighter 80%" among the Theme Colors)
2. Modify the macro so that the formatting previously created is applied to a number of rows according to the user's choice, alternating it with non-formatted rows: only even rows must be formatted.

Note: for simplicity, always apply the formatting starting from row **1**.

Test the macro, trying to insert different numbers of rows to be formatted. Finally, save the changes and close the file.

EXERCISE 8.16 - Sales chart

The file **Exercise 8.16 - Sales Chart.xlsm** consists of only one worksheet, which contains a series of data concerning sales and a histogram chart. The company you are consulting for asks you to implement an automated system to quickly change the type of graph from histogram to line and vice versa, based on the user's choice. In cell **G2**, data validation has already been set together with a list of the two different types of charts.

You are asked to:

1. Record a macro to change the type of chart from column to line chart.
2. Record a second macro to change the type of chart from line to column chart.
3. Use the code of the two macros recorded to create a single macro, which allows changing the type of chart according to the user's choice in cell **G2**. If the user does not select a chart type (blank cell), a warning message must be displayed.
4. Assign the macro that results from the merging of the macros created in steps 1 and 2 to a button, which must be positioned to the right side of cell **G2**.

Test the macro. Finally, save the changes and close the file.

EXERCISE 8.17 - Add worksheets

Open the file **Exercise 8.17 - Add worksheets.xlsm**. Among the activities of a business, it is often necessary to add new worksheets to the current workbook, and to rename them according to the name of the customer analyzed, drawn from a list.

You are asked to:

1. Create a macro that adds a new worksheet to the current workbook, in the last position (it is recommended to start with registered code).
2. Modify the macro so that the newly added worksheet is renamed according to the name present in the cell selected in the **Customer list** worksheet, which contains the names that must be used. Before adding the new worksheet, it is necessary to check whether:
   - The selection consists of only one cell
   - The selected cell is not empty

   If these conditions are not met, an error message should be displayed to the user that clearly indicates the type of problem encountered.
3. Assign the macro to a button on the worksheet.
4. Test the macro by selecting cell **B3**. What happens? Insert an additional check to avoid the "Name already in use" run-time error.

Test the macro by trying all possible cases. Finally, save the changes and close the file.

EXERCISE 8.18 - Sales pivot

In the **Exercise 8.18 - Sales Pivot.xlsm** file, the **Pivot** worksheet contains a Pivot table that has been created using the data in the **SalesData** worksheet. To facilitate data consultation and export, you are asked to write a macro that creates three worksheets corresponding to the three regions (North, Middle, and West). In these three worksheets, it is necessary to only copy values, not to recreate the entire Pivot table.

You are then asked to:

1. Create, as a first step, a specific macro capable of setting the filter on a specific Region. Based on your selection, you need to create a new worksheet with the name corresponding to the Region and copy the data from the pivot table (including row and column headings) into it.
2. It is also necessary to avoid creating the Region worksheet if it already exists.
3. Now, create a second overall macro that uses/calls the previous one to perform the same operations with the other two Regions (do not duplicate the code!).
4. At the end of the overall macro execution, **A1** must be the active cell in the **Pivot** sheet, the pivot table must not be filtered, and the copy area must not be active (i.e. the dashed border around the selection **B4:F9** must not be still visible).
5. Associate the overall macro with a button on the **Pivot** sheet.

Note: remember that macros can have parameters (input arguments) like the functions, so the specific macro can get the Region name as an input value from the overall macro.

Test the macro. Finally, save the changes and close the file.

EXERCISE 8.19 - Insert rows

To simplify the job of users, who often must insert new rows within a dataset in Excel, you are required to:

1. Create a macro named **Insert_row** in the file **Exercise 8.19 - Insert Rows.xlsm**, which inserts a row above the current position, using the recorder to get the code.
2. Assign the macro to the "double click on the mouse button" event, creating an appropriate macro in Sheet1 (Data).
3. Modify the macro so that the row is inserted in the position where the double click occurred.

Note: the sub that manages the row insertion must receive the value of the row of the current active cell / the position of the double click as input from the macro that manages the "double click" event.

Test the macro. Finally, save the changes and close the file.

EXERCISE 8.20 - Stock Exchange (summary exercise)

A stock exchange operator asks you to automate the Excel file **Exercise 8.20 - Stock Exchange.xlsm** in which a worksheet with a chart and some worksheets with data from the Stock Exchange are present. Data formats are not suitable for analysis; therefore, they must be changed. The operator wants data to be copied, on user's choice, from one of the original worksheets in the analysis worksheet and formatted appropriately. Each worksheet is named by a different Stock Exchange: **DJI**, **FTSEMIB**, and **NDX**.

You are asked to:

1. Create a macro that performs the following steps:
   a) Copy data from one of the worksheets (e.g., **DJI**) and paste them in the **Chart** worksheet, starting from cell **A1**
   b) Transform the text so that it is distributed over different columns, considering that data are not in the correct format, and that decimals use a comma as separator
   c) Sort data by date, in an ascending order
2. Assign the macro to a button, positioned in the **Chart** worksheet.
3. Modify the macro so that:
   a) It cleans up the contents of columns **A:G** of the **Chart** worksheet
   b) The user is asked which stock exchange index should be displayed
   c) The user is asked which column should be used in the chart (listing them all in the question text)
   d) Make sure that the **Chart** worksheet is updated according to the user choices, including the chart (Note: to achieve this point, it is advisable to first record a macro to change the data series and the title of the chart, **Macro_ChangeSeries_Original**)
   e) Verify that the user has not entered an empty string, neither for the stock exchange index, nor the column. In this case, you must notify the user with an error message and exit the procedure
4. Make sure that any error generated by entering a non-existent name is managed. In the event of an error, the user must be notified with a message.

Note: to simplify the code, in the **Chart** worksheet the column headings of the values High, Low, Close etc. are all named Ranges, as well as the cells containing the value series (check for cell names and ranges in the Name Manager window on the Formula tab of the Ribbon!).

Test the macro. Finally, save the changes and close the file.

Unit 9. More Functions and Solver

Topics of this unit

Topics: ROUND, INT, RAND, RANDBETWEEN, HLOOKUP, PPMT, IPMT, RATE, VA, NPV, IRR, TEXT, CONVERT, NETWORKDAYS functions, Data tables, advanced filter, Solver add-in.

EXERCISE 9.1 - Hot deals

The website TV Madness, which sells online televisions and related products, has decided to celebrate its first 10 years of activity, offering discounts to its customers on many products from among its catalog, with discount rates going from 30% to 90%, changing every four hours.

The file **Exercise 9.1 - Hot deals.xlsx** contains three worksheets, namely, **List**, **Discount**, and **Historical**. The **List** worksheet contains the data of all the products that will be discounted in the next few hours. The **Discount** worksheet contains the area where the discount rates for each product for the next 24 hours will be saved. The **Historical** worksheet contains the discount rates variation between each time interval and the previous one in the last 48 hours. Values are expressed in euros.

You are asked to:

1. In the **Discount** worksheet, use a function to generate randomly the discount rate for each product and for every time scheduled in the "Raw rates" area. To prevent the values from changing after each operation, copy all the discount rates and paste the values in the same cells.
   The discount rates planned by the management of the TV Madness website are between 30% and 90%. Then use a function in the Correct rates area of the **Discount** worksheet that shows as a result:
   - 30% when the discount rate is equal to or less than 30%
   - 90% when the discount rate is equal to or greater than 90%
   - The discount rate already calculated in all other cases
2. Before applying the discount, the TV Madness management decided to round the product prices down to the nearest integer. In a new column of the **List** worksheet named **New price**, round down the price of each product.
3. In a new column of the **List** worksheet named **Discounted price**, calculate the discounted price for each product using the correct discount rate at 9.00 AM and rounding down again to the nearest integer.
4. In the **Historical** worksheet, calculate the average variation of all the products for all the ranges, in absolute value.

Apply appropriate formatting and organize the data in a suitable manner to ensure maximum readability, and give a neat and professional appearance to the worksheets.

Save the changes and close the file.

EXERCISE 9.2 - Blue Vision

Blue Vision, a company operating in the telecommunications sector, must buy new equipment for its most important production plant. The cost of the new equipment amounts to 2.5 million euro and the company's management is considering three different solutions: all require an initial cost of 2.5 million euros, but each one has a different payment plan, both in terms of duration and of cash flows.
In order to choose the best solution, it is necessary to calculate the interest rate to be used to discount the cash flows of each solution: to this end, the management of the Blue Vision decided to use the weighted average cost of all debts, based on the total annual cost.
The file **Exercise 9.2 - Blue Vision.xlsx** contains two worksheets: the **Debt** worksheet contains the data of all the current debts of the Blue Vision (four different fixed rate mortgages and a line of credit at the bank); the **Projects** worksheet contains the cash flows of the three solutions to be evaluated. Values are expressed in euros.

You are asked to solve the following problems:

1. In the **Debt** worksheet, using the appropriate functions:
   - Calculate the interest rate of each of the four mortgages (cells **B5:E5**)
   - Calculate the annual cost of each of the four debts (cells **B9:B13**); with regard to the line of credit consider an annual cost of 350,000 euros
   - Calculate the weight of the annual cost of each debt with respect to the total cost (cells **C9:C13**)
   - Use a function to show the interest rate of each debt in cells **D9:D13**
   - Calculate the weighted average interest rate (in cell **B15**), using the weights just calculated and the related interest rates
2. Copy in the **Projects** worksheet the weighted average interest rate just calculated, so that it remains linked to the original value. Then, calculate for each project, the net present value and the internal rate of return.

Apply appropriate formatting and organize the data in a suitable manner to ensure maximum readability, and give a neat and professional appearance to the worksheets.

Save the changes and close the file.

EXERCISE 9.3 - Gold

Anthony Nowitzki lives in Rome and, since 2004, invested part of his savings in gold. Now the bank has offered him a new investment plan; first, Mr. Nowitzki wants to calculate the actual value in euros of his investment in gold, and then evaluate the bank offer.

In the **Exercise 9.3 - Gold.xlsx**, there are three worksheets, namely, **Gold**, **Exchange rates, and Exchange rates**. The **Gold** worksheet contains the average price of gold in dollars/ounce (USD/ounce) from 2004 to 2014, and the amount of gold (in grams) held by Mr. Nowitzki during the same period. The **Exchange rates** worksheet contains the average values of the exchange rate in euros/dollar in the same period. The **Investment** worksheet contains the details of the investment offered by the bank. Values are expressed in euros.

You are asked to solve the following problems:

1. In a new column of the **Gold** worksheet, convert into ounces the amount of gold held by Mr. Nowitzki, rounding the result to two decimal places.
2. Then, calculate the value in euros of the amount of gold held by Mr. Nowitzki, using the values of the exchange rate EUR/USD in euros of the **Exchange rates** worksheet.
3. Mr. Nowitzki would like to hold his investment in gold, but would also like to understand how the value of the investment changes based on the price of gold and on the amount of gold held. Therefore, perform an analysis in the **Gold** worksheet creating a two-variable data table that shows the value of gold, considering all combinations of gold price USD/ounce (from 1,000 to 1,800, with increments of $1,000/ounce) and grams of gold held (from 3,000 to 4,400, with increments of 200 grams). Note: To create the table use 2014 data.
4. The investment offered by the bank to Mr. Nowitzki includes a series of monthly payments of 250 euros for 10 years to be paid at the beginning of the month, each one invested at an interest rate of 6.50%. Calculate, in the **Investment** worksheet, the future and present values of the investment.
5. Mr. Nowitzki has the opportunity to decide for a monthly payment lower or higher than the one suggested by the bank; also the interest rate of the investment could change. Then, perform an analysis in the

Investment worksheet creating a two-variable data table that shows the present value of the investment, considering different combinations of monthly payment (from 150 to 350 euros, with increments of 25 euros) and interest rate (from 3% to 9%, with increments of 0.5%).

Apply appropriate formatting and organize the data in a suitable manner to ensure maximum readability, and give a neat and professional appearance to the worksheets.

Save the changes and close the file.

EXERCISE 9.4 - Personal loan

Richard Weber asked his bank for a loan of 40,000 euros to buy a small boat. The Loan worksheet of the **Exercise 9.4 - Personal loan.xlsx** file contains the terms of the loan offered by the bank, which is a duration of 48 months and an 8.50% fixed annual interest rate. Furthermore, there are a preliminary credit checks that cost 350 euros, and a mandatory multi-risk insurance with a single 550 euros premium.

You are asked to:

1. Calculate the personal loan monthly installment (to be paid at the end of each period) then, create the amortization schedule of the loan in the already prepared area of the worksheet. In particular:
   - Enter the identification number of each installment in the **Installment ID number** column
   - Copy the amount of the monthly installment in the **Payment** column
   - Calculate the principal payment and the interest payment for each installment of the loan
2. Then, calculate the total interests to be paid and the effective annual interest rate of the loan.

Apply appropriate formatting and organize the data in a suitable manner to ensure maximum readability, and give a neat and professional appearance to the worksheets.

Save the changes and close the file.

EXERCISE 9.5 - New car

John Smith wants to buy a new car worth 35,000 euros. He cannot pay in cash, so he has three alternatives: a bank loan, a loan from a finance company, and a leasing.

The file **Exercise 9.5 - New car.xlsx** contains the conditions of the three solutions, with the duration, interest rate, frequency of installments, cost of the file, and the possible advance payment; for the leasing solution, there is also the value of the final redemption of the good.

You are asked to help John Smith decide which solution is the most cost effective, solving the following problems:

1. Calculate the monthly payment for each of the three solutions, considering that the cost of the file and the eventual advance payment are not part of the funded cash.
2. Calculate the total cost of each of the three solutions, including the cost of file.
3. Calculate the effective annual interest rate and the net present value of each solution, using a 2% interest rate and considering that the cost of the file and the eventual advance payment should be paid at the beginning of the first period, whereas final redemption in the leasing should be paid with the last installment.
4. Make sure that the values of cells **B3:D3** (solution name) corresponding to the lowest net present value is automatically formatted with a fill of your choice.

Apply appropriate formatting and organize the data in a suitable manner to ensure maximum readability, and give a neat and professional appearance to the worksheets.

Save the changes and close the file.

EXERCISE 9.6 - Gluten-free products

Red's management, a wholesaler of gluten-free products, is testing a new tool to forecast the sales of each product in the following week. Every Friday afternoon, the management receives the actual sales data of each product, compares them with the forecast made the previous week, and finally elaborates the forecast for the next week.

In the **Exercise 9.6 - Gluten-free products.xlsx** file, you can find two worksheets, namely, **Products** and **Parameters**. The **Products** worksheet contains the expected sales of each product made last week and the actual sales of the week just ended; the **Parameters** worksheet contains the data required to calculate and evaluate the sales forecast for the next week.

In order to help Red's management, you are asked to:

1. Calculate, in a new column of the **Products** worksheet called **Next week**, the sales expected for next week for each product in the list, without using other columns to perform the operation. The Next week forecast is calculated by rounding down to the nearest integer the result of the following formula:
   Section parameter × Actual sales + (1 − Section parameter) × Expected sales
   The expected sales are those of the previous week, and the section parameter is a value that changes based on the section the products are exposed (section parameters are available in the **Parameters** worksheet).
2. Calculate, in a new column called **Deviation**, the percentage variation between the actual sales and the expected sales.
3. In a new column with the heading **Forecast evaluation**, use a function that returns as a result, for each product, an evaluation of last week's forecasts precision (from very bad to very good) according to the deviation just calculated (considering its absolute value), using the data available in the **Parameters** worksheet.
4. Starting from cell **L8** of the **Products** worksheet, use an advanced filter to show the data of products with the deviation between the actual and expected sales between 5% and 15% (bounds included) and with product type Pasta or Frozen Foods.

Apply appropriate formatting and organize the data in a suitable manner, to ensure maximum readability, and give a neat and professional appearance to the worksheets.

Save the changes and close the file.

EXERCISE 9.7 - Condo fees

The administrator of the Horizons condominium must allocate among all the residents the costs of the year that just ended. .

In the **Exercise 9.7 - Condo fees.xlsx**, there are two worksheets, namely, **Residents** and **Expenses**. The **Residents** worksheet contains the list of all the residents with some information about their apartments, the services used, and the consumption for the heating during the year in terms of gallons of oil. The **Expenses** worksheet contains the total values of different kinds of expenditures (in euros), the criteria for the allocation of the maintenance of the lift cost (to be divided based on the floor), and the criteria for the allocation of the satellite TV (cost based on the stair).

To help the administrator of the condominium, you are asked to calculate in the **Residents** worksheet:

1. The expense for the heating allocated to each resident, rounded to the nearest integer, considering that the cost of the oil is 1.4 euros per liter.
2. The expenses for the lift allocated to each resident, considering that the total expense for the lift maintenance should be divided equally among all the residents of the same floor. The expense of each resident should be rounded to the second decimal place.
3. The expense for the satellite TV of the residents that have it installed, considering that the expense is different based on the stair of the apartment. For the residents that do not have the satellite TV installed, the result should be an empty cell.
4. The general expenses quota allocated to each resident, considering that it should be allocated based on the square meters of the apartment. The expense allocated to each resident should be rounded to the second decimal place.

Apply appropriate formatting and organize the data in a suitable manner to ensure maximum readability, and give a neat and professional appearance to the worksheets.

Save the changes and close the file.

EXERCISE 9.8 - Car purchase

Your friend Luke is fond of cars, and would like to run simulations on some car purchase options. He has already selected four models of gasoline cars and would like your help to assess what the best purchase would be.
The **Options** worksheet of the file **Exercise 9.8 - Car purchase.xlsx** includes:
- In cell **B1**, the approximate availability of cash to buy the car (all values are expressed in euros)
- In cell **B2**, the estimated cost of a liter of gasoline
- In cell **B3**, the estimated annual mileage in kilometers
- In cells **A6:A9**, the four cars selected as "finalists" (in order not to influence your analysis, however, he does not want to tell you the exact model and therefore he has indicated them simply by the letters A, B, C, and D)
- In cells **B6:B9**, the car purchase cost
- In columns **C**, **D**, and **E**, other annual costs related to the car (insurance, road tax, and maintenance)
- In column **F**, the consumption expressed in kilometers per liter of gasoline

You are asked to:

1. Enter in column **G**, with the heading **Three-year cost**, the total cost for the purchase and maintenance of each car over a three-year period.
2. Highlight, with colors of your choice, the name of the car (A, B, C, or D) with the highest total cost and the one with the lowest cost. The highlighting must update itself automatically as data change in column **G**.
3. In the same worksheet, insert a data table that, taking as reference the car with the lowest total cost, calculates the total cost according to the different gasoline cost assumptions (from 1.4 to 1.9 euros with increases of 0.1 euros each) and kilometers driven per year (from 10,000 to 20,000 with increases of 1,000 kilometers each).
4. After having carried out these evaluations, Luke is convinced that the best car for his needs is that with the lowest purchase cost. Now he has to figure out how to pay for it, given that the cash on hand is not enough. The **Loan** worksheet contains the data of the loan offered by the bank to pay for the car. Copy the value corresponding to **Three-year cost**

of the cheapest car in cell **B3**; then, calculate the monthly payment to be paid at the beginning of each period for a 3-year fixed rate loan, according to the rate reported in cell **B4**.

5. As the rate is very high and Luke is afraid he cannot afford it, he asks you to make a simulation, in the **Loan** worksheet, to see the sum he should ask the bank to have a monthly payment equal to the amount that he thinks he can afford, i.e., 500 euros.

6. Insert one function, in cell **C1** of the **Options** worksheet, that assesses whether the cash available to Luke, added to the figure just calculated to have a loan whose monthly payment is 500 euros, is sufficient to cover the amount needed to purchase the chosen car (i.e., that with the lowest purchase cost). If the amount is sufficient to cover the requested amount, the function will have to return as a result the text "Purchase allowed"; otherwise, it will have to return the text "Review choice, or find another xxx euro", where xxx represents the missing amount to obtain the total cost, rounded to the nearest two decimal places.

Apply appropriate formatting and organize the data in a suitable manner to ensure maximum readability, and give a neat and professional appearance to the worksheets.

Save the changes and close the file.

EXERCISE 9.9 - Promotional Campaign

The management of a company that produces and sells electricity wants to launch some new commercial offers with a flat rate, which should guarantee a sure cash inflow. The expected duration of the promotional campaign is 6 months. These new offers include the subscription of contracts that bind customers to a fixed monthly payment for 5 years.

In the **Exercise 9.9 - Promotional Campaign.xlsx** file, you will find data and values prepared by the sales department of the company. Three types of contracts have been created: AllFlat Basic, AllFlat Medium, and AllFlat Pro, which offer different characteristics with regard to the price, the maximum monthly consumption in kW·h, the cost per kW·h within and above the contractual limit.

A series of data is also available in the worksheet. In particular:
- The main specifications of the contracts: duration, price, maximum consumption, and cost (values are expressed in euros)
- A second section that includes some clauses of the contract: the percentage of overrun estimated for each type of contract, average consumption in kW·h, and average consumption in kW·h over the limit of the contract
- The estimated number of customers per type of contract
- The cost of production of each kW·h for the company
- The estimate of the total number of kW·h to provide based on the average consumptions, percentage of overruns, and number of estimated customers
- The unitary management cost of each contract for the company (which includes general, support, commercial, and administrative costs), and the total cost for each type of contract calculated using both the monthly management cost and the cost of the electricity

In a separate table (Cash Flow), you will find the calculation of the Monthly Net Cash Flow deriving from the promotion, calculated as the difference between the revenues and the total monthly costs, as well as the half-year overall Net Cash Flow.

Our goal is to find out the combination of monthly prices and cost per kW·h over the maximum consumption thanks to the promotional campaign which

manages to provide a cash flow of 50 million euros, respecting the following conditions:
- The cost of the kW·h over the maximum consumption must be less than or equal to 0.6 euros
- The maximum price of the three contracts has to be less than or equal to:
  - 100 euros for the Basic contract
  - 180 euros for the Medium contract
  - 230 euros for the Pro contract
- The monthly price of each contract has to be an integer.

Apply appropriate formatting and organize the data in a suitable manner to ensure maximum readability, and give a neat and professional appearance to the worksheets.

Save the changes and close the file.

EXERCISE 9.10 - German course

In the **Exercise 9.10 - German course.xlsx** file, there are results of the final assessment of the German courses held this year at the Deutsche-Institut school.

You are asked to:
1. Clean up from extra spaces the Evaluations in the **Information** worksheet, using a proper function.
2. In the **Final assessment** worksheet, insert a formula in column **E** that gives as a result the Evaluation achieved by each student, referring to the data available in the **Information** worksheet.
3. Again in the **Final assessment** worksheet indicate for each student, using a function:
    a. In column **F**, who was the teacher of the course
    b. In column **G**, the course level that everyone has attended
4. In column **H**, use a function to calculate, for insufficient students only, the price that would be required to attend the course again, keeping in mind that if the failure was not severe (grade 50 or above), the student is entitled to a 30% discount. For prices, refer to the figures available in the **Information** worksheet.
5. The director of the school has arranged in the **School expenses** worksheet a plan to understand how to maximize the revenues of the school. In the worksheet there are missing data, which you can find in the **Information** sheet. Use a function to fill the hourly rate of the teachers and the price of the courses in columns **E** and **G**.
6. Use an Excel feature that allows you to calculate, in cells **F2:F5** of the **School expenses** worksheet, the optimal number of students per class that allows to maximize the revenues of the school, respecting these constraints:
    - Students cannot be less than 15 and more than 27 per class
    - The number of students must be an integer
    - The total number of students cannot exceed the maximum allowed

Apply appropriate formatting and organize the data in a suitable manner to ensure maximum readability, and give a neat and professional appearance to the worksheets. Save the changes and close the file.

EXERCISE 9.11 - Overtime

Open the **Exercise 9.11 - Overtime.xlsx** file. A customer has commissioned to our small company the implementation of a project to be carried out in a very short time over the weekend (hence only achievable by using overtime). The HR department has interviewed all the employees to understand who could be assigned to the project: the list of employees who have given their availability is present in the **Project** worksheet. In addition to the list of employees available to perform the work, the **Project** worksheet contains:
- The overtime hourly wage for each employee (which depends on the individual contracts of employment) in column **B**. Values are expressed in euros
- The maximum number of overtime hours (as per the contract) still available in the current month for each employee in column **C**
- The number of hours needed to complete the project (cell **B17**)

The cells referring to the total number of hours assigned (**B18**) and to the overall cost (**B20**) already contain some formulas that will update as soon as the hours of work for each employee will be inserted.

Your task is to calculate in column **D** the overtime hours to be assigned to each employee, minimizing the overall cost incurred by the company for the project commissioned by the customer, while respecting a number of constraints imposed by the management. In particular, the constraints to be observed are the following:
- The total number of hours assigned must be equal to the number of hours needed
- The number of hours assigned to each employee must not exceed the corresponding maximum number of overtime hours still available in the current month
- The number of hours assigned to each employee must be an integer
- The number of hours assigned to each employee must be equal to or greater than 10

Apply appropriate formatting and organize the data in a suitable manner to ensure maximum readability, and give a neat and professional appearance to the worksheets. Save the changes and close the file.

EXERCISE 9.12 - Home video

You work for a company that deals with the adaptation and distribution of several movies for the home video market in the Italian territory. The company has the problem of optimizing shipments departing from the three warehouses (located one each in Milan, Rome, and Naples) to the company's headquarters, from where they are distributed widely to the individual branches and dealers. The problem is complicated by the different costs, from warehouse to branch, and the numerous logistical constraints (maximum capacity of storage, due to the size of the warehouses, and of shipping due to the load capacity of the truck). The management has instructed us to conduct a study to assess the best combination (i.e., the one that allows minimizing costs) for the monthly shipment of about 50,000 titles on Blu-ray discs from warehouses to the company headquarters.

To solve the problem, in the file **Exercise 9.12 - Home video.xlsx**, you have the initial data: the number of Blu-ray discs (BD) that will be sent to each branch, the cost of shipment from each company's warehouse, and logistics constraints. We find these data already collected in the worksheet **Shipping costs**: the shipping costs in cells **B4:D15**, the number of Blu-ray discs requested by each branch in **E4:E15**, and the in-stock availability in **F17:H17**.

Several functions have already been set, to perform the calculations when the numbers of the Blu-ray discs to be sent are added:

- The sum of the Blu-ray discs required by each branch (in **E16**)
- The number of Blu-ray discs that will be sent to each branch (in **I4:I15**), from each warehouse (in **F16:H16**), and the total of the Blu-ray discs that will be shipped (**I16**)
- The difference in inventories (in **F18:H18**)
- The total availability of stock and inventory in **I17** and **I18** (the "&" operator was used to display "Tot" before the figure)
- Finally, the total costs in **I19** (with **SUMPRODUCT**)

You are asked to set the Solver so to help you find the correct numbers of Blu-ray discs to be shipped from each warehouse to minimize the cost of shipping, respecting the demands and logistical constraints. In particular:

- The number of Blu-ray discs to send to each branch (**E4:E15**) must be equal to the required number (**I4:I15**)
- The inventory (**F18: H18**) must be >=0

- The number of Blu-ray discs to be sent (**F4:H15**) must consist of integers

Apply appropriate formatting and organize the data in a suitable manner to ensure maximum readability, and give a neat and professional appearance to the worksheets.

Save the changes and close the file.

EXERCISE 9.13 - Hotel Eden (summary exercise)

The director of Hotel Eden, located in a famous ski resort in the Italian Alps, wants to analyze the data of reservations for the 2020-2021 winter season.

In the **Exercise 9.13 - Hotel Eden.xlsm**, there are three worksheets, namely, **Reservations**, **Prices**, and **Mortgage**. The **Reservations** worksheet contains the list of all the reservations confirmed until now for the winter season. The **Prices** worksheet contains the data of room prices based on time of year and the type of service; the **Mortgage** worksheet contains the data of a fixed rate mortgage offered by the bank to the Hotel Eden management to achieve some extension work. Values are expressed in euros.

To help the director of the Hotel Eden you are asked to:

1. Calculate, in a new column of the **Reservations** worksheet called **Days**, the days of stay of each customer, considering the expected check-in and check-out dates.
   In a new column of the same worksheet called **Season**, calculate in which season will be the stay, based on the check-in date.
   Calculate, in the same worksheet, the number of working days in the time span considered (using the oldest and most recent check-in date on the worksheet, using appropriate Excel functions).

2. In a new column of the **Reservations** called **Bill**, calculate using a single nested function, the bill that each customer will pay for the stay, on the basis of the season, the number of people, the days of stay, and the prices available in the **Prices** worksheet, considering that the price changes according to the season and to the type of service.
   In a new column of the **Reservations** worksheet called **Discounted bill**, apply a 20% discount to the bill of each customer for his stay if the following conditions are met:
   a) Check-in date before 2/15/2021
   b) Stay of at least 3 people
   c) Age equal to or less than 30 or equal to or greater than 55

Then, apply a formatting to the **Reservations** worksheet so that the values of the **Customer** column are automatically formatted with a fill of your choice when the bill for the stay has been discounted.

3. In a new worksheet called **Totals**, calculate the average days of stay of customers with age between 30 and 55 (bounds included), for each country of origin; make sure that the function returns the text "N.A." when it is not possible to calculate the average for a country.
In the same worksheet calculate, using a function, the total bill for customers with check-in date in March 2021, for each booking channel. Note: to perform the calculation use the values of the **Discounted bill** field.

4. The owners of the Hotel Eden have decided to achieve some extension work for a total cost of 5.1 million dollars. The operation had access to a state funding that fully reimburses the interest paid in the first three years of the mortgage.
Then, in the **Mortgage** worksheet calculate:
   a) The monthly installment of the fixed rate mortgage offered by the bank
   b) The total interests paid in the first 3 years of the mortgage
   c) The principal paid pack in the first 3 years of the mortgage

5. Using the data of the **Reservations** worksheet, create in a new worksheet called **Pivot**, a pivot table that shows the total bill spent by the Hotel Eden customers (use the values of the **Discounted bill** field) by check-in date and type of service. Then:
   - Group the check-in dates by months
   - Sort the values of the **Check-in date** field into the following order: Dec, Jan, Feb, Mar, Apr
   - Make sure that, for each value of the **Check-in date** field the age of each customer is displayed and grouped into 10 years' intervals (18-27, 28-37 etc.)
   - Modify the default row and column headings as "Months" and "Service"
   - Set the **Season** field as a filter of the pivot table

Finally, create a macro named Format, saving it in the current workbook that performs the following tasks in the **Reservations** worksheet:
- Apply a light fill color of your choice to the column headings
- Sort the list by the **Days** field, in a descending order
- APPLY the "dddd dd mmmm" format to the values of the **Check-in date** (excluding the heading)

Apply appropriate formatting and organize the data in a suitable manner to ensure maximum readability, and give a neat and professional appearance to the worksheets.

Save the changes and close the file.

EXERCISE 9.14 - TechMind contest (summary exercise)

TechMind, company selling technology products in the United States, has organized a contest for the first 300 customers who in the last week have spent more than 650 dollars in one of its stores. The contest involves:
- Extraction of 15 winners who will receive one of the prizes offered by TechMind (it is possible that a customer wins one or more prizes)
- Extraction of 20 winners who will receive a coupon equal to the expenditure they made, rounded to the nearest thousand dollars (it is possible that a customer win one or more prizes)
- The award of a coupon to all the 300 customers, on the basis of their age

In the **Exercise 9.14 - TechMind contest.xlsx** file, there are three worksheets, namely, **List**, **Winners**, and **Prizes**. The **List** worksheet contains the data of the 300 customers participating in the contest. The **Winners** worksheet contains the tables to enter the contest winners. The **Prizes** worksheet contains the list of 15 prizes with their full description and their value (in euros).

You are asked to solve the following five problems:

1. In the **Winners** worksheet, extract the winners of the 15 prizes in the table with the heading **Prize winners**. Use a function to generate, in the **Winner ID** column, a random number that represents the Customer IDs of the 15 winners of the contest.
   Once the Winner IDs have been generated, overwrite the formulas with the values corresponding to the results. By using the appropriate functions, show near to each Winner ID:
   - The name and surname of each winner
   - The description of each of the 15 prizes
   - The value of each prize

2. Still in the **Winners** worksheet, extract the winners of the 20 coupons in the table with the heading **Coupon winners**. Use a function to generate randomly, in the **Winner ID** column, the Customer IDs of the 20 winners of the contest.

Once the Winner IDs have been generated, overwrite the formulas with the values corresponding to the results. Using a single nested function, calculate the value of the coupon to give to each winner, rounding the value to the nearest thousand dollars.

3. Calculate the value of the coupon to be given to all participants in the contest based on their age. In a new column of the **List** worksheet with the heading **Coupon**, use a function that returns as a result, for each customer taking part in the contest:
   - 200 if the age is less than 23
   - 150 if the age is between 23 and 55 years (bounds included)
   - 100 if the age is greater than 55

   TechMind wants to send to each participant a personalized message with the amount of the coupon, the name of the store where they can pick it up, and the expiration date of the coupon (90 days after today).
   The message should be placed, for each participant, in a new column of the **List** worksheet with the heading **Message**.
   Taking as an example, the participant Dolly Moss of Charleston, born on 03/29/1974, and assuming that today's date is 1/19/2015, the message to be created using a single nested function should be the following: "Dear Dolly Moss, you can pick up at the Charleston store your $150.00 coupon, that you will be able to spend within Friday, 04/19/2021".

4. Apply a **formatting** to the **List** worksheet, so that the values of the **Name** and **Surname** field are automatically formatted with a fill of your choice when the age of the participant is greater than 55 years. The format should automatically change following any changes in the data.
   Copy the table of the **List** worksheet in a new worksheet called **Filter** and use an advanced filter to show, filtering the list in-place, the data of the participants:
   - Born in the sixties, who spent more than 3,000 dollars, and more than 50 purchases made during the last year
   - Born in the eighties, who spent more than 5,500 dollars, and less than 20 purchases made during the last year

5. In a new worksheet called **Analysis**, calculate for each state of the participants in the contest, the total expenditure and the average purchases made during the last year, both for participants born after 12/31/1980. Make sure that, when it is not possible to calculate the average purchases last year, the result is "No purchases made".

   Then, create a mixed chart with two axes in the **Analysis** worksheet, showing the total expenditure and the average purchases made last year, for each State. Add a meaningful title to the chart and to the two vertical axes, and move the chart to a new worksheet.

Apply appropriate formatting and organize the data in a suitable manner to ensure maximum readability, and give a neat and professional appearance to the worksheets.

Save the changes and close the file.

EXERCISE 9.15 - PluriPlast (summary exercise)

PluriPlast Ltd. is a manufacturing company producing spare parts for cars, especially plastic parts such as bumpers. The **Presses** worksheet of the **Exercise 9.15 - PluriPlast.xlsm** file contains data related to PluriPlast's molding floor machinery (injection presses for plastic molding). In particular, the Production line field shows the production line where the press is physically located. In the **Data** worksheet you can find two tables containing, respectively:
- the production capacity of each press model
- the productivity data of each production line of the last year

More precisely, the columns in these two tables have the following meanings:
- **Raw materials processed (Kg/hour)** shows the Kg of raw material that can be processed by each press model in an hour
- **Hours of production** shows the total number of working hours in the last year, for each production line.
- The column **% of exploitation** shows the average productivity of the production line, which is the percentage of hours of production during which the presses have actually processed the raw material into semi-finished products. (Productivity is never at 100% for many reasons: mold change, temporary press malfunction etc.)

The **Supply** worksheet contains the list of raw material orders placed in the last few months. The **Costs** worksheet contains data required to perform the analysis of costs originating from the use of the presses. Values are expressed in US dollars.

You are therefore asked to:

1. Calculate in a new column of the **Presses** worksheet, the quantity of raw material processed by each press in the year (in Tons), after having listed all the necessary data from the **Data** worksheet corresponding to each press model.

2. In a new column of the **Supply** worksheet called **Months for delivery**, calculate for each order the difference between the order date and the scheduled delivery, expressed as the number of months elapsed.

Then, in a new column called **Delivery delay (working days)**, calculate the number of working days elapsed between the scheduled and actual delivery dates. In case the delivery is yet to arrive, the function should return as a result an empty cell.

3. In a new worksheet named **Totals**, calculate for each supplier the total quantity ordered with delivery scheduled after December 31, 2016, based on the data available in the **Supply** worksheet.

   In the same worksheet, calculate the average quantity of the orders actually delivered, for each production line, in March 2017 alone; make sure that the message "No delivery" appears when a production line had no deliveries in the month of March.

   Copy the table of the **Supply** worksheet in a new worksheet called **Filter**, and use an advanced filter to show, filtering the list in-place, regarding the orders:
   - With quantity equal to or greater than 4,000, belonging to the B line and scheduled for delivery between 12/1/2016 and 3/31/2017 (bounds included)
   - With quantity greater than 5,000 belonging to the C line and scheduled for delivery after 2/15/2017

4. The management of PluriPlast decided to improve the production efficiency of the presses. The goal is to minimize the total cost incurred by the company through a more efficient use of the productive resources. The **Costs** worksheet contains a table with the following information for each press:
   - The hourly cost (**Press cost**)
   - Last year's working hours (**Hours of production**)
   - The maximum number of hours the press can work (**Maximum hours of production**)
   - The percentage of exploitation (**% of exploitation**)

   The management wants to identify the combination of working hours of each press for which the total cost incurred by PluriPlast is minimized. While looking for the solution, it is important to take into account the following conditions:

- The percentage of exploitation of each press must be between 55.6% and 81.5% (included)
- The hours of production should be integer numbers
- The hours of production of each press must be lower than or equal to the corresponding maximum hours of production
- The average percentage of exploitation must be greater than or equal to 68%

5. Using the data available in the **Supply** worksheet, create in a new worksheet called **Pivot**, a pivot table showing the total quantity by supplier and by scheduled delivery date. Then, group the scheduled delivery dates by months and set the **Line** field as filter of the table. Now, draft a pivot chart to represent the content of the pivot table, and then move it into a new worksheet.

   Finally, create a macro named **Format** (saving it in the current workbook) that performs the following tasks in the **Supply** worksheet:
   - Apply to the values of the column **Order date** (excluding the header) the format "dddd mm/dd/yyyy"
   - Apply a light fill color of your choice to the column headings (cells **A1:H1**)
   - Sort the list by scheduled delivery date (from the oldest to most recent one)

Apply appropriate formatting and organize the data in a suitable manner to ensure maximum readability, and give a neat and professional appearance to the worksheets.

Save the changes and close the file.

Unit 10. Database Functions and Chart Options

Topics of this unit:

Use and creation of templates, SUM function with 3D references, Database functions: DSUM; DMIN; DMAX; DCOUNT; DAVERAGE, commenting, Compare and Merge Workbooks command, advanced chart options.

This unit is specifically dedicated to the preparation of the ECDL/ICDL Advanced Spreadsheets certification.

EXERCISE 10.1 - *Payroll office*

You are a professional and you are collaborating with the reorganization of a small business payroll office (Logos3 Ltd.). Values are expressed in US dollars.

You are asked to:

1. Create a new template of expense statement for the employees of the company. Entries can be invented at will. Save the new template with the name **Expenses report.xltx**.
2. Look, among the models available in Excel, for an invoice template. Create a new workbook from the template chosen, and save the file with the name **Invoice.xlsx**. Customize the file created by the template using your own data (name etc.).

Apply appropriate formatting and organize the data in a suitable manner to ensure maximum readability, and give a neat and professional appearance to the worksheets.

Save the changes and close the file.

EXERCISE 10.2 - Sport shoes

Open the file **Exercise 10.2 - Sport shoes.xlsx**. The file contains the sales data for the last year of a company specialized in the production of running shoes. The company sells its products through a network of distributors in Spain, France, and Italy. In the three worksheets available in the file, you find data aggregated by type of shoes relative to the number of products sold in each of the three countries. The tables available in the three worksheets are identical, varying only for the number of products sold. The company asks for your help in processing the data, to obtain the values of the total sales of the year and some additional information.

You are asked to solve the following problems:

1. In the three worksheets, use the Excel functions to calculate the total number of shoes sold in each of the three countries, for each type of shoes and for each quarter.
2. Insert a new worksheet called **Europe Total**, which is an exact copy of one of the three existing sheets. Then, delete the sales values in the new worksheet (i.e., the contents of cells **B2:F7**), without affecting other elements of the worksheet.
3. In the worksheet **Europe Total**, calculate the total products sold by quarter and type, based on the data contained in the other three worksheets.
4. In the same worksheet, use a function to calculate the maximum value of sales achieved by different types of shoes (referred to the annual European total).
5. Use a function that shows as a result, with reference to the maximum value, the type of the corresponding product.

Apply appropriate formatting and organize the data in a suitable manner to ensure maximum readability, and give a neat and professional appearance to the worksheets.

Save the changes and close the file.

EXERCISE 10.3 - Budget

The CFO of a company that provides internationalization services to other companies is preparing the costs budget of the Milan and Paris offices. The file **Exercise 10.3 - Budget.xlsx** is a shared workbook that contains the costs budget of next year's four quarters of the Milan office: the CFO sent it to the Paris office director, who entered all the expected costs for his office and sent back the **Exercise 10.3 - Budget Paris.xlsx** file. Both files are shared.

You are asked to help the CFO solving the following problems:

1. Open the **Exercise 10.3 - Budget.xlsx**, compare and merge it with the **Exercise 10.3 - Budget Paris.xlsx** file. Then, save the merged workbook and remove the sharing.
2. Working on the merged workbook, calculate the total costs of each quarter for the Milan and Paris offices in cells **B15:I15**.
3. Enter a comment in cell **B1** with the text "Show to the CEO before approving" and make sure that it is always visible in the worksheet.
4. Activate and track changes so that all the changes made by any person and at any time are highlighted.

Apply appropriate formatting and organize the data in a suitable manner to ensure maximum readability, and give a neat and professional appearance to the worksheets.

Save the changes and close the file.

EXERCISE 10.4 - District competition

You work for the administrative office of New York Town Hall, which is responsible for processing data for the competitions for the recruitment of new employees and internal mobility. You have received the file **Exercise 10.4 - District competition.xlsx** that contains the raw data of 10 candidates that came to the last step of selection for an important position in your district, intended for employees of US cities' Town Halls around New York. You need to perform calculations to determine who is, based on numbers, the best candidate, and at the same time providing a flexible tool to the examination board to review the data before the final interviews.

Therefore, you are asked to:

1. Calculate the overall score, as follows:
    - The test score +
    - Ten points if the candidate is already an employee of the New York City Town Hall +
    - Ten points if the candidate was born in the seventies
2. Record a macro in the current workbook named **Sort_score** that allows sorting the list of the Candidates worksheet based on the overall score, in a descending order.
3. Record another macro named **Sort_name** that allows sorting the list based on the Last name and then Name together, both in ascending orders.
4. Assign the macros to two button or shapes on the worksheet.
5. Save the file in the correct format to contain macros, as **Exercise 10.4 - Competition macro.xlsm**.

Apply appropriate formatting and organize the data in a suitable manner to ensure maximum readability, and give a neat and professional appearance to the worksheets.

Save the changes and close the file.

EXERCISE 10.5 - Admission office

John Smith is the director of the university's admissions office and wants to analyze the admission requests coming from international students.
The file **Exercise 10.5 - Admission office.xlsx** contains the list of students who have applied for admission to the university in the last two weeks and who have passed the assessment test. The **Requests** worksheet contains, for each candidate, the name and surname, date of birth, high school final score, assessment test score, income bracket, and any scholarship that they could be awarded in case of registration.

You are asked to help John Smith to analyze the admission requests solving the following problems:

1. In the file you just opened track changes is activated: accept all the changes that were made in the document, then disable track changes and remove the sharing.
2. In a new worksheet called **Analysis**, calculate using a database function, the number of deserving students identified according to the following characteristics:
    a. Assessment test score greater than 910, income bracket equal to or less than 8, and possible scholarship, or:
    b. High school final score equal to or greater than 95, assessment test score greater than 960, and income bracket equal to or less than 5.
3. In the same worksheet, calculate the average assessment test score for the students born in 1996 or 1997; female, coming from Spain or Italy; and high school final score greater than 90.
4. Enter a comment in the cell with the heading **Scholarship** in the **Requests** worksheet, with the message "Check family income". Make sure the comment is always visible in the worksheet.
5. Using the **Historical** worksheet data, create a mixed chart with two axes that simultaneously show the number of economics bachelor students admitted and the average assessment test scores for each year considered. Then:
    a. Give a meaningful title to both axes
    b. Remove the chart title and the legend

c. Set 84 as the minimum value of the axis with the average admission test score
d. Set the following minimum and maximum values for the axis with the number the Economics bachelor students admitted: 2,100 and 2,800
e. Set the image **Exercise 10.5 - Books.jpg** as the background of the entire chart
f. Move the chart in a new worksheet

Apply appropriate formatting and organize the data in a suitable manner, to ensure maximum readability, and give a neat and professional appearance to the worksheets.

Save the changes and close the file.

EXERCISE 10.6 - Distributors

Open the file **Exercise 10.6 - Distributors.xlsx**. The file contains data for the distributors in Lombardy for the products of a paper mill.

You are asked to:

1. Compare and merge the files **Exercise 10.6 - Distributors.xlsx** with the file **Exercise 10.6 - Distributors - Copy.xlsx** (the values in cells **D5**, **D8**, and **D9** should be updated). Then, remove the "shared" option from the workbook.
2. Use a Database function to assess the situation of the distributors of Milan, Como, and Varese, which in recent times are delaying deliveries. The function must return one of the following results:
   - "Call urgently distributors in other cities" if the total of the shortage for the cities of Milan, Como, and Varese is over 5,000 pieces
   - "Wait for the next deliveries" if the shortage is less than 2,000 pieces
   - "Urge distributors" in other cases
3. Insert a chart that allows to view the data for the products ordered delivered and the shortage for all distributors in the list. Change the display unit of the values axis to thousands.

Apply appropriate formatting and organize the data in a proper manner to ensure maximum readability, and give a neat and professional appearance to the worksheets.

Save the changes and close the file.

EXERCISE 10.7 - Car dealer

Open the file **Exercise 10.7 - Car dealer.xlsx**. The file contains data for an Italian car dealer. In particular, the **Price list** worksheet contains the list of models for sale, whereas the **Sales** worksheet gives the detail of cars sold last month. In the **Loans** worksheet, finally, you find data related to some financing proposals that the dealer offers its customers.

You are asked to:

1. Insert in cell **B1** of the **Sales** worksheet a function that displays the current date, so that it is automatically updated.
2. Enter in cell **E1** a function that displays the month of the date present in **B1**.
3. Insert a function in the cells of the field "Base price" to show the price of each model, according to what is present in the **Price List** worksheet.
4. In the **Total Price** field, calculate the total price (base + accessories) for each car sold.
5. In the worksheet **Sales by model**, calculate the number of units sold and the total value of the sales for each of the models for sale. Sort the table according to the collection total in an ascending order.
6. In the same worksheet, create a column chart that represents the total revenues for each model. Make sure that the columns of the chart are represented by the image of a car (use the image file **Exercise 10.7 - Car.jpg** available among the files of the exercise).
7. In the **Loans** worksheet, enter a function that calculates the installment due from customers for different financing proposals, assuming a fixed rate and the monthly payment of installments to be paid at the beginning of the period.
8. In the worksheet **Sales by agent**, show the list of sellers of the dealer based on the data of the worksheet **Sales** and removing duplicates. Sort the list by last name of the seller in an ascending order. Then, calculate the total sales (in euros) for each one of the sellers.
9. In the same worksheet, calculate the possible bonus to be paid to each seller, according to the following rules:
    - If the total sales is less than € 100,000, no prize (the result must be a blank cell)

- If the total sales is between € 100,000 and 300,000, a prize of 1,000 euros
- If the total sales is greater than € 300,000, premium equal to 0.7% of total sales, rounded to the nearest hundred euro, with a maximum of 3,000 euros

Apply appropriate formatting and organize the data in a suitable manner to ensure maximum readability, and give a neat and professional appearance to the worksheets.

Save the changes and close the file.

EXERCISE 10.8 - Fruit & Vegetables

Open the file **Exercise 10.8 - Fruit and vegetables.xlsx**. You work for a small fruit and vegetables company, and the owner asks you to help automate billing processes.

You are asked to:

1. Make sure that in the merged cells **F8:H9**, it is possible to select one of the names of customers using a drop-down list in the cell. The list of customers is available in the **Customers** worksheet.
2. Make sure that, when the name of a customer is selected, the merged cells **F11:H11** automatically shows the customer's address. If no customer is selected, the cell should remain empty.
3. Similarly, the merged cell **F13:G13** should automatically show the customer city, and show nothing if no customer is selected.
4. The merged cells **F15:H15** must show, in the same way, the VAT number of the customer, and show nothing if no customer is selected.
5. Make sure that in cells **C19:C47**, it is possible to select one of the items in the catalog by means of a drop-down list in the cell. The list of items is available in the **Items** worksheet.
6. When one of the items is selected from the list, the corresponding cells in the same row (Code, Unit, and Price) should automatically be filled with the corresponding values. If no item is selected, the corresponding cells must not show anything.
7. Fill in cells **G19:G47** with useful formulas to calculate the total, given the price (which will automatically be populated by selecting the item), multiplied by the amount (which will be compiled by hand in column **E**), minus any percentage discount (which in case will be compiled by hand in column **H**). The formula must not show any value as long as you do not enter the ordered quantity.
8. Calculate in cell **G49**, the sum of the amounts due. In cell **G50**, calculate VAT (i.e., 22% of the sum just calculated). In cell **G52**, calculate the total including VAT.
9. Make sure that only the cells with the light blue filling can be completed once the sheet is protected. It must not be possible to modify all the other cells.

10. Record a macro in the current workbook to complete the following steps:
    - Delete the contents of the cells with light blue filling
    - Protect the sheet so that only the cells with the light blue filling can be selected and compiled. Do not insert any password
    - Select the cell where you will select the name of the customer
11. Assign the macro to a button or a shape on the worksheet.
12. Save the file in the correct format to contain macros, as **Exercise 10.8 - Fruit macro.xlsm**. Test the macro.

Apply appropriate formatting and organize the data in a suitable manner to ensure maximum readability, and give a neat and professional appearance to the worksheets.

Save the changes and close the file.

EXERCISE 10.9 - Albert Einstein

Open the file **Exercise 10.9 - Albert Einstein.xlsx**. The file shows the grades obtained in mathematics by students of the 4th H of high school Albert Einstein. Your friend Mario, in fact, teaches mathematics, but he is not very good with computers, and would like to automate a series of operations on the register of votes. For that, he asks for your help.

In particular, he asks you to help him solve the following problems:

1. Calculate, in cells **F4:F23** and **J4:J23**, the average per four months. In cells **K4:K23**, calculate the final average, as the average of the two four months' averages.
2. In cells **L4:L23**, enter a function that returns the final result achieved by each student, as follows:
   - **Promoted**, if the final average is greater than or equal to 6
   - **Postponed**, if the final average is between 5 (included) and 6 (not included)
   - **Rejected** if the final average is less than 5
3. Format the cells in the **Result**, so that the three results are automatically formatted with a different fill color (e.g., green for Promoted, yellow for Postponed, red for Rejected). Formatting should update automatically as data change.
4. Rename **Sheet1** with the name **4H**.
5. Record a macro in the current workbook, named **Sort_students**, which sorts students in an ascending order according to the last name, then the first name simultaneously. Save the file in the correct format to contain macros, as **Exercise 10.9 - Einstein macro.xlsm**.
6. Create a button using a WordArt at will, with the text "Sort". Insert a rectangle around the WordArt. Group the two objects. Assign the macro you just created to the grouped object.
7. Add a column after the **Name**, with header **Full name**. In this column, enter a function to return the last name and the name of each student together, separated by a space.
8. Insert a 3D grouped bar chart that shows the **Full names** of the students and the final average. Change the fill color of the bar relative to the highest average (e.g., in green) and to the lowest one (e.g., in red).

9. Set the image **Exercise 10.9 - Marks.jpg** as the chart background, setting transparency at 75%.
10. Insert a new column to the left of that of the last name. Add the header "Code" in cell **B3**. In cells **B4:B23**, enter a function to build a code for each student, in the following way (all caps):
    - The first 3 characters of the Last name
    - The number of characters of the Last name
    - The last 2 characters of the Name
11. Enter a comment in cell **B3**, which explains how the code has been created.
12. In cell **A26**, enter the text "List updated:". In cell **D26**, enter a function that states the current date, so that it is automatically updated as the date changes.
13. In cell **A27**, enter the text "Number of students:". In the cell **D27**, count the number of students in the class, using appropriate Excel function.
14. Protect the workbook so that it can only be opened by entering the password "GradEs4H".

Apply appropriate formatting and organize the data in a suitable manner to ensure maximum readability, and give a neat and professional appearance to the worksheets.

Save the changes and close the file.

EXERCISE 10.10 - SEFCO (summary exercise)

SEFCO Inc. (Security, Efficiency, & Control) is a company producing control valves for electric and hydraulic systems.

The file **Exercise 10.10 - SEFCO.xlsm** has two worksheets, namely, **Valves and New prices**. The **Valves** worksheet contains the data of a sample of 300 control valves produced by SEFCO with their price, the quantity sold last year, and the stock available; the **New prices** worksheet contains the tables needed to calculate the sample new control valves prices based on the quantity sold and list price.

You are asked to solve the following problems:

1. In a new column of the **Valves** worksheet called new price, calculate using a single nested function, the new price to be applied to each product of the sample, considering that the new price must be calculated on the basis of data available in the **New prices** using the following formula:
   List price + Price increase − Discount based on quantity sold
   Apply a formatting to the cells of the Product ID column, so that the product ID is automatically formatted with a fill of your choice when the product price is one of the 50 products with higher new price. The format should automatically change if there is any change in the data.

2. In a new worksheet called **Totals**, calculate the number of products with the list price between 1,000 and 5,000 euros, for each type of product.
   In the same worksheet, also calculate the total quantity sold last year for products priced between 1,000 and 5,000 euros, for each type of product.

3. Using the data of the **Totals** worksheet, create a mixed chart with two axes showing simultaneously the number of products and the quantity sold, both with the list price between 1,000 and 5,000 euros. Once the chart has been created:
   - Give a significant name to the chart and the axes
   - Remove the legend
   - Set a maximum value of 35 in the axis showing the number of products

- Set a maximum value of 90,000 in the axis showing the quantity sold, and visualize data in thousands (without modifying the data source)
- Apply the **Exercise 10.10 - Valve.png** image as a background of the chart

4. In the **Valves** worksheet calculate, using the database functions:
    - The total quantity of products of the Butterfly Valve sold last year, with a list price greater than 5,000 euros and a stock of at least 50
    - The average stock of products of the Butterfly or Ball Valve types, with price between 2,000 and 6,000 euros (bounds included) and with a quantity greater than 3,000 sold last year
    - The highest and lowest quantity of products sold with list price greater than 4,000 euros and a stock between 50 and 150 (bounds included)

5. Enter a comment in the cell with the heading "Product ID" of the list of the **Valves** worksheet with the message "Update all the IDs", and make sure that the comment is always visible in the worksheet.
Activate the sharing of the workbook and track changes.

Apply appropriate formatting and organize the data in a suitable manner to ensure maximum readability, and give a neat and professional appearance to the worksheets.

Save the changes and close the file.

Unit 11. Financial Applications

Topics of this unit:

Financial functions: YIELD, XIRR, TBILLYIELD, NPV, IRR, XNPV, PPMT, IPMT, date and time functions: COUPPCD, COUPDAYBS, COUPDAYS, COUPNCD statistical functions: MEDIAN, STDEV.S, VAR.S, COVARIANCE.S, CORREL, KURT, SKEW, SLOPE, INTERCEPT, RSQ, Data analysis add-in.

EXERCISE 11.1 - Premium Bonds

A client of Premium Investments, the company you work for, asked you to evaluate the yield of two fixed-rate bonds before deciding on the best one to buy. Open the **Exercise 11.1 - Premium bonds.xlsx** file. The **Bond** worksheet contains all the data required for the evaluation: current purchase price, redemption date, coupon frequency, face value, and annual nominal yield. Both bonds are in euros.

You are asked to:

1. Set the current date as purchase date of both bonds, so that it is automatically updated day by day.
2. Calculate in cells **B10** and **E10**, the value of the periodic coupon (semi-annual in both cases).
3. Using Excel functions, calculate in cells **B13:B15** and **E13:E15**, the last coupon date, the days since the last coupon and the accrued interest. Where requested, use the "Actual/360" basis.
4. With the available data calculate the yield to maturity of both bonds in cells **B18** and **E18** using the REND function.
5. Apply a format to cells **B18** and **E18** so that the cell corresponding to the highest yield to maturity is highlighted with a fill color of your choice. The format should automatically change following any changes in the gross amount values.
6. Create the table with all the coupon maturities and the cash flows dates for both bonds starting from cell **A24**, keeping in mind that in the financial functions it is important that all cash inflows are positive and all cash outflows are negative. Use a function to calculate each date of the two bonds.
7. With the new available data calculate the yield to maturity of both bonds in cells **B19** and **E19** using the XIRR function.
8. Apply a format to cells **B19** and **E19** so that the cell corresponding to the highest yield to maturity is highlighted with a fill color of your choice. The format should automatically change following any changes in the gross amount values.

Apply appropriate formatting and organize the data in a suitable manner, to ensure maximum readability, and give a neat and professional appearance to the worksheets.

Save the changes and close the file.

EXERCISE 11.2 - Coupon&Coupon

You are asked to evaluate the yields of zero coupon bonds. Open the **Exercise 11.2 - Coupon&Coupon.xlsx** file. The **Zero coupon** worksheet contains all the data required to evaluate two zero coupon bonds with different maturities. Both bonds are in euro.

You are asked to:

1. Calculate the yield to maturity of a zero coupon bond with maturity date lower than 12 months: in cells **B4:B6** are specified the purchase date, the redemption date and the market price of the bond.
2. With the available data calculate the yield to maturity of the bond in cell **B8** using the TBILLYIELD function.
3. Create the table with all the coupon maturities and the cash flows dates starting from cell **A15**, and then calculate the yield to maturity of the bond using the XIRR function.
4. Apply a format to cells **B8** and **B10** so that the cell corresponding to the highest yield to maturity is highlighted with a fill color of your choice. The format should automatically change following any changes in the gross amount values.
5. Evaluate now the yield of the second zero coupon bond, with maturity date greater than 12 months. Insert the current date as purchase date, so that it is automatically updated day by day.
6. With the new data calculate, using a function, the yield to maturity of the bond in cell **E8**.

Apply appropriate formatting and organize the data in a suitable manner, to ensure maximum readability, and give a neat and professional appearance to the worksheets.

Save the changes and close the file.

EXERCISE 11.3 - FRN

Open the **Exercise 11.3 - FRN.xlsx** file. The **Bond** worksheet contains the data of two floating rate notes, both linked to Libor rates and purchased on 6/25/2017, of which you have to calculate the yield to maturity. The annual nominal coupon yields are calculated as follows:
- Bond 1: **2% + 2 * Libor 3M**
- Bond 2: **2.3% + Libor 6M**

The **Libor** worksheet contains the expected values of the Libor 3M and Libor 6M rates for the period 2017-2030.

You are asked to:

1. Calculate the value of the next semi-annual coupon (with respect to 6/25/2017) for each of the two bonds in cells **B10** and **E10**, using a function returning automatically the right Libor rate based on the year of the purchase date.
2. Using Excel functions, calculate in cells **B13:B15** and **E13:E15** the last coupon date, the days since last coupon and the accrued interest. Where requested, use the "Actual/360" basis.
3. Create the table with all the coupon maturities and the cash flows dates for both bonds starting from row **23**, following these instructions:
    a. Use Excel functions to calculate the dates of all cash flows (but the first one, corresponding to the purchase date)
    b. Make sure that 44 dates are automatically calculated (up to row **66**). When you need less than 44 dates, the cells not used must be blank
    c. To calculate each cash flow (but the first one) use a single nested function considering the right Libor rate based on the year and adding the redemption value (face value) to the last cash flow
    d. Make sure that 44 cash flows are automatically calculated (up to row **66**). When you need less than 44 cash flows, the cells not used must be blank
4. With the available data, calculate the yield to maturity of the two bonds in cells **B19** and **E19**.
5. Apply a format to cells **B19** and **E19** so that the cell corresponding to the highest yield to maturity is highlighted with a fill color of your choice.

The format should automatically change following any changes in the gross amount values.

Apply appropriate formatting and organize the data in a suitable manner, to ensure maximum readability, and give a neat and professional appearance to the worksheets.

Save the changes and close the file.

EXERCISE 11.4 - Reverse floater

Open the **Exercise 11.4 - Reverse floater.xlsx** file. The **Rev_floater** worksheet contains all the data required (cells **B4:B11**) to calculate the yield to maturity of a reverse floater bond: issue date, purchase date, redemption date, purchase price, face value, coupon frequency. In the worksheet, you can find also the expected values of the Euribor 3M rate for the period 2017-2026.
The reverse floater bond to evaluate has the following characteristics:
- The value of the first two coupons after the issue date is fixed, calculated based on a 6.25% interest rate
- The value of each following coupon is calculated with the formula **5.15% - 2 * Euribor 3M**
- The bond has an annual minimum yield of 2%: then each result of the previous formula lower than 2% must be replaced with 2%

Calculation of the yield to maturity of the bond must be done with respect to the purchase date (11/18/2017).

You are asked to:

1. Using Excel functions, calculate in cells **B14:B16** the last coupon date, the days since last coupon and the accrued interest. Where requested, use the "Actual/360" basis.
2. Create the table with all the coupon maturities and the cash flows dates of the bond starting from cell **A24**. Use Excel functions to calculate the dates of all the cash flows (but the first one). To calculate each cash flow use a single nested function, returning the right Euribor 3M rate based on the year of each cash flow.
3. With the available data, calculate the yield to maturity of the bond in cell **B19**.

Apply appropriate formatting and organize the data in a suitable manner, to ensure maximum readability, and give a neat and professional appearance to the worksheets.

Save the changes and close the file.

EXERCISE 11.5 - *Capital budgeting*

The company you work for wants to invest in new technologies. Open the **Exercise 11.5 - Capital budgeting.xlsx** file, containing three worksheets with data regarding three different investment plans to evaluate. All cash flows are in US dollars.

You are asked to:
1. In cell **B22** of the **Project1** worksheet, calculate using a function, the net present value of the project, considering that in the Years column are the numbers of years starting from the beginning of the project (t0 = now, t1 = at the end of first year, t2 = at the end of second year, etc.).
2. Using a function, calculate in cell **B24** the internal rate of return of the project
3. In the **Project2** worksheet, you can find data regarding the second project to evaluate, consisting in a series of cash flows in given dates. Using the most appropriate functions, calculate the net present value and the internal rate of return of the project in cells **B22** and **B24**.
4. Using data tables, create a table in the **Project2** showing the net present value of the project for all the possible values of the annual discount rate from 1% to 20% (1% changes).
5. Using a single function, calculate in cell **F19** of the **Project3** worksheet the net present value of the project considering that:
   a. For each year, a different interest rate should be applied, using data in the table of columns **I** and **J** of the worksheet. Use a function to return the discount rate values in the cells of column **C**
   b. Each cash flow has to be discounted for the whole period using the same discount rate (e.g., a cash flow occurring in 2023 has to be discounted with a 6.25% discount rate without considering other interest rates)
   c. If necessary, create new columns to facilitate calculations

Apply appropriate formatting and organize the data in a suitable manner to ensure maximum readability, and give a neat and professional appearance to the worksheets. Save the changes and close the file.

EXERCISE 11.6 - Super Leasing

You work for Super Leasing, a small office and furniture leasing company. Open the **Exercise 11.6 - Super Leasing.xlsx** file. In the **Plan** worksheet, you have to create the structure of a repayment plan that can be used for any leasing contract.

You are asked to:

1. Calculate the monthly payment and the total cash outlay of a leasing contract in cells **B6** and **B7**, based on the following data (to be inserted in cells **B1:B4**):
   a. Principal: 90,000 US dollars
   b. Annual interest rate: 7.55%
   c. Term (years): 4
   d. Residual value: 15,000 US dollars
2. Calculate now the leasing amortization schedule starting from cells of row **13**, calculating in each row the number of the monthly installment, balance, principal, interest, and monthly installment. In creating the schedule, keep in mind that the tool should allow amortization schedules with a maximum term of 8 years; when the term in lower or equal to 8 years, cells not needed must be empty.
   In order to facilitate the creation of the amortization schedule, some cells have already been filled.
3. Set cell **B1** so that the maximum principal is equal to 110,000 US dollars
4. Set cell **B3** so that the maximum possible term is 8 years
5. Protect the worksheet (without any password) so that the only cells that can be edited are those in cells **B1:B4**.

Apply appropriate formatting and organize the data in a suitable manner to ensure maximum readability, and give a neat and professional appearance to the worksheets.

Save the changes and close the file.

EXERCISE 11.7 - *Stock performance*

Open the **Exercise 11.7 - Stock performance.xlsx** file. The **Stock** worksheet is empty and should be filled with the historical quotes of stocks of the Alpha company to analyze. All quotes are in euros.

You are asked to:
1. Import in the **Stock** worksheet, starting from cell **A1**, the file **Exercise 11.7 - Stock.txt**, containing the historical quotes of stocks of the Alpha company.
2. Create a line chart of the Adj close field values, move it to a new worksheet named **Chart** and give it a meaningful title.
3. In a new worksheet named **Stats**, using Excel functions and data of the Adj close field, calculate:
    a. mean
    b. median
    c. standard deviation
    d. variance
    e. minimum value
    f. maximum value
    g. kurtosis
    h. skewness

   Consider that the Alpha stock quotes are a sample of all the historical quotes.
4. Now, calculate the descriptive statistics of the Adj close field using the Data Analysis tool. Save the results of this operation in a new worksheet named **Stats2**.
5. In two new columns of the **Stock** worksheet with the headings **SME30** and **SME90**, calculate the 30 and 90 days simple moving average.
6. Create a line chart of the Adj close, SME30 and SME90 fields (consider only the values of the 2015–2017 period), move it to a new worksheet named **SMEChart**, and give it a meaningful title.

Apply appropriate formatting and organize the data in a suitable manner to ensure maximum readability, and give a neat and professional appearance to the worksheets. Save the changes and close the file.

EXERCISE 11.8 - Stock analysis

Open the **Exercise 11.8 - Stock analysis.xlsx** file. The worksheets **Stock1**, **Stock2**, and **Stock3** are empty and should be filled with the historical quotes of stocks of Alpha, Gamma, and Delta companies to analyze.

You are asked to:

1. Import in the **Stock1**, **Stock2**, and **Stock3** worksheets, starting from cell A1, the **Exercise 11.8 - Stock_1.txt**, **Exercise 11.8 - Stock_2.txt**, and **Exercise 11.8 - Stock_3.txt** files containing the historical quotes of Alpha, Gamma, and Delta companies.
2. In a new column of the **Stock1** worksheet with the heading %**Alpha**, calculate the percentage variation of the stock price with respect to the previous day (use data of the Adj close field). Do not calculate the variation of 1/1/2007.
3. In the **Stock2** worksheet, calculate the mean and the standard deviation of the Gamma stock using the values of the Adj close field (consider that the Gamma stock quotes are a sample of all the historical quotes).
4. Create a chart of the Gamma stock quotes that shows its evolution, average quote, average quote plus the standard deviation, and the average quote minus the standard deviation. Move the chart in a new worksheet named **Chart**.
5. Copy the cells of columns **A** (Dates field) and **F** (Adj close field) of the **Stock1** worksheet corresponding to the 1/2/2014 to 1/12/2017 period in a new worksheet named **Norm**. Give the heading Alpha to the column with the Alpha stock quotes in the **Norm** worksheet.
6. Then, use a function to return in **C** and **D** columns of the **Norm** worksheet (with the headings Gamma and Delta) the quotes of Gamma and Delta stocks from the **Stock2** and **Stock3** worksheets of the 1/2/2014 to 1/12/2017 period. Note: dates of Gamma and Delta stocks quotes could be different from those of the Alpha stock, so make sure that if the function does not find the searched value it replaces it with the value of the previous date.
7. In three new columns of the **Norm** worksheet with the headings **NAlpha**, **NGamma**, and **NDelta** normalize the quotes of the three stocks, setting the value 100 for the 1/2/2014 date.

8. Create a chart showing the evolution of the normalized quotes of the three stocks. Move the chart in a new worksheet named **Chart2**.

Apply appropriate formatting and organize the data in a suitable manner to ensure maximum readability, and give a neat and professional appearance to the worksheets.

Save the changes and close the file.

EXERCISE 11.9 - Regression

Open the **Exercise 11.9 - Regression.xlsx** file. The **Stock** and **Index** worksheets are empty and should be filled with the historical quotes of the Omega company and main market index.

You are asked to:
1. Import in the **Stock** worksheet, starting from cell **A1**, the **Exercise 11.9 - Stock.txt** file, containing the historical quotes of the Omega stock.
2. Import in the **Index** worksheet, starting from cell **A1**, the **Exercise 11.9 - Index.txt** file, containing the historical quotes of the market index.
3. Copy the cells of columns **A** (Date field) and **F** (Adj close field) of the **Index** worksheet in a new worksheet named **Analysis**. Give the heading **Index** to the column with the Alpha stock quotes in the **Analysis** worksheet.
4. Then, use a function to return in column **C** of the **Analysis** worksheet (with the heading Omega) the quotes of the Omega stock from the **Stock** worksheet. Note: dates of the Omega stock quotes could be different from those of the index, so make sure that if the function does not find the searched value, it replaces it with the value of the previous date.
5. In the **Analysis** worksheet the following indicators, calculate:
    a. mean (of the Omega stock)
    b. standard deviation (of the Omega stock)
    c. covariance between the Omega stock (y) and the index (x)
    d. correlation between the Omega stock (y) and the index (x)
6. In the **Analysis** worksheet, calculate using Excel functions, the slope, intercept, and R-squared of the regression line between the Omega stock (y) and index (x).
7. Create a scatterplot of the Omega and index quotes; then, show the regression line equation and the R-squared value on the chart.

Apply appropriate formatting and organize the data in a suitable manner to ensure maximum readability, and give a neat and professional appearance to the worksheets.

Save the changes and close the file.

EXERCISE 11.10 - Market Analysis (summary exercise)

You work for Market Analysis, a financial consulting company. You were asked to answer the requests of some clients who need to evaluate some investments. To help those clients, make their investment choices you have at your disposal the **Exercise 11.10 - Market Analysis.xlsx** workbook containing:
- The data of two bonds to evaluate (**Bonds** worksheet)
- The data of an investment in the real estate market (**Investment** worksheet)

All values are in euros.

You are asked to solve the following questions:

1. Calculate, in the **Bonds** worksheet, the yield to maturity of the two bonds, a fixed rate bond and a zero coupon bond. If necessary, create the table with all the maturity dates and the cash flows for both bonds. In this case, make sure that the tables are ready to be used also for other bonds and that the cells do not show error messages, but empty cells. If necessary, use the "Actual/360" basis.
Then, apply a format to cells wherein the yield to maturity of the two bonds has been calculated such that the cell corresponding to the highest yield to maturity is highlighted with a fill color of your choice. The format should automatically change following any changes in the gross amount values.

2. The **Investment** worksheet contains data of an investment to purchase a property and rent it to a company. Evaluate the investment calculating the net present value and the internal rate of return.
Then, find for which value of the discount rate the net present value is equal to 100,000 euros.

3. In two new worksheets named **Stock** and **Index**, starting from cell **A1**, the **Exercise 11.10 - Stock.txt** and **Exercise 11.10 - Index.txt** files, contain the historical quotes of the Alpha company and the market index.

In the **Index** worksheet, calculate in a new column with the heading **SME50**, the 50 days simple moving of the index (use data of the Adj close field).

In the **Index** worksheet, calculate using Excel functions and data of the Adj close field, the following descriptive statistics:
   a. mean
   b. median
   c. standard deviation
   d. kurtosis
   e. skewness

Consider that the imported quotes are a sample of all the historical quotes.

4. Copy the cells of columns **A** (Dates field) and **F** (Adj close field) of the **Index** worksheet in a new worksheet named **Analysis**. Assign the heading **Index** to the column with the index quotes in the **Analysis** worksheet.

   Use a function to show in column **C** of the **Analysis** worksheet (with the heading **Alpha**), the quotes of the Alpha stock from the **Stock** worksheet. Note: dates of Alpha stock quotes could be different from those of the index, so make sure that if the function does not find the searched value, it replaces it with the value of the previous date.

5. Perform a regression analysis in the **Analysis** worksheet: calculate, using Excel functions, the slope, intercept, and the R-squared of the regression line between the Alpha stock (y) and index (x).

   Create a scatterplot of the Alpha and index quotes; then, show the regression line equation on the chart.

Apply appropriate formatting and organize the data in a suitable manner to ensure maximum readability, and give a neat and professional appearance to the worksheets.

Save the changes and close the file.

Unit 12. Data Analysis and Reporting

Topics of this unit:

Lookup & reference functions: INDEX, INDIRECT, OFFSET, information function ISNUMBER, data validation, form control setting (checkbox and scroll bar), options of the Paste command (Paste as linked picture).

EXERCISE 12.1 - Turnover

Open the **Exercise 12.1 - Turnover.xlsx** file. The **Turnover1**, **Turnover2**, and **Turnover3** worksheets contain data regarding the turnover of a company selling its products in six different countries. The **Lists** worksheet contains the list of the six countries, list of the products considered, and list of the year for which the turnover is available. Both bonds are in euros.

You are asked to:
1. Use a function in cell **B2** of the **Turnover1** worksheet that shows the value of the turnover of product 3 in Spain.
2. Use a function in cell **B2** of the **Turnover2** worksheet that shows the value of turnover of product 4 in Brazil in 2015. The function must consider the four tables of the worksheet simultaneously and must allow choosing the table in which the value should be searched.
3. In the **Turnover3** worksheet, set cells **B1**, **B2**, and **B3** such that it is possible to select from three different drop-down menus the country, year, and product desired. In the **Lists** worksheet, you can find the list of the countries, of the years and products.
4. In cell **B5** of the **Turnover3** worksheet, use a function to show automatically the turnover value corresponding to the country, year, and product selected in the three drop-down menu in cells **B1**, **B2**, and **B3**. Also, make sure that when no values have been selected in cells **B1**, **B2**, or **B3**, no error messages are shown but an empty cell.

Apply appropriate formatting and organize the data in a suitable manner to ensure maximum readability, and give a neat and professional appearance to the worksheets.

Save the changes and close the file.

EXERCISE 12.2 - Orders

Open the **Exercise 12.2 - Orders.xlsx** file. The **Orders** worksheet contains a sample of 100 orders of a company operating in the food and beverage sector. All monetary values are in euros.

You are asked to:

1. Create a new worksheet named **Query**; then, insert the heading **Order ID** in cell **A1**. In cell **A2**, make sure it is possible to select an order ID from a drop-down menu with all the order IDs from the **Orders** worksheet. Use the order IDs list copied in a new worksheet named **Lists** and sort in an ascending order.
2. In cell **B1** of the **Query** worksheet, make sure it is possible to select from a drop-down menu one of the headings of **Orders** worksheet table. Put the fields list in the **Lists** worksheet.
3. Use a function in cell B2 of the **Query** worksheet to return automatically the value of the **Orders** worksheet table corresponding to the order ID and the field heading selected. Note: in setting the function, do not modify the table, move, or copy the data and columns.
4. Also, make sure that when no values are selected in cells **A2** or **B1** (or both), in cell **B2** an error message is not shown but a blank cell.

Apply appropriate formatting and organize the data in a suitable manner to ensure maximum readability, and give a neat and professional appearance to the worksheets.

Save the changes and close the file.

EXERCISE 12.3 - *Gifts*

Open the **Exercise 12.3 - Gifts.xlsx** file. The company you work for has decided to ship some gifts to some of its clients. The **Gifts** worksheet contains the list of products to ship.

You are asked to:
1. Set the cells of a new column of the **Gifts** worksheet with the heading **Company** such that it is possible to enter the name of a company to ship the gift to in each of the column. Make sure that it will not be possible to enter in the cells duplicate values. In case a duplicate value is entered, the following error message must pop up: "Company already entered. Ship the gift to another company".
2. Set the cells of a new column of the **Gifts** worksheet with the heading **Number of packs** such that in each of them it is possible to enter, for each company, the number of packs to be shipped. The values entered in the cells must respect the following rules:
    a. The values entered must be numeric
    b. The total of packs shipped to all the companies must be equal or lower than 30
3. Set the cells of a new column of the **Gifts** worksheet with the heading **Product ID** such that it is possible to enter the ID of the shipped product in each of the column. The values entered in the cells must respect the following rules:
    a. The entered ID must be at a maximum 6 characters long
    b. No spaces are allowed in the entered IDs
    In case a wrong ID is entered, the following error message must pop up: "Enter IDs at a maximum 6 characters long and without spaces"

Apply appropriate formatting and organize the data in a suitable manner, to ensure maximum readability, and give a neat and professional appearance to the worksheets.

Save the changes and close the file.

EXERCISE 12.4 - Product IDs

Open the **Exercise 12.4 - Product IDs.xlsx** file. The **Products** worksheet contains a short list of orders of the Food&Beverage ltd., a company selling food and beverage products all around the world. Its management decided to change all product IDs, and wants to understand how to avoid the entry of wrong IDs in the worksheet.

You are asked to:

1. Set the cells of a new column of the **Products** worksheet with the heading **Product ID 1**, such that only IDs beginning with "PR18" can be entered. Then, set the error message "Enter only IDs beginning with PR18". After having set the cells, try entering some IDs of your choice to test how it works.
2. Set the cells of a new column of the **Products** worksheet with the heading **Product ID 2**, such that only IDs beginning with "PR18" or "XN7W" can be entered. Then, set the error message "Enter only IDs beginning with PR18 or XN7W". After having set the cells, try entering some IDs of your choice to test how it works.
3. Set the cells of a new column of the **Products** worksheet with the heading **Product ID 1**, such that only IDs beginning with "PX2D" or "5GS3" and with a maximum length of 10 digits can be entered. Then, set the error message "Enter only IDs beginning with PX2D or 5GS3 and with a maximum length of 10 digits". After having set the cells, try entering some IDs of your choice to test how it works.

Apply appropriate formatting and organize the data in a suitable manner to ensure maximum readability, and give a neat and professional appearance to the worksheets.

Save the changes and close the file.

EXERCISE 12.5 - Counties and offices

Open the **Exercise 12.5 - Counties and offices.xlsx** file. The **Employees** worksheet contains a list of some employees that should be transferred to work in another office. The **Offices** worksheet contains the lists of the offices of the company.

You are asked to:

1. Set the cell of a new column of the **Employees** worksheet with the heading **Country**, such that in each cell it is possible to select from a drop-down menu one of the three countries in which the company has an office (Italy, USA, or France).
2. Then, set the cell of a new column of the **Employees** worksheet with the heading **Office**, such that in each cell it is possible to select from a drop-down menu one of the available offices. Note: the list of the available offices in these drop-down menus must change based on the Country selected in the cell of the Country field: for example, selecting Italy in the Country field, in the drop-down menu of the Offices field, only the values Florence, Milan, Naples, Rome, and Turin must be shown.
3. Now, set the cells of a new column of the **Employees** worksheet with the heading **Departure**, such that in each of them it is possible to insert the departure date of the employee for the new office based on the following rules:
    a. The date inserted is valid only if it is not a Sunday or a Saturday
    b. The date of departure must be maximum 30 days after today's date
    Set in the cells the following error message: "Departure dates should be maximum in 30 days (no Sundays and no Saturdays)".

Apply appropriate formatting and organize the data in a suitable manner to ensure maximum readability, and give a neat and professional appearance to the worksheets.

Save the changes and close the file.

EXERCISE 12.6 - Variable period

Open the **Exercise 12.6 - Variable period.xlsx** file. The **Period** worksheet contains a list of some employees that should be transferred to work in another office. The **Offices** worksheet contains the lists of the offices of the company.

You are asked to:

1. Make sure in cell **F2**, it is possible to select from a drop-down menu one of the months available in column **A**.
2. Make sure in cell **F2**, it is possible to select from a drop-down menu one of the following numbers, without creating a list in a new worksheet or in the **Period** worksheet: 3, 6, 9, 12. Each of these numbers represents the months to add to the month selected in cell **F2** to obtain the period to analyze.
3. Use a function in cell **F5** to calculate the total sales in the selected period. For example, selecting June 2014 as the starting month and selecting 3 as the number of months, the period to consider to sum the sales is June 2014 to September 2014 (extremes included).

Apply appropriate formatting and organize the data in a suitable manner to ensure maximum readability, and give a neat and professional appearance to the worksheets.

Save the changes and close the file.

EXERCISE 12.7 - Choose your category

Open the **Exercise 12.7 - Choose your category.xlsx** file. The **Products** worksheet contains data regarding the sales, costs, and profit margin of some products of the company you work for. All values are in US dollars.

You are asked to:

1. Set cell **I1** such that it is possible to select from a drop-down menu one of the following values: Sales, Costs, and Margin. If possible, do not use references to cells of the worksheet, but enter the values using appropriate Excel functionality.
2. In column **E** of the **Products** worksheet, use a function to show for each product the value corresponding to the value selected in cell **I1**.
3. Create a chart that, based on the value selected in cell **I1**, shows the values of the sales, costs, or margin. Selecting another value in cell **I1** must change the values shown in the chart automatically.

Apply appropriate formatting and organize the data in a suitable manner to ensure maximum readability, and give a neat and professional appearance to the worksheets.

Save the changes and close the file.

EXERCISE 12.8 - Chart with bands

Open the **Exercise 12.8 - Chart with bands.xlsx** file. The **Sales** worksheet contains your company sales values in 2017. For 2017, the management has decided two sales levels within which to consider satisfactory monthly sales (100 and 200).

You are asked to:

1. Create a chart that shows the company sales in 2017 (line chart) and the range between the minimum and maximum levels (area chart).
2. Set a checkbox that, if selected, shows the range between the minimum and maximum levels in the chart, and that, if not selected, hides it.
3. Move the checkbox inside the chart box.

Apply appropriate formatting and organize the data in a proper manner to ensure maximum readability, and give a neat and professional appearance to the worksheets.

Save the changes and close the file.

EXERCISE 12.9 - Scroll bar

Open the **Exercise 12.9 - Scroll bar.xlsx** file. The **Products** worksheet contains data of 100 products of your company. The management asks you to create a tool that allows comparing 10 products at a time.

You are asked to:

1. Copy, starting from cell **L2**, the headings of the main table, from Product to Value 5. The values of the headings must remain linked to the main table cells.
2. Insert a scroll bar (Form control), which allows you to show ten values. Link the form control to a cell of the worksheet.
3. Use a function to return, starting from cell **L3**, the name of the product and the values of the other fields. Make sure that the values of ten rows are shown based on the value of the scroll bar.
4. Create a line chart that shows the current values of the Value 2 and Value 5 fields of the ten products selected.

Apply appropriate formatting and organize the data in a suitable manner to ensure maximum readability, and give a neat and professional appearance to the worksheets.

Save the changes and close the file.

EXERCISE 12.10 - Dashboard (summary exercise)

You have to create a dashboard to compare the macroeconomic data of some European Countries. Open the **Exercise 12.10 - Market Analysis.xlsx** workbook containing:

- The **Gdp**, **Debt**, **Debt-gdp**, and **Pop** worksheets, with data regarding the Gdp, public debt, public debt/Gdp ratio, and population in the European countries and in some other countries
- The **Control** worksheet, containing lists and data to be used as reference to create the dashboard
- The **Calc1** worksheet containing the table to perform the main calculations
- The **Dashboard** worksheet, ready to host the dashboard

You are asked to solve the following questions:

1. In cells **C4**, **F4**, and **C13** of the **Calc1** worksheet, make sure it is possible to select from a drop-down menu one of the countries of the list found in the **Control** worksheet. Select a country of your choice in each of the three cells. In cell **F13**, make sure it is possible to select from a drop-down menu the value "European Union (27 countries)" or the value "Euro area (17 countries)". Select one of the two values.
Then, make sure that in cells **C5**, **F5**, **C14**, and **F14** appear the text "Value in" followed by the reference year (set in cell **B4** of the **Control** worksheet).

2. Use a function to show in cells of the ranges **C6:C9**, **F6:F9**, **C15:C18**, and **F15:F18** of the **Calc1** worksheet, the values corresponding to Gdp, public debt, public debt/Gdp ratio, and population of the selected Countries. Where needed, use a function to select the right column, without entering the number of the column in the function.

3. Make sure that in the cell ranges **I6:I9**, **I15:I18**, and **I24:I27** are shown the names of the Countries selected in cells **C4**, **F4**, **C13**, and **F13**. The values must change automatically when new values are selected in the cells.

Using a function, show in cells of the ranges **J6:R9**, **J15:R18**, and **J24:R27** the values corresponding to the Country and to the year selected. Where needed, use a function to select the right column, without entering the number of the column in the function.

4. In a new worksheet named **Calc2**, create a table showing the public debt/Gdp ratio of the different Countries in the reference year and the corresponding values, sorted from the greatest to smallest. Use the list of the Countries of the Control worksheet and a function to return the values corresponding to each Country. In a new worksheet named **Calc3**, create a table showing the public debt/Gdp ratio of the different Countries in the reference year and the corresponding values, sorted from the smallest to greatest.
Apply to the values of each table a formatting using data bars.

5. Create two line charts using data of the **Calc1** worksheet showing the evolution of Gdp and of the public debt/Gdp ratio; then, move them to the **Dashboard** worksheet.
Copy the **B1:F18** area of the **Calc1** worksheet and paste it as a linked picture in the **Dashboard** worksheet. Then, copy and paste as image in the **Dashboard** worksheet data of the ten Countries with the highest public debt/Gdp ratio ("Top 10") and data of the ten Countries with the lowest public debt/Gdp ratio ("Bottom 10").
Organize the data in the **Dashboard** worksheet such that they are readable.

Apply appropriate formatting and organize the data in a suitable manner to ensure maximum readability, and give a neat and professional appearance to the worksheets.

Save the changes and close the file.

SECTION 2.

COMMENTS AND FUNCTIONS

Comments and functions unit 1

EXERCISE 1.1 - Quarterly sales (commented)

Tools needed to solve the exercise:

SUM function, percentage calculation, chart creation.

Comment point 1

To calculate the totals you need to use the SUM function. The totals per region may be calculated in cells **F2:F4**, as adding new columns of data (or calculations) to a table should be done without leaving empty columns inside the table.

This would prevent Excel to consider the table in a unified way and cause problems with features such as sorting, filtering, or pivot tables, which work on tables meant as unitary element.

Therefore, placing the totals by geographical area in cells **G2:G4**, for example, leaving column **F** empty, would be a mistake. In cell **F1**, it is necessary to insert a header of the new column of data or calculations that you are entering, for example "Total" (or "Annual sales total per region"). To make this happen, you can insert a SUM function in cell **F2**, with the syntax =SUM(B2:E2); then, copy it into the cells below with the Copy and Paste commands, or by using the auto fill feature.

The totals per quarter should be calculated under the table, and in this case, it is necessary to leave a blank line between data and totals.

In case of sorting or filtering of the table, in fact, the totals of the column (as in this case the totals per quarter) would not be considered by Excel as a part of the table, whereas any row total (as in this case the totals for geographical area) or data added in new columns should be sorted and filtered along with the other columns.

That is why, the previous totals were entered in column **F** and not in **G**. The totals per quarter should be calculated again using a SUM function. In addition, in this case it is appropriate to insert a label in cell **A6** (e.g., "Total" or "Total per quarter") to facilitate the readability of data. The formula to enter in cell **B6** is =SUM(B2:B4).

Be careful not to include in the sum also cell **B5**, which is empty but not part of the data to be added. Once inserted the correct formula in **B6**, you can copy it to cells **C6:F6** using the Copy and Paste commands or the auto fill feature, to calculate the totals of the other quarters and, in **F6**, the grand total (that is the annual total required by the exercise).

Comment point 2

The calculation of the percentage of each value with respect to the total is made with a simple formula of division between the value and the total. It is not necessary to use any Excel function.

Then, after entering in the cell **G1** a label (e.g., "% incidence"), you can proceed in **G2** calculating the percentage of the value of Italy (in cell **F2**) with respect to the total (contained in **F6**).

The division formula necessary to perform this calculation is therefore =F2/F6. To copy the formula into the cells below, to calculate the percentage of the other two geographical areas, in this case it is necessary to use the logic of Excel absolute references. If we insert the formula in **G2**, as we have written, and copy it in the cells below, we would get in cells **G3** and **G4** a #DIV/0! error.

This depends on the fact that, as both references **F2** and **F6** are relative, when the formula is copied to other cells the references are updated depending on where the formula is copied.

In this case, however, the reference to cell **F6** should remain fixed when the formula is copied into the cells below (i.e., should always refer to cell **F6** that contains the total), whereas the reference **F2** should be free to change (becoming **F3** and **F4** in the cells below, to indicate correctly the values of the respective regions).

To make sure that the reference to cell **F6** does not change if copied down, it is necessary to make it partly absolute, by blocking the reference to row **6** (creating what is called a mixed reference). The correct formula to be written in **G2** is therefore =F2/F$6.

The dollar sign is what it takes to make an absolute reference, and in this case it is used only on the part of the reference (row **6**) to be blocked to allow copying down the formula. The addition of an extra dollar before the **F** in this case would not affect the formula (i.e., writing =F2/$F$6), meaning that it would not change the result, but it would be completely useless to also block the column reference.

Comment point 3

To create a chart you should first select the data to display and their labels (which will form the legend or the description of the categories of the chart). In this case, therefore, it is necessary to select cells **A1:A4** and, with the CTRL key, cells **F1:F4** (cells **A1** and **F1** can be omitted). Then, choosing the appropriate command to insert a pie chart, it will be created with the sections corresponding to the three selected values and the legend that shows the three regions.

If you also select cell **F1**, the chart will show a title corresponding to the contents of that cell (e.g., "Total"). The title can be customized to be clearer (e.g., "Sales per region").

If the title is not shown, you can add it with the appropriate command, and then customize it.

To show the value corresponding to each section of the pie you can use the Add Data Labels command. The labels of a pie chart can show different elements including the value or the percentage corresponding to each section.

Comment about formatting and organizing data

The formatting of data on the worksheet is an important part of the operations in Excel. Formatting, in fact, is not just coloring or adding borders, but is the whole set of operations that allows making data more readable, thus the worksheet more effective.

To start, you need to consider the problem of numerical formats. What do the numbers in the worksheet represent? Units, currency, or other? In this case, the exercise clearly indicates that they represent US dollar currency; then, you need to format properly all the cells containing numeric values (except percentages), choosing the Currency format with $ symbol (and two decimal places, which are shown by default choosing this format).

For the cells that contain the percentage values (**G2:G4**), the best format is just the Percentage format, which multiplies the value shown in the cell by 100 and displays the % symbol. So, for example, the value 0.522887 (or similar) shown in cell **G2** is displayed as 52%. In this case, it is appropriate (although usually not strictly necessary) to display at least one decimal place, as all the numbers resulting from the calculation of the percentage are not integers. In cell **G2**, then 51.3% will be displayed.

In addition to the number formatting, which is essential, you should make sure that the table headings are highlighted with respect to the data. Therefore, cells **A1:G1** should be formatted to differentiate them from those below. It is enough to use a bold format, but if you prefer you can also use fill colors or font colors and borders to make the effect more attractive from a visual standpoint, remembering that the ultimate goal is to maximize readability and not coloring the worksheet as much as possible. Even the totals can be highlighted, for example with a simple bold.

You should not use too many different styles (bold, italic, underline, etc.), many different colors, and borders to avoid creating an effect of confusion that would worsen the readability of the worksheet instead of improving it.

Also concerning the chart, it is necessary to ensure the readability: legend and data labels should be clearly visible, the title should be clear and well located, and size of the chart should be appropriate. Also in this case it is not purely a matter of appearance, but these operations are needed to ensure a perfect readability to data represented in the chart.

Comment about data backup

Once that you have carried out all the operations required from the exercise, you need to save changes to the file (using the Save command).

This operation should be carried out constantly, not only if and when expressly requested from the exercise, but as a good practice in one's work with Excel (and with any computer application), so as to secure the work from any problem.

However, once you have done the exercise, to store the complete file you need to save your changes and, at this point, you can close the file.

EXERCISE 1.2 - Four elections (commented)

Tools needed to solve the exercise:

SUM function, percentage calculation, chart creation.

Comment point 1

To solve this question, simply insert a SUM function in cell **B11**, and then copy it into the cells by side.

Comment point 2

It is a simple column chart, to be inserted after selecting cells **A3:A9** (labels) and **E3:E9** (values).

Comment point 3

To calculate the percentage values you must use the formula of division, paying attention to absolute references. As we want to write a single formula in cell **B15** and then copy it to any other cell in the table, we will have to lock the reference to the row that contains the total creating a mixed reference, as follows: =B3/B$11 (where **B3** contains the value of Party1 in 2000 election, while **B11** contains the total number of votes for the same election).

In this case, the addition of a second dollar symbol, before the **B** of the reference **B$11**, would not be irrelevant but wrong: by inserting it, we would prevent the possibility to copy the formula horizontally (we should rewrite the formula in **C15, D15,** and **E15**).

By entering the dollar symbol only before the reference of the row (**11**), the formula is not only correct, but can also be copied both horizontally and vertically, completing the table in a few seconds.

The principle of the absolute, relative, and mixed references in Excel is critical and should be fully understood, especially when you need to work with large amounts of data. It is impossible to rewrite a formula 100, 1,000, or a million times, and that is why Excel provides a system that, if understood, allows to write a single formula and copy it to all the other similar cells, may them be 3, 3000, or 3 million.

EXERCISE 1.3 - Income (commented)

Tools needed to solve the exercise:

SUM, MAX, MIN, AVERAGE functions, chart creation, percentage calculation.

Comment point 8

In this case, the calculation of the percentage values always refers to a single total, which is the grand total calculated at the point 6, located in the **Income** worksheet. The formula for calculating the result in cell **B2** of the **Percentages** worksheet is =Income!B2/Income!$B$17.

The worksheet name followed by the exclamation point is necessary because cells **B2** and **B17** referenced in the formula are located in another worksheet (**Income**).

The absolute reference **$B$17** (not mixed as in other earlier exercises) in this case is necessary because the formula must be copied both to the right and downward, while the denominator of the division must always refer to the same cell **B17**.

That is why, you must use the double dollar sign, to block both the row and the column reference. Any other solution (**B17**, **$B17**, **B$17**) would produce error messages or incorrect results when the formula is copied from cell **B2** of the **Percentages** worksheet to all other cells of the table.

EXERCISE 1.4 - Cinema

Tools needed to solve the exercise:

Sorting, SUM, MAX, MIN, AVERAGE, COUNTA functions, simple formulas (division), percentage calculation, chart creation.

EXERCISE 1.5 - Courses (commented)

Tools needed to solve the exercise:

SUM, MAX, MIN, AVERAGE, ABS, IF functions, simple formulas (subtraction), percentage variation calculation, chart creation.

Comment point 2

To calculate the variation in the number of students, it is sufficient to use a subtraction. In cell **D4**, the formula will be =C4-B4. We do not need any absolute reference: in this way, by copying the formula downward you will get the desired results for all courses and the total.

Comment point 3

To calculate the percentage variation, it is necessary to use a more complex formula than the previous one, but still without the use of any function. The general syntax of the formula to calculate the percentage variation requires a

subtraction between the most recent and oldest values, then a division by the oldest value. In this case, therefore, the formula in **E4** will be =(C4-B4)/B4.
Alternatively, having already calculated in **D4** the numerical value corresponding to the variation, you can use the formula =D4/B4. Then, the result should be formatted with a percentage format, and the formula may be copied down without the addition of any absolute reference.

Comment point 4

To transform numeric values, positive or negative, in their absolute values (all positive numbers), the Excel function ABS can be used. The formula to be used in **F4** is =ABS(E4) that transforms any numerical value contained in cell **E4** in a positive number; then copy down the formula through cell **F9**.

Comment point 6

To make sure that Excel returns a certain result in case a specific condition occurs, and another if the condition does not occur, you can use the IF function.
In this case, the function to be entered in cell **B17** is =IF(C11>B11,"Increase","Decrease").
Therefore, if the condition inserted in the logical_test argument (C11>B11) occurs, the function returns the contents of the value_if_true argument (i.e., the text "Increase").
Otherwise (that is, when **C11** is less than or equal to **B11**), it returns the contents of the value_if_false argument, i.e., the text "Decrease".
Clearly, the logical_test of the function could also be set up to check if the value in cell **D11** (or **E11**) is positive, with the same arguments value_if_true and value_if_false.
In this case, simplified to allow you to review the IF function in a linear way, the event that the number of members of the second year is the same as that of the previous year is not covered.
Or rather, this hypothesis is compared with the case "Decrease", which occurs when the enrollments of the second year are not higher than those of the former.
In the exercises of the following units, the IF function will be used in a finer (and more complex) manner, to consider all possible cases (even when there are more than two) and provide an adequate outcome.

Comment point 7

In this case, the column chart must represent two sets of data, corresponding to the values of each course for the two years under consideration.

The values of the two series should be shown side by side in the chart, so they can be compared (as requested by the exercise).

The selection of the data required to create this chart corresponds to the cell range **A3:C9**. Category labels, values, and names of the series are all close, then you can select them at the same time, without using the CTRL key.

Among the different versions of the column chart, you must choose one with "grouped" columns and not "stacked". The latter type of chart makes it possible to compare the total values of the series rather than individual values (in fact the differences are less visible), whereas the exercise asks to compare the values of each course in the two years considered.

Sometimes, the fact that the category labels or names of the series in a chart are made by numbers (as in this case with the years which represent the name of the series) can be a problem, as Excel may not correctly distinguish the components to represent in the chart and the ones to use as labels or names, giving a misrepresentation.

In this exercise, rather simple, the problem does not arise. In the upcoming exercises, there will be more complex cases, in which it will be necessary to act in a different way.

EXERCISE 1.6 - Population by age (commented)

Tools needed to solve the exercise:

SUM, MAX functions, percentage variation calculation, chart creation.

Comment point 4

The exercise asks to create a column chart that represents the total value of the population from 2005 to 2014.

The special feature in the creation of this chart is that the category labels (that is, those that should be shown below the horizontal axis of the chart and that indicate what each bar represents) are numbers, which is the years 2005 to 2014, as the data to be displayed (the values of the population). In these cases, Excel is often not able to understand autonomously the difference between the values to display and the labels.

If you respected the general rule, which suggests selecting data and labels before you create the chart, you would get a chart that incorrectly contains two sets of data: the correct one (the values to display) and an incorrect one (the years, that are not data but labels).

When the labels are numbers (often years), it is best to select only the data to display (without labels), then create the chart and finally add the labels at a later time.

To do this, in the exercise, you should select only cells **B106:K106**, then create the chart.

Once you have done this, you need to add the category labels (that would otherwise remain shown as numbers from 1 to 10) using the "Select data" command, then using the Edit button in the horizontal axis labels and selecting the cells **B3:K3**.

Once you have done this, the chart can be completed with a proper title (e.g., "Italian population, 2005-2014").

The legend may then be deleted as, having a single set of data, the title of the chart is illustrative and the legend is redundant.

Comment point 5

The problem of the labels consisting of numbers is repeated in the next step, further complicated by the fact that in this case not only the category labels are numbers (years), but also the names of the series (that is what should appear in the legend: 30, 60, 90).

Also, in this case, therefore, the most efficient solution deviates from the general rule that would lead to select all items before creating the chart (data, category labels, and names of the series).

As in the previous point, it is better to select only data (cells **B34:K34**, **B64:K64**, **B94:K94**, holding down the CTRL key after selecting the first cell range), then create a line chart.

After this, you need to change the labels of the horizontal axis, exactly as above (the cells to be selected are **B3:K3**).

Finally, you need to change the names of the series (which are currently displayed in the legend as Series1, Series2, and Series3) so as to show 30, 60, and 90.

To do this, you can always act in the Select Data dialog box, using the Edit command in the Legend Entries (Series) pane.

In the Series name box of Series1 you must type 30, then 60 for the Series2, and 90 for Series3.
Once you have done this, you need to add a title to the chart (e.g., "Trend comparison by age").

EXERCISE 1.7 - Sales data (commented)

Tools needed to solve the exercise:

SUM function, simple formulas (subtraction, multiplication, division), percentage variation calculation, sorting, chart creation.

Comment point 4

To separate the receipts and VAT you must consider that the receipts are made from the turnover + VAT, which in this case is 22% of the same turnover. The operation necessary to obtain the turnover from receipts is thus a division of the receipt by 122, then multiplying by 100. The formula in **F2** in this case will therefore be =C2/122*100 (alternatively it could be =C2/1.22). Once you have the result in **F2** you can copy the formula in the cells below to get the correct results, without the inclusion of any absolute or mixed reference.

To calculate VAT in cell **G2**, you can multiply the turnover by 22%, as in the solved file (=F2*22%), or subtract the revenues from receipts (=C2-F2): the result will be the same.

Comment point 5

To sort the list by the percentage variation it is sufficient to select any single cell among those that contain the values considered (**E2:E13**), then use the quick sort command on the Data tab: Sort largest to smallest.

To sort it is not necessary nor appropriate to select all the cells containing the percentage variation, nor even select the entire table or other parts of it.

Comment Formatting and organizing data

The formatting in this case must cover all the values of receipts, variation, turnover, and VAT, which should be expressed in Currency format with the symbol $ (including related totals).

The percentage variation should instead be expressed in a percentage format, preferably with one or two decimal places.

The headers of the table should be highlighted with respect to the data: just use bold, or you can also use fill colors and borders as long as you do not overdo it by making the table messy and difficult to read. Even the totals can be highlighted with bold formatting.

EXERCISE 1.8 - Exams (commented)

Tools needed to solve the exercise:
Operation on worksheets (adding, deleting, renaming), COUNTA, COUNT, AVERAGE, MAX, MIN, functions, simple formulas (subtraction), chart creation.

Comment point 3
To calculate the number of exams in the program, you can use a COUNTA function referring, for example, to the names of the exams available in the Data worksheet: =COUNTA(Data!B2:B25).
To calculate the number of passed exams, you can use a COUNT function referring to cells that may contain the grades obtained: =COUNT(Data!C2:C25). In this way, numbers actually present in the cells will be counted (i.e., the grades), and the result will update when more grades will be added. The result would be the same, in this specific case, using the COUNTA function instead of COUNT. The latter function, however, is more correct, as you need to count the grades (which in this case are surely numbers) it excludes with certainty – in addition to the empty cells – any type of value (e.g., text) that may be inserted, voluntarily or not, in the cells affected by the count.
To calculate the number of exams to take, you can simply perform a subtraction between the number of exams in the program and the number of exams taken. It would be also possible to use the COUNTBLANK function, topic of the exercises of later units.
To calculate the average grade, you can use an AVERAGE function on the cells that contain or may contain the grades: =AVERAGE(Data!C2:C25). In this way, adding other grades, the average result will be updated accordingly.
To calculate the number of exams with honors, you can use a COUNTA function in cells that may contain the "com laude" statement: =COUNTA(Data!D2:D25).

To calculate the maximum and minimum grades you can use the MAX and MIN functions on the cells that contain the grades: =MAX(Data!C2:C25) and =MIN(Data!C2:C25).

EXERCISE 1.9 - Balance sheet

Tools needed to solve the exercise:
Simple formulas (subtraction), SUM, IF functions, chart creation.

EXERCISE 1.10 - TV shows

Tools needed to solve the exercise:
SUM, IF functions, percentage calculation, chart creation.

EXERCISE 1.11 - Cigarettes

Tools needed to solve the exercise:
AVERAGE, MAX, IF functions, chart creation.

EXERCISE 1.12 - Families

Tools needed to solve the exercise:
MAX, MIN, AVERAGE functions, sorting, chart creation.

EXERCISE 1.13 - Beer and wine

Tools needed to solve the exercise:
AVERAGE, IF functions, percentage variation calculation, chart creation.

EXERCISE 1.14 - Three elections

Tools needed to solve the exercise:
SUM, ABS, IF functions, percentage calculation, percentage variation calculation, sorting, chart creation.

EXERCISE 1.15 - Athletics (commented)

Tools needed to solve the exercise:
Numerical formatting, MAX, IF functions, sorting, chart creation.

Comment point 4
To make sure that the IF function returns a blank cell, you must use the syntax "" (double quotes without anything in between), in this case in the argument value_if_false.

Please note that in a case like this, or in which the result of a function is an empty cell (""), even if the cell does not show any value, by performing a count with a function COUNTA the cells are however counted, because in the cell there is a result of a function. In contrast, using a COUNTBLANK function these cells are not counted because, although they appear empty, they are not.

EXERCISE 1.16 - Bills

Tools needed to solve the exercise:
SUM function, percentage calculation, chart creation.

EXERCISE 1.17 - Turnover analysis

Tools needed to solve the exercise:
IF function, percentage variation calculation, sorting, chart creation.

EXERCISE 1.18 - US and foreign sales (commented)

Tools needed to solve the exercise:
SUM function, chart creation.

Comment point 2

For the chart in step a), it is sufficient to create a simple column chart (either 2D or 3D) selecting cells **B3:G3** and **B7:G7**. In addition to adding a meaningful title, some appropriate customizations are: the elimination of the legend (often useless when a column or bar chart represents only one set of data), and the change in the number format on the value axis so that it does not show any decimal place (in fact the repetition of "00" for each tick mark is not significant and makes the whole chart less readable). Moreover, with the aim to improve readability, you can change the main unit of measurement from 50,000 (default) to 100,000. All these options can be changed by clicking the right mouse button on the item to change (e.g., the value axis) and choosing the format [name of the item selected].

For the chart in step b), it is sufficient to select cells **B3:G4**, then insert a line chart (e.g., lines with indicators). Among the possible customizations, as well as adding a meaningful title, you can evaluate the elimination of legend and change of the number format on the value axis to show no decimal place, as in the chart in step a).

The cells to select for chart c) are those of the range **A3:G5**. In this case, you should use a chart with stacked values (e.g., a column chart, as suggested in the text of the exercise) to highlight the total value of the US and abroad markets, while maintaining the display of two values in each column of the chart. Also here, some customization on the value axis can be useful for readability (main unit and number of decimal places, as in the chart in point a)). The legend in this case is fundamental to understand which color corresponds to the values of the US market and the foreign market.

For chart d), you must select cells **A4:A5** and simultaneously, with the CTRL key, **H4:H5**. Then, insert a pie chart. You must then customize the data labels, choosing to show the percentages on the sections of the pie. The legend can either be maintained or not displayed (but in this case, the name of the category should be shown on the sections of the pie, which in this case corresponds to US and abroad).

The two charts in e) have the same data source, i.e., cells **A3:G5**, which should be selected before you insert the chart. It is in both cases a common line chart; it is the subsequent customizations that differentiate the e)/i from e)/ii chart. In the first case, the different sales growth between the US and abroad must be highlighted: this is achieved by restricting the maximum of the scale of values, or by setting minimum and maximum values that are as close as possible, while ensuring the proper display of the chart. In this case, it is appropriate, for example, to set the maximum (i.e., the highest value shown on the vertical axis) at 400,000. In the second chart, on the contrary, if you want to flatten the difference it is necessary to raise the maximum limit, e.g., to 1,000,000. You can also move the legend below the chart, to flatten it even more. As can easily be seen from the solved file, the effect of the two charts is very different although they represent the same data.

EXERCISE 1.19 - Rainfall (commented)

Tools needed to solve the exercise:
AVERAGE, SUM, IF functions, chart creation, operations on worksheets (rename), percentage calculation.

Comment about formatting and organizing data
The empty/unused worksheets, such as **Sheet3** in this file, must be deleted to ensure proper organization and readability of the data.

EXERCISE 1.20 - UFO

Tools needed to solve the exercise:
Sorting, SUM, MAX, MIN, AVERAGE functions, chart creation, operation on worksheets (rename), percentage calculation.

EXERCISE 1.21 - Accidents

Tools needed to solve the exercise:
Sorting, SUM, MAX, AVERAGE, COUNTA. IF functions, chart creation, operations on worksheets (rename), percentage calculation.

EXERCISE 1.22 - Music sales (commented)

Tools needed to solve the exercise:
SUM, IF functions, operations on worksheet (rename), chart creation, percentage calculation, numerical formatting, sorting, page setup.

Comment point 10
The page print settings are accessible from the tab Page Layout (group of commands Page Setup / Orientation icon and group of commands Scale to Fit / Width and Height icons) or File - Printer / Orientation and No scaling / Fit sheet ... buttons.

EXERCISE 1.23 - Seven dwarfs

Tools needed to solve the exercise:
Simple formulas (subtraction), percentage variation calculation, IF, MAX, MIN, AVERAGE, COUNTA functions, chart creation.

EXERCISE 1.24 - Expenses (commented)

Tools needed to solve the exercise:
Simple formulas (addition, multiplication), SUM function, percentage calculation, chart creation.

Comment point 5
To create a pie chart representing the percentage values compared with a total you do not need the values already in percentage, nor the total value: just select the values to be displayed (in this case cells **J18:L18**) with their labels (in this case **J4:L4**) and create the chart. Once you create the pie, you can display data labels, on each section, as percentages (which are calculated automatically by Excel for this type of chart, without the need to calculate them in the worksheet).

EXERCISE 1.25 - Three musketeers

Tools needed to solve the exercise:
Operation on worksheets (rename), SUM, MAX, MIN, AVERAGE, IF, COUNTA functions, numerical formatting, chart creation, percentage calculation.

EXERCISE 1.26 - Murders

Tools needed to solve the exercise:
SUM, AVERAGE, MAX, MIN, IF, COUNTA functions, percentage variation calculation, chart creation, percentage calculation.

EXERCISE 1.27 - City council (commented)

Tools needed to solve the exercise:
MAX, MIN, SUM, IF functions, percentage calculation, chart creation.

Comment point 1
To calculate the maximum and minimum one must consider that the cells containing the data are not contiguous with each other and that the column headers already present in the sheet make sense that in columns **C, E, G,** and **I** data will be inserted that do not have to enter in the calculation of minimum or maximum.
Therefore, in this case, the arguments of the formula are the individual cells and not a selection of one single range of cells: in **J4** the formula will be =MAX(B4,D4,F4,H4), whereas in **K4** it will be =MIN(B4,D4,F4,H4).

EXERCISE 1.28 - Parliamentary groups

Tools needed to solve the exercise:
SUM, MAX, MIN, ABS, IF functions, percentage calculation, percentage variation calculation, chart creation.

EXERCISE 1.29 - Regional chief towns (commented)

Tools needed to solve the exercise:
Sorting, chart creation, AVERAGE, ABS, IF functions, simple formulas (division, multiplication), percentage calculation, operation on worksheets (rename, delete).

Comment point 1
Formatting numeric data and column headings as the first activities on **Sheet1**, in the logic of organizing the data to ensure maximum readability, when you copy the table from lines **3** to **9** (post sorting) on **Sheet2** you create a table already organized, which then requires no additional formatting work.

Comment point 4
The population density measures how many people live in one square kilometer, which in **L6** will be =I6/J6.

Comment point 5
It is an application of the IF function wherein the test involves the use of the symbol ≥ that in Excel is designated as >=; the formula in cell **M6** is therefore =IF(L6>=1000,"High density","-").

Comment point 7
The calculation of square kilometers of urban green can be done in two ways, on the basis of the available data. In the first case, you can utilize the information of the number of square meters of greenery per inhabitant and the number of inhabitants per municipality; as the simple multiplication provides the data in square meters, it is also necessary to divide the result by 1,000,000 to switch from sqm to km^2. The formula in **O6** is then: =E6*I6/1000000

In the second case, you can multiply the percentage of green compared with the total surface area per the overall km^2, but given that in column **D** values are not numbers between 0 and 1 (the % Excel format) but numbers between 0 and 100, data must be transformed in real percentage dividing by 100. The formula in **P6** is then: =D6/100*J6.

Comment point 8
Enter the average in cell **Q28** for consistency with the existing content in the row.

Comment point 9
As the reference of the cell containing the average must not vary in the formula, it is necessary to use a mixed reference, blocking with $ the line coordinate, the **R6** cell is therefore:
=IF(Q6<Q$28,"Acceptable approximation","").

EXERCISE 1.30 - Population (commented)

Tools needed to solve the exercise:
Percentage variation calculation, SUM, MAX, MIN, AVERAGE, IF functions, chart creation.

Comment point 1
To format numbers in the required manner, you need to choose the Number type of formatting, setting the comma as thousands separator and no decimal places. This can be done using the commands in the Home tab of the Ribbon, in the Numbers group.
To calculate the percentage variation, you need to set the formula of subtracting the values of the most recent and oldest, all divided by the oldest value. In the specific case, the formula will be =(M4-B4)/B4. You must then set the Percentage format with two decimal places.

Comment point 2
To calculate the total population in the first year you must set a SUM function in cell **B33** (or lower, still leaving at least one blank row between the data and the total), and then copy it to the right until column **M**, corresponding to the last year considered. The function to be included in **B33** is =SUM(B4:B31), recalling that in the syntax of Excel colons mean "from ... to" and are used to indicate cell ranges. The formula does not require the use of absolute references, as it must be copied to the right and the range **B4:B31** will be adapted from Excel, according to the system of relative references, to consider the data in each column of the year considered. In cell **A33**, it is appropriate to include a header that allows understanding the data that we have calculated (e.g., "Total population").
The same applies to the MAX and MIN functions, which can be inserted in the rows immediately subsequent to that in which the total was inserted. The function to be inserted in **B34**, for example, will be =MAX(B4:B31), whereas

in **B35** it will be =MIN(B4:B31). After this, you can copy the formulas to the right until column **M**.

The exercise also asks to calculate the number of countries considered. In this case, it is necessary to use the COUNTA function, which just serves to count the number of values, which can be numeric, text, or dates (while, e.g., the COUNT function counts only the numeric values of a list). It is therefore possible to insert the function, e.g., in cell **B37**:
=COUNTA(A4:A31).

Comment point 3

To create the chart, you must select the data to be displayed. As already experienced in other earlier exercises, as the labels of the value axis are numbers (the years 2002 to 2013), it is better not select them before creating the chart (as you would usually do, if they were not numbers). The initial selection will therefore be the range **B33:M33**, which is the one that contains the total population for each year. Once you have selected these cells, you can insert the chart with an appropriate command, choosing a line chart as required (e.g., the "lines with indicators" variant).

To ensure that the chart displays on the value axis the corresponding years (and not the generic indication 1-2-3 etc.), you must use the Select Data command, then edit the labels of the horizontal axis and select the cells that contain the years (**B3:M3**).

The chart should then be moved to another worksheet. To do this, you can use the "Move Chart" command, available in the contextual menu that you get by right clicking on the chart. Here, you can choose the option New sheet and type the name "EU Population Chart".

The difference between this method and, e.g., the insertion of a new worksheet and subsequent displacement of the chart with the Cut and Paste commands resides in the fact that with the Move Chart command you obtained a worksheet that contains only the chart (not displaying the usual grid with the cells).

Conversely, by inserting a worksheet and then moving the chart you get a more traditional display (with the cells and the graphic overlay), more useful if you need to enter more data in the worksheet.

To make sure that the legend will not be shown, simply click it and press the Delete key on the keyboard.

A generic title should already be shown on the chart, then just customize it by typing a meaningful title (e.g., "Total EU population"). In case the title is not shown, it can be added to the chart with the appropriate commands, which can be found on the Ribbon.

To set the minimum value on the axis value (the vertical axis of the chart, in this case), you can use the Format Axis command, which is obtained with a right click on the axis, and then enter the value 475000000 in the box provided. To change the format of the line, finally, also, in this case a right mouse click on it is sufficient and the choice of the command Format Data Series. Here, you find all the available line options, including color and shading, as required by the exercise.

Comment point 4

In the **Population 15-24** worksheet, you need to insert an AVERAGE function in cell **B33** (again separated by at least one row from the data), as follows: =AVERAGE(B4:B31). The function can then be copied to the right to obtain the result for each one of the years considered.

In column **N**, after entering the header **Youngsters 2013**, you must enter an IF function (in cell **N4**) with the following syntax: =IF(M4>=M$33,"Many young people","Few young people"). The test of the function evaluates whether the percentage of young people of Belgium in the year 2013 (cell **M4**) is greater than or equal to the average of 2013 (cell **M33**). If it is true, the function returns the result "Many young people", otherwise "Few young people". The cell reference **M$33** is mixed (with absolute reference on the row 33) so that by copying the formula downward, the comparison is always made with the cell **M33**. If the reference was relative, in fact, by copying the formula it would become **M34**, **M35**, and so on.

The reference to cell **M4**, instead, is relative because when copying the formula downward, it will have to change to consider in each row the value of the corresponding country.

Comment point 5

In cell **H3** of the **Forecast** worksheet, you need to insert a header, such as "Variation 2010-2040". In cell **I3**, you can type "Variation 2010-2060".

In the cells below, it is necessary to calculate the percentage variation, using the formula already seen: (the newest value−oldest value)/oldest value.

In this case, the "newest" value is that of 2040 in column **H**, and that of 2060 in column **I**, while in both cases the "oldest" value is the one of 2010. The formula in **H4** will therefore be =(E4-B4)/B4, while in **I4** it will be =(G4-B4)/B4. Both formulas do not require absolute references and can be copied downward as they are, to return the required results.

To create the chart, in this case, you can select all the elements regularly before inserting the chart (ideal procedure).

The correct selection includes therefore the value axis labels (**A4:A30**) and at the same time, holding down the CTRL key, the values to be displayed (cell **H4:I30**).

The type of chart to choose is "grouped columns" (either 2D or 3D), which allows to compare the values of the two selected series (in this case the change from 2020 to 2050 and that from 2020 to 2070), showing them side by side in the column representation.

To change the position of the legend, it is sufficient to right click on it and choose "Format Legend", then change the appropriate option.

Formatting to be applied to get a legible, neat, and professional result concerns first the number formats (application of Number and Percentage format where required or where appropriate). You can also make the worksheets more readable highlighting the titles, headings, and totals with the use of bold, borders, and fill colors.

Comments and functions unit 2

EXERCISE 2.1 - Home loans (commented)

Tools needed to solve the exercise:
Data import from text file, percentage variation calculation, Conditional Formatting, chart creation, IF, AND functions, nested functions.

Comment point 1
Data in the **Exercise 2.1 - ECB_home_loans.txt** file are delimited by a semicolon and have the comma as a decimal separator and the point as thousands separator. To import them into the spreadsheet, we must use the Get External Data/From Text command and, during the import wizard, we must specify that they are delimited data (step 1), separated by a semicolon (step 2), and that the separators used in the file are the comma as a decimal separator, and the point as thousands separator (Advanced option in step 3). It should be noted that to avoid possible errors in the import process, it is always advisable to specify both separators in the third step of the import wizard, even if the data do not have both (as in this case).

Comment point 2
The calculation of the percentage variation of each value of the Euro area compared with the previous value does not need any functions: it is sufficient to create a formula that divides the value of the **Euro area** field by the previous value. For example, the formula in cell **H2** is the following:
=(G2/G3)-1
The formula we just set would return an error in cell H143 (#DIV/0!), because the formula divides the last value of the **Euro area** field (cell **G143**) by an empty cell (cell **G144**). Then, it is necessary to use an IF function to make sure that when the cell of the **Euro area** column in the row below is empty, the text "Not available" appears. As an alternative, it would be possible to use the IFERROR function, which will be used in the exercises of the next units.

Comment point 3

To the values of the **% Euro area** column three different conditional formatting commands should be applied: the command "Greater than" in the Highlight Cells Rules category sets the automatic formatting for cells with positive changes ("Format cells that are greater than 0"). The command "Less than" in the same category allows to set the automatic formatting for cells with negative changes ("Format cells that are less than 0"). The command "Equal to," always in the same category, allows to set the automatic formatting for the cells containing the value "Not available". Remember that to apply properly the conditional formatting, it is advisable first to select all the values to be formatted, excluding the column heading.

Comment point 4

Before creating the chart, we need to select the data of the considered period (column **Period**) and countries (columns **Spain**, **Italy**, and **Netherlands**). Then, add a title to the chart, and finally, move it to another worksheet using the "Move chart" command.

Comment point 5

To calculate if the percentage variations of France and Italy are both positive, we must use an AND function nested in an IF function.

Two conditions are to be verified: "the variation of France is positive" and "the variation of Italy is positive". The IF function must have "Both positive" as a result when they are both true, so it is necessary to use the AND function. The test argument of the IF function in cell **I2** is the following:
AND((D2/D3)-1>0,(E2/E3)-1>0)

Finally, we have to enter the previous IF function in a second IF function that checks if in the cell of the **% Euro Area** column there is the value "Not available": if so, the function must return once again the value "Not available", if not it must use the IF function seen previously. Therefore, the IF function in the cell is the following:
IF(H2="Not available","Not available",IF(AND((D2/D3)-1>0,(E2/E3)-1>0), "Both positive",""))

EXERCISE 2.2 - Internet users (commented)

Tools needed to solve the exercise:
Data import from text file, percentage calculation, SUM, IF, AND functions, nested functions, sorting, chart creation, conditional formatting.

Comment point 1
To import data contained in the file **Exercise 2.2 - Internet and mobile phone users.txt**, use the Import external data/From text command. During the import process, it is necessary to specify that data are delimited by the semicolon symbol (steps 1 and 2), and which are the separators used in the file, that is the comma as decimal separator and the point as thousands separator.
It should be remembered that the Advanced command is used to indicate the settings used in the imported file, and not the settings of the computer. If this step was skipped, the figures would be imported into the worksheet as text and sometimes even as dates, making it difficult (if not impossible) the following conversion to numbers.

Comment point 2
To calculate the percentage values of the new **% Internet** and **% phones users** columns, it is necessary to divide the users of each country (i.e., mobile phones users) by total users (i.e., the total mobile phones users), calculated using the SUM function. It must be noted that to copy correctly the formula in the cells below, the reference to the range inserted in the argument num1 of the SUM function must be mixed or absolute. Using mixed references, then typing the formula =C2/SUM(C$2:C$213) in cell **F2**, you can copy it to the column on the right and downwards, without rewriting the formula.

Comment point 3
After sorting the table for mobile phones users, in a descending order (Sort by **Mobile phone users**, from the largest to smallest), the cells to be selected to create the chart are those of the columns **Country** and **Mobile phone users** (the first 16 rows, which is the headings and data for the first 15 countries). Move the chart to a new worksheet with the Move chart command, then select only the column representing the figure of Italy and use the command Format Data Point to set a different fill color.

Comment point 4

Conditional formatting must be applied twice, first to the values of the **Internet users** column and then to the values of the **Mobile phone users** column: it must be remembered that to apply correctly conditional formatting to a large number of values, it is better to select first all the column values excluding the heading, then apply the desired conditional formatting. In both cases, the default formatting of the Top 10 items category (Top/Bottom rules) has been applied, with the choice of a custom fill.

Comment point 5

In order to check the countries that are in the top 20 positions of the ranking both as Internet and mobile phone users, it is necessary to use an IF function setting up a double condition in the test argument. In this case, the two conditions must verify if the country ranking of each country is equal to or less than 20 both as internet and mobile phone users: if both conditions are TRUE, the function must have "Top ranking" as a result, otherwise nothing. The function in cell **H2** is the following:
=IF(AND(A2<=20,E2<=20),"Top ranking","")

EXERCISE 2.3 - Top sellers (commented)

Tools needed to solve the exercise:
Data import from text files, sorting, AVERAGE, IF, AND, COUNTBLANK COUNTA functions, nested functions, Conditional Formatting, filter, Paste command options, creation of a chart with two axes.

Comment point 1
To import the .txt file, the first step is to open a new Excel workbook. After that, you can use the procedure Text Import Wizard.
After choosing the file that contains the data, it is necessary to indicate the type of data you are importing: in this case (as in most cases, for text files) it is delimited data, as you can easily understand observing the preview shown at the bottom of the dialog box (the values, which start from row 10, are clearly separated by semicolons).
In the second step, you need to select the correct delimiter (semicolon), clearing the default one (tab or tabulator). Once selected the correct delimiter, the preview will show data divided into columns.

Being a German file, it uses European decimal and thousands separator (comma and point are reversed compared with the English notation). It is therefore necessary to specify the manner in which the values should be imported into Excel files. To do this, you must click on the Advanced button in the third step of the procedure, then in the dialog box indicate the comma as a decimal separator and the point as thousands separator.
Once you have confirmed and completed the procedure Text Import Wizard, import the table starting at cell **A1**.
Once the import is completed, it can be noted that the values in column **F** (Price) could not be recognized as numbers, but imported as text (right-aligned), probably due to the presence of the sign €, misinterpreted as text by Excel. In this case, you have to activate the "Replace" command and proceed with the following steps to ensure that prices are correctly interpreted as numerical values:
- Select the cells **F2:F50**
- Replace the comma (,) with the point (.)
- Replace the € symbol with nothing (leave the box "Replace with:" empty)

Now you can format cells **F2:F50** with the Currency format, choosing € Euro (€ 123) as the currency symbol and leaving two decimal places.

Comment point 3

To sort the table, at the same time, based on the values of the column **PART NUMBER** and then of the **Quantity** column, both in descending order, it is preferable that the active cell is placed within the table to be sorted, without manually selecting it all.
Choosing the Custom sort command, you can fill in the dialog box by choosing the first criterion in the first line (in this case **PART NUMBER**), from Z to A for a descending order. To enter the second criterion, which is subordinate to the first, you need to add a level and select **Quantity** in "Then by". As this is a numeric variable, you should sort from the largest to smallest for a descending order.

Comment point 4

You should use the AVERAGE function applied to the values of prices column (selecting only the cells that contain the data, not the entire column and not the header in row **1**), placing it below the list with at least one line of separation (for readability and to avoid that the formula is involved e.g., in filters or sorting).

Comment point 5
To meet the demand you should use an IF function. As the possible results are three (more than those allowed by a simple IF function, which has only two possible outcomes), you must use a nested IF function in another IF. Indeed, in general you need many IF functions nested one inside the other as the number of alternatives to consider minus one: three alternatives are provided by two nested IF functions.
The first condition to be tested, in this case, is that Quantity is between 150 and 220 (inclusive). Excel does not accept a syntax that represents the concept of "between" (like 150≤Quantity≤220), so the test should be divided into two inequalities that have to occur simultaneously. To construct a test of this kind is therefore necessary to use the function AND, in this way: AND(E2>=150,E2<=220). The second condition to be tested is a simple inequality, Quantity>220 (without the symbol = because the extreme is already included in the other test).
The formula to be written in cell **G2** and then copy down is as follows:
=IF(AND(E2>=150,E2<=220),"Almost Top Seller",IF(E2>220,"Top Seller","")).

Comment point 6
You must use the Conditional Formatting. After selecting the relevant cells (**G2:G50**) you can choose the type of conditional formatting rules Highlight cells, Equal to ... indicating in the dialog box the text that shall set off the formatting (Top Seller) and choosing the color scheme preset (Fill green with dark green text).

Comment point 7
To count how many **AAID** are not "Top Seller" or "Almost Top Seller" simply count how many empty cells are present in the range **G2:G50** using the COUNTBLANK function.
To count how many cells are "filled" with Top Sellers or Almost Top Sellers, however, it is not sufficient to directly use the COUNTA function, because the presence of the IF function in cells, although it returns a result "empty" (""), means that the cell is counted as containing a value (the result of the formula). It is therefore necessary to subtract from the total count of the cells (made with COUNTA) the number of empty cells:
=COUNTA(G2:G50)-COUNTBLANK(G2:G50)
As usual, the table of counts should be placed at least one row away from the table containing the data.

Comment point 8
To filter the list you need to activate the tool Filter from the ribbon. In this case, the filter has to act on three fields simultaneously:
- Column **F**: Number filters - Between… "is greater than or equal to" 101 AND "is less than or equal to" 147
- Column **B**: Text filters – Begins with… "begins with" AA
- Column **E**: Number filters - Greater than or equal … "is greater than or equal to" 100

Comment point 9
Once you have renamed one of the available sheets in the workbook (e.g., **Sheet2**) in **Large quantities**, you can copy the filtered table in **Sales data** sheet and paste it from the cell **A1** in sheet **Large quantities** using the Paste command with the option "paste values - values and source formatting (E)" that preserves any formatting and paste the results of the formulas instead of the formulas themselves.

Comment point 10
It is about creating a mixed chart (bars for Quantity and line for Price), with double vertical axis (**Price** on secondary axis / right one). You start by selecting the three variables of interest, including headers (range **D1:F7**). Then, insert a clustered column chart and then, after selecting the series Price, change the chart type only for the latter series turning it into line and transferring it on the secondary axis.
After selecting the series Price on the chart it is also possible, by right-clicking, to access the context menu from which to add data labels.

Comment point 11
You must use the Conditional Formatting. After selecting the relevant cells (**F2:F7**) you can choose the type of conditional formatting Top/Bottom Rules, Top 10 items…indicating in the dialog box the number of cells to format (two) and the custom format.

EXERCISE 2.4 - Alphabet Inc.

Tools needed to solve the exercise:
Data import from the Web, sorting, MAX, MIN, IF, AVERAGE, OR, COUNTBLANK functions, nested functions, Conditional Formatting, chart creation, filter, Paste command options (Values).

EXERCISE 2.5 - Show

Tools needed to solve the exercise:
Simple formulas (multiplication, subtraction), IF, AND functions, nested functions, Conditional Formatting.

EXERCISE 2.6 - Productivity

Tools needed to solve the exercise:
IF, AND, OR, COUNTBLANK, COUNTA functions, nested functions, Conditional Formatting.

EXERCISE 2.7 - Customer care

Tools needed to solve the exercise:
Data import from text file, IF, AND, OR, AVERAGE functions, nested functions, sorting, Conditional Formatting.

EXERCISE 2.8 - ISTAT (commented)

Tools needed to solve the exercise:
Data import from text file, Replace command, chart creation, filter, COUNTBLANK, IF, MIN, MAX functions, nested functions, Conditional Formatting, sorting.

Comment point 5

To solve this question, you should use the Replace command, entering in the "Find what" box the value 0 and nothing in the "Replace with" box. In addition, you need to select the "Match entire cell contents" option before performing the replacement with the "Replace All" command.

EXERCISE 2.9 - Planets (commented)

Tools needed to solve the exercise:
Data import from text file, Replace command, sorting, MAX, MIN, AVERAGE, COUNTBLANK, AVERAGE, AND, IF, MAX, MIN, nested functions, Conditional formatting, filter, percentage calculation, chart creation.

Comment point 1

During the import process from the file **Exercise 2.9 - Solar system.txt** file, we must specify the correct separators, setting the comma as decimal separator and a point as the thousands separator. It should be noted that the numerical values of the Orbital period field are already set correctly (they have the point as the decimal separator), but the separators are not modified because the values are considered text by Excel, thanks to the symbol of the day "d".

The data cleaning requires the use of the Replace command: pay attention to the presence of any extra spaces in cells with the values to be replaced, which must be removed during the process. For example, to remove the symbols "d" in the column **Orbital period**, we should use the Replace command to remove the space that precedes each symbol (thereby setting " d"), to avoid possible problems recognition of the values by Excel after the replacement. For the calculation of the maximum, minimum, and average, we used the MAX, MIN, and AVERAGE functions.

Comment point 2

The conditional formatting set on the values of the **Mean distance from Sun** and the **Equatorial diameter in km**, fields require two different conditions for each field. In both cases, a couple of formatting rules of the Top/Bottom rules category is applied: the First 10 and Last 10 items elements, both set to the value 2.

To identify the two planets with the largest diameter and with the lowest orbital velocity are, we need to use an IF function with a second IF function nested into it. The possible output of the function are three: "Largest diameter", "Lowest orbital velocity" and nothing (""). A single IF function would not be enough, whereas the use of two IF functions leads to three possible outputs. It should be noted that in the test of the two IF functions, we have used the MAX and MIN functions to find, respectively, the planet with the highest diameter, and with the lowest orbital velocity.

Comment point 3

The calculation of the percentage of the mass of each planet with respect to the total mass of all the planets was performed by calculating first the total mass in cell **B11** (SUM function), and then setting a division between the mass of the planet and the total mass. In this case, it would also be correct to skip the first step and calculate the total mass of all the planets directly in the formula; for example, in cell **C2**:
=B2/SUM(B$2:B$10)
The pie chart used in the solution allows you to effectively represent all data.

Comment point 4

During the import process from the **Exercise 2.9 - Planets.txt** file, we must set the comma as a delimiter, and specify the correct separators, setting the comma as decimal separator and the point as the thousands separator. To calculate how many planets do not have the inclination data and the size of the orbit, a COUNTBLANK function was used. Once it has been set, unlike e.g., the filters, it allows us to make the calculation without modifying the table, without sorting the data or visualizing only a part of them.

Comment point 5

In the Revolution column, we must use an IF function with the test set to verify that the revolution period of each planet is above the average of the revolution periods of all the planets, using the AVERAGE function. Pay attention to the cell references used, which must be compatible with the copy of the function in the cells below; in particular, it is necessary that the cell references of the AVERAGE function are mixed or absolute.

In the Comparison column, it is necessary to use another IF function, but in this case in the test argument it must be verified simultaneously that the revolution period is between 300 and 450, and that the mass is between 0.01

and 1, using the AND function. All conditions to be verified can be inserted in the same IF function; e.g., the test argument of the function test in cell **L2** is the following:
AND(D2>300,D2<450,B2>0.01,B2<1)

EXERCISE 2.10 - Home Sweet Home (commented)

Tools needed to solve the exercise:
Data import from text file, sorting, nested functions, function COUNTBLANK, function SUM, percentage calculation, filter, chart creation, Conditional Formatting.

Comment point 1
Data in the **Opera quotations.txt** file are delimited by a semicolon. To import them into the spreadsheet it is necessary to use the Get External Data/From Text command and, during the import wizard, specify that the data are delimited (step 1) and separated by a semicolon (step 2).

Comment point 2
The price per m^2 is normally given by the division between the Price and the number of m^2, except when there is a single or double garage, in which case the expression "Price of the garage to be estimated" must appear in the cell. Inside the argument test of the IF function, it is therefore necessary to insert an OR function, to verify if there a single (first argument) or a double garage (second argument).
The apartments without a garage, either single or double, have an empty cell in the **Garage** column. To quantify their number, use the COUNTBLANK function.

Comment point 3
When calculating the percentage price of each apartment on the total price pay attention to the use of references. In the formula, the price of a single apartment cell must in fact contain relative references, while the total price cell must contain the "$" symbol on the row reference, to allow the copying down of the formula while not allowing changes in the row of the total price.

Comment point 4

The expression "Small size" should appear in the Size column if two conditions occur simultaneously: one linked to the number of rooms (which must be equal to 1) and one linked to the size of the apartment (which must be equal to or less than 30 m^2). Inside the logical test of the IF function, it is therefore necessary to insert an AND function, to verify if both conditions are true.

In order to format with an optional fill color, the cells containing the expression "Small", you must use the conditional formatting with the "Equal to" option inside "Highlight Cells Rules".

To show "OK" when the price of the apartment has been higher than the area's average price, the logical test of the IF function must verify whether the individual price of the apartment has been higher than the average of the prices. Pay attention to the use of references.

While creating the graph, as it is required to use the addresses of the apartments as labels of the category axis, and the addresses are quite long, it is better to use a Bar chart rather than a Column one.

Comment point 5

The commission is generally 1.5% of the selling price, except in two cases: a) when the selling price of the apartment is the highest of the list and b) when the selling price per m^2 of the apartment is the highest of the list. It is therefore necessary to use a first IF function, in whose logical test check the first of the two conditions. If the condition does not occur (argument "Value_if_false"), it is necessary to use a second IF function, in whose logical test check the second of the two conditions. If also the second condition does not occur (argument "Value_if_false" of the second IF function), the commission will be equal to 1.5%, which corresponds to the general case.

Comments and functions unit 3

EXERCISE 3.1 - Drugstores (commented)

Tools needed to solve the exercise:
Remove Duplicates command, SUM, COUNTIF, SUMIF, AVERAGEIF functions, chart creation, sorting, Subtotal, percentage calculation.

Comment point 1
After creating the new worksheet named **Functions**, you need to create a table with the list of the districts where the examined drugstores are located. To do this, copy in column A of the new worksheet the entire contents of the **District** column, then use the Remove duplicates command to make sure that the label of each district is shown just once.
Then, insert in cell **B1** the label **N. drugstores** and in **B2** the COUNTIF function needed to count the drugstores of each district. Pay attention to the use of mixed references in the range of values to be counted.

Comment point 2
In a way similar to that done for the counting in the previous point, after entering into cell **C1** the heading **Total turnover**, use the SUMIF function in cell **C2** to calculate the total turnover for each district.
For the same reasons described in the previous paragraph, it should be noted the use of mixed references this time is used in both the range of values (to verify the criteria and values to sum).

Comment point 3
Following the same approach described for point 2, you can calculate the average turnover per district using the AVERAGEIF function.

Comment point 4
The most appropriate way to graphically show the percentage of a series of values is a pie chart. This is one of those types of charts that displays the percentage values without having to calculate them first in a new column of the spreadsheet.

The cells to be selected for the chart, namely, those containing the data to be represented and the corresponding text labels, are the ranges **A2:A5** and **C2:C5**. After creating the pie chart, to show the items you need (title, legend, percentages, etc.) use the options available and the chart formatting.

Comment point 5
To show series of values very different from each other, like the number of drugstores and the average turnover, so that both are visible in the plot area, one of the series should be represented on the secondary axis.
The creation of a mixed chart with two axes requires three steps: the creation of a chart with all the series of data to be represented, the shift of one of the two series on the secondary axis, and the modification of the chart type for the series on the secondary axis. In this case, it is therefore necessary to create the chart (e.g., a column chart) selecting both series of data and also their labels, namely, the ranges of cells **A2:B5** and **D2:D5**: due to the scale diversity one of the series is practically indistinguishable; therefore, it must be shifted on the secondary axis by using the command Format data series and activating the option Secondary axis. As a result, the columns of both series will now be overlapped. You therefore need to click with the right key of the mouse on a column of one of the two series, select the command Change series chart type, and choose the type of chart you want (e.g., to area). To complete, customize the chart by inserting the most appropriate elements, like the title, the name of the series and so on.

Comment point 6
Once the data have been copied to the new worksheet **Total**, sort the table by district and, after selecting the entire table, use the Subtotal command. To calculate the total sales for each district, you must apply the following settings:
- At each change in: District
- Use function: Sum
- Add subtotals to: Turnover

Comment point 7
Following the best practice for the appropriate organization of the data within the worksheet, when inserting the total turnover you have to leave a blank row at the end of the table. In cell **B18**, enter then the SUM function.

After entering the label % in cell **D1**, calculate the percentage of the turnover for each drugstore by entering the formula =B2/B$18 in cell **D2**. Pay attention to the use of mixed references for the denominator. To complete the task, copy the formula in all other cells in the column and apply the Percentage formatting to show the results properly.

EXERCISE 3.2 - Men at work (commented)

Tools needed to solve the exercise:
SUMPRODUCT, SUMIF, COUNTIF functions, links to cells, Conditional Formatting, Remove Duplicates command.

Comment point 1
First, create the space before the table, inserting three blank rows. Enter in cells **D1:G1** the text labels with the column headings, and in cell **C2** the text label **Unit price**. Considering the request of the accounting manager, the values to enter in cells **D2:G2** should be linked to the corresponding cells of the table in the **Price list** worksheet, with a formula that in **D2**, for instance, should be ='Price list'!B2.

Comment point 2
The total expenditure for each of the purchases made during the quarter is given by the sum of the costs incurred for each type of material, in the row of the purchase made on any specific date. Having available the amount (in the row corresponding to each single purchase) and the unit prices (in row **2**) you can therefore proceed, row by row, by calculating the sum of the products between each amount and the corresponding unit price. The formula to be used in cell **H5** is the following: =SUMPRODUCT(D$2:G$2,D5:G5)
Pay attention to the use of mixed references (absolute on the rows) for the range **D2:G2** (where there are the unit prices), and the use of relative references for the range of the amounts related to each single purchase (**D5:G5**): in this way it is possible to copy and paste the formula into all cells from **H6** to **H16**, quickly completing all the calculations.

Comment point 3
To highlight automatically a series of cells based on a specific criterion, you must use the Conditional Formatting options.

Considering that the request is to format cells belonging to a column that is different from the one containing the values on which the criterion should be verified, it is necessary to use the formatting rule that uses a formula to determine which cells to highlight. After selecting the entire range **A5:A16** and choosing to insert a conditional formatting using a formula to determine which cells to format, the formula =H5>300 has to be inserted. Before confirming, you must also define the format settings as required.

Comment point 4

After creating the new worksheet **Quantity**, insert the column headings for the types of material purchased (row **1**), and the list of the months of the quarter under consideration (column **A**).

In cell **B2**, enter the SUMIF function to calculate the total amount for the type of material and the month considered. The function in cell **B2** is therefore the following: =SUMIF(Purchases!$C$5:$C$16,$A2,Purchases!D$5:D$16).

Note the specific use of the $ symbol in the different arguments of the function:

- To make absolute the range (row and column) in which to test the criterion
- To make absolute only the column for the cell containing the criterion, which will therefore be different for each row but not for the different columns of the same row
- To make absolute the row references of the range of cells to be summed, which will therefore be the same for each type of material

Setting in this way the references to be used in the SUMIF function, you can copy the content of the cell **B2** in all other cells in the range **B2:E4**.

Comment point 5

After copying cells from **A5** to **A16** of the **Purchases** worksheet, paste them in the **Quantity** worksheet starting from cell **A7**, then use the Remove Duplicates command to obtain a list of unique values. Now insert in cell **B7**, the COUNTIF function to count the names in column **A** of the table available in the **Purchases** worksheet.

Paying attention to the correct use of the relative and absolute references, the final formula will be =COUNTIF(Purchases!A$5:A$16,A7), then it can be copied into the cells below to complete the exercise.

EXERCISE 3.3 - Car insurances (commented)

Tools needed to solve the exercise:
IF function, nested functions, Conditional Formatting, sorting, Subtotal, chart creation.

Comment point 1
After entering heading labels in cells **F1** and **G1**, use the following formulas in the cells below:
- =D2/C2 starting from cell **F2**, then copying the formula down to cell **F20**
- =E2/D2 starting from cell **G2**, then copying the formula down to cell **G20**

Comment point 2
Copy in a new worksheet, the entire table available in the **Statistics** worksheet, or create a duplicate of the Statistics worksheet, naming it **Totals**. As the results have to be calculated for each area, before proceeding with the subtotals you need to sort the table by Area (ascending order).
Then, after selecting a single cell within the table or after selecting the whole table, use the Subtotal command with the following settings:
- At each change in: Area
- Use function: Average
- Add subtotals to: Circulating cars + Car accidents + Costs

Comment point 3
In a new row below the table available in the **Statistics** worksheet, insert the SUM function at the bottom of columns **C**, **D**, and **E** to obtain the total of the values in the respective ranges of cells.

Comment point 4
In the cells at the bottom of columns **F** and **G**, copy the formula used in the cells above.

Comment point 5
Starting from cell **H2** use the function:
=IF(F2>F$22,IF(G2>G$22,"* €","*"),IF(G2>G$22,"€","")).
Observe the nested structure of the tests performed and the use of the absolute references on the cells of the totals.

The first thing to verify (with the test of the first IF function) is the percentage of accidents: if it is higher than the overall rate (available in cell **F22**), two other circumstances might occur. If the average cost per accident is also higher than the overall average cost, in cell **H2** both symbols * and € will be shown. If this second condition is not met (i.e., only the accident rate is higher than the overall average) only the symbol * will be shown.

To finish, if the test on the percentage of accidents is not met, the test on the average cost per accidents is repeated: if this cost is higher than the overall average cost, only the symbol € is shown. If not, i.e., none of the test is satisfied, an empty cell will be shown.

To achieve the same result another approach was also possible, checking first if the accident rate and the average cost per accident are both higher than the respective overall average values. Otherwise, each of the two conditions would have to be tested individually. The function resulting from this second approach is the following:
=IF(AND(F2>F$22,G2>G$22),"*€",IF(F2>F$22,"*",IF(G2>G$22,"€","")))

Comment point 6

To highlight the name of the city with the highest average cost, it is necessary to use the formatting rule that uses a formula to determine the cells to format. After selecting the entire range **A2:A20**, create therefore a new conditional formatting rule by entering the formula =G2=MAX($G$2:$G$20). Before confirming, set the formatting options to be applied to those cells that meet the criteria.

Comment point 7

To make clearly visible in a chart series of values with different orders of magnitude, as the average cost per accident and the number of circulating cars, it is necessary to represent one of the two series on the secondary axis.

First, select the cells of both series of values with the cells containing their respective text labels (namely, the ranges **A2:A20**, **C2:C20**, and **G2:G20**) and insert a column chart. Due to the diversity of scale, it is normal that the elements of the Average cost per incident series are almost not visible.

Clicking with the right key of the mouse on one of the columns of the visible series, activate the option for the Secondary Axis in the Format data series pane: as an effect, the columns of both series will be overlapped. It is therefore necessary to change the chart type of one of the two series to make the data readable. Click therefore again with the right key of the mouse on one of the columns of the "Average cost per incident" series, and choose the type of chart that you want. To complete, customize the chart by inserting the most appropriate elements (title, name of the series, legend etc.) and move the chart in a new worksheet by using the Move chart command.

EXERCISE 3.4 - Exam

Tools needed to solve the exercise:
ABS function, percentage variation, Conditional Formatting with formula, IF and AVERAGE functions, cell links, creation of a chart with trend line.

EXERCISE 3.5 - Clothing Store

Tools needed to solve the exercise:
COUNTIF and SUMIF functions, Remove Duplicates command, Mixed chart with two axes, Conditional Formatting with formula, filter, sorting, Subtotal.

EXERCISE 3.6 - Beauty Business

Tools needed to solve the exercise:
Conditional formatting, SUMIF, AVERAGEIF, SUMPRODUCT functions, creation of a chart with a trend line, Subtotal.

EXERCISE 3.7 - Cosmetics Shop

Tools needed to solve the exercise:
Conditional Formatting, percentage variation calculation, cell links, SUMIF, AVERAGEIF functions, percentage calculation.

EXERCISE 3.8 - International Education

Tools needed to solve the exercise:
Conditional Formatting, SUM, SUMIF, AVERAGEIF functions, percentage calculation, creation of a mixed chart with two axes, sorting, Subtotal.

EXERCISE 3.9 - Dinner with classmates (commented)

Tools needed to solve the exercise:
Conditional Formatting, SUMIF, AVERAGEIF, SUMPRODUCT functions, creation of a mixed chart with two axes, Remove Duplicates command, sorting, Subtotal, simple formulas (sum, division).

Comment point 1
After calculating in column **G**, the total hours of commitment, a conditional formatting has to be applied to cells in the Name column (**A2:A26**), based on a test performed on the corresponding cells containing the total hours of commitment (column **G**).

Comment point 2
A summary table as the one requested, has to be positioned in accordance with the best practice to be followed when organizing the data in a worksheet. The best choice relies on keeping consistency in the alignment of the columns (so that ideally there is continuity when reading the data) and, of course, on leaving an adequate space from the source table.
Then, the conditional formulas SUMIF and AVERAGEIF have to be used to calculate the sum and the average, by aggregating the values when the Gender (column **B**) correspond, respectively, to **M** or **F**.

Comment point 3
It is possible to create the second summary in a way similar to the one described in the previous point.
After that, you have to select the cells containing the data to be presented graphically (**C33:E34** file solved) inserting then the chart. It should be noted that as data series the two labels **M** and **F** are proposed. Before proceeding to apply the options requested in the exercise, it is therefore necessary to reverse the series with the categories using the Switch rows/columns command in the Design tab. At this point, it will be possible to add the secondary axis and to

change the chart type for one of the two series. Finally, you will have to set all other aspects concerning the chart layout (titles, legend etc.).

Comment point 4

To create the list with the names of all the cities, it is convenient to use the Remove duplicates command, by acting on a copy of the data available in column **C** of the **Calculations** worksheet. It is then possible to calculate the average income by using the AVERAGEIF function, aggregating the amounts in column **F** of the **Calculations** worksheet (Total income from work field) when the town corresponds to the label listed in the new list created in the **Towns** worksheet.

To calculate the subtotals, it is important to remember the need to sort the table (previously copied and pasted from line **12** of the new worksheet) based on the Town field. To complete the exercise, it is necessary to set the function Average in the subtotal for both the required fields (Hours dedicated to work and Hours dedicated to home/family) and compact the view of the data so that only the subtotals (average for each town) and the grand total (Grand Average) are visible.

Comment point 5

Knowing the income from work and the hours dedicated to work, the calculation of the hourly wage is given by the division income/hour.

To know the individual supposed overall income it is necessary, for each classmate, to multiply the total hours of commitment to the hourly wage just calculated. The total supposed overall income of the entire class will be the sum of all the individual supposed overall income.

The single function that allows performing the two stages of the calculation just described is the SUMPRODUCT function, where you need to specify two arguments, corresponding, respectively, to the cell in column **G** and the range of cells in column **H**.

EXERCISE 3.10 - Wages (commented)

Tools needed to solve the exercise:

ABS function, percentage variation, Conditional Formatting, Remove Duplicates command, COUNTIF, AVARAGEIF, SUMIF functions,

Conditional Formatting with formula, sorting, Subtotal, Mixed chart with two axes.

Comment point 1

To calculate the difference in absolute terms, use the ABS function, which turns into positive numbers also negative differences. The percentage variation in absolute terms is calculated by dividing the difference just calculated (which is already in absolute terms) for the previous year's wage, which is the oldest value.

To format the cells as requested use the option "Rules First/Last" of the conditional formatting.

Comment point 2

To calculate the information required using COUNTIF, AVERAGEIF, and SUMIF functions, it is preliminarily necessary to create, in the Analysis sheet, a list of the job titles, making sure that the label of each job title is shown only once. The appropriate command for this purpose is Remove Duplicates.

When creating the three functions, remember to pay particular attention to the references, which in the argument "criteria" must be relative as job titles change, while the arguments containing ranges do not have to change.

Comment point 3

To calculate the number of employees with a current annual wage greater than 45,000 US dollars, use the COUNTIF function, paying attention to the fact that the value within the argument "criteria" should be in quotation marks ("> 45000").

To highlight the badge numbers of employees with a current annual wage greater than 45,000 US dollars, you must use a conditional formatting with formula. The condition that must be applied to the range of cells A2:A51 is the following =E2>45000. It is important to put relative references on cell E2 as, otherwise, the whole range A2:A51 would be simultaneously highlighted or not, depending on the content of the single cell E2.

Comment point 4

As it is required to calculate the subtotal of salaries for each job title, it is necessary to preliminarily sort the data by job title. It is possible to use a single subtotal selecting both columns related to the wage in the area "Add subtotal to:".

Comment point 5
To create the chart, you can start by selecting cells A1:C7 of the Analysis worksheet and creating, for example, a histogram. Then, we suggest to select the series "Average wage", click with the right mouse button and select "Change Series Chart Type" inside the window that appears, you can then choose for one of the two series a Line chart and add a Secondary axis.

Comments and functions unit 4

EXERCISE 4.1 - Emerald (commented)

Tools needed to solve the exercise:
Simple formulas (multiplication), PMT, FV functions, Conditional Formatting, Paste command options (Transpose), Goal Seek.

Comment point 1
When using the PMT function, you should pay attention to the temporal coherence between the arguments; for this purpose, within the PMT function in the cell **E2**, it is necessary:
- To divide the annual interest rate by 4 to calculate the quarterly rate
- To multiply the number of years by 4 to calculate the number of periods for which you will pay the installment
- To insert in the "PV" argument the amount of requested funding
- To insert as argument "Type" the value 0 (or omitted) as the installments are paid at the end of the period.

For the calculation of the total cash outlay, it is necessary to multiply the quarterly installment just calculated by the number of times the installment will have to be paid, i.e., the number of years multiplied by 4.

Comment point 2
The answer to this question requires the use of the conditional formatting with formulas as it is asked to format specific cells (those containing the name of the bank) in the case of a condition that occurs not in those cells themselves, but in other ones (those containing the total payment).
It is necessary to select the range of cells containing the names of the banks and, in the section "Use a formula to determine which cells to format" of the Conditional Formatting, enter the following formula: =F2=MAX(F$2:F$5).
F2 must in fact be a relative reference, while the range should be formed by mixed references (or possibly absolute references).
Note also that, as the total cash outlays are negative numbers, the lowest outlay corresponds to the maximum value in the range.
After entering the formula, it is then necessary to set the required format.

Comment point 3

The data asked for the copy are those present in the range **A1:F2**. Once selected, use the Copy command, then move to the cell **A1** of a new worksheet and use the Paste Special command with the Transpose option. After doing this, rename the worksheet with the name **Installment goal**.

To remove the conditional formatting rules, you need to select the cells involved and use the command "Clear rules from selected cells", in the Conditional Formatting menu.

Comment point 4

To answer the question you must use the Goal Seek, to be set with the following criteria:
- Set cell: **B5**
- To value: -15,000
- By changing cell: **B3**

It is necessary to pay attention to the fact that the value 15,000 represents a cash outflow (the installment to be paid), so a negative sign must precede it.

Comment point 5

While entering the data in the **Patent** spreadsheet, it is necessary to pay particular attention to the fact that the payment, constituting a cash outflow, should be placed as a negative number.

Even in the FV function, as already seen for the PMT function, it is necessary to pay attention to the temporal coherence between arguments. You must therefore:
- Divide the annual interest rate by 12 to calculate the monthly rate
- Multiply the number of years by 12 to calculate the number of periods for which the payment will be made
- Insert as "Pmt" the amount of the monthly payment
- Insert as "Type" the value 0 (or omitted) as the payment are at the end of the period.

EXERCISE 4.2 - Smart Courses (commented)

Tools needed to solve the exercise:
Simple formulas (multiplication, division), naming cells, IF, SUM functions, scenarios.

Comment point 1
To change the name of a cell, you must use the Name Manager, in the Formulas tab: identify the name to be changed and, using the Edit button, assign the required name.

Comment point 2
As the salary of the teacher changes depending on their seniority, it is necessary to use an IF function for the calculation of the total rate, with the logical_test: B7="junior".
If the result of the test is TRUE, the function has to multiply the number of days by the junior teacher rate. If the result of the test is FALSE, the function has to multiply the number of days by the senior teacher rate.
It is also necessary to pay attention to the use of cell references in the arguments value_if_true and value_if_false, which must be relative with regard to the duration of the courses and mixed (with the $ symbol on the row reference) with regard to the rates.

Comment point 3
For the calculation of the rent, it is necessary to multiply the total number of days expected for each type of course by the cost of daily rent of the classroom, paying attention to the use of references: relative with regard to the duration of the courses and mixed (with the $ symbol on the row reference) with regard to the daily rent.

Comment point 4
After calculating the total rate as the sum of general costs, teacher rate, and cost of the rent, in the column **Cost per participant**, it is necessary to divide this value by the number of participants.
The text specifically requires to use in the formula the name previously assigned to the cell ("Participants"), and not the cell reference (in this case **B4**); the formula in cell **H7** will therefore be =G7/Participants.
Remember that the names of the cells, when used in the formulas, are equivalent to absolute references.

Comment point 5

To create a new scenario, it is necessary to use the command **Add** in the **Scenario Manager** box. After naming the scenario as required, you have to indicate as variable cells those for which a variation is foreseen, i.e., **B1** and **B2**. After clicking OK, you have to enter the values that the variable cells must take in the scenario: 350 for the cell **B1** and 530 for the cell **B2**.

Comment point 6

The required scenario analyzes the hypothesis of an increase in the number of participants and, at the same time, an increase in rental costs due to the need of a larger classroom. The variable cells are therefore **B3**, which in the scenario must be equal to 200, and **B4**, which must be equal to 40.

Comment point 7

After creating the scenarios, you are now required to use the command **Summary** to show, in a new worksheet, the variation of the result cells in different scenarios. The result cells are those for which you want to show the result as the variable cells change. The exercise asks to show the change of the total cost and the cost per participant, for different types of courses: the result cells is thus the full range **G7:H9**.

However, before proceeding with the Scenario Summary, it is necessary to assign a name to all variable and result cells, to be easily identifiable in the summary, which otherwise would show the cell references (e.g., $B$3) with considerable interpretation difficulties and scarce readability.

Therefore, assign a name to the following cells: **B1** (e.g., Junior_rate), **B2**, **B3**, **G7** (e.g., Total_cost_ basic), **H7** (e.g., Participant_cost_basic), **G8**, **H8**, **G9**, and **H9**. Remember that in the point 1, you have already assigned the name "Participants" to cell **B4**.

At this point, it is possible to proceed with the **Scenario Summary**. After clicking on the command **Summary**, in the next box, you have to select the result cells (**G7:H9**).

EXERCISE 4.3 - Credits and debts (commented)

Tools needed to solve the exercise:
Simple formulas (multiplication, division), IF, PMT, FV functions, nested functions, Goal Seek, chart creation.

Comment point 1
When using the PMT function, it is essential to draw your attention to the temporal coherence among the arguments; the loans on the sheet **Mortgages** have a different frequency of payment of the installments and it is necessary, depending on the frequency, to set different arguments within the PMT function.
In addition to the arguments Pv (**B$8**) and Type (0 or omitted as payments are at the end of the period):
  a) In the case of six-monthly installments, the annual interest rate must be divided by 2 and the number of years multiplied by 2
  b) In the case of the monthly installments, the annual interest rate must be divided by 12 and the number of years multiplied by 12
  c) In the case of quarterly installments, the annual interest rate must be divided by 4 and the number of years multiplied by 4

With an IF function, inquire first if the frequency is six-monthly: if true, proceed with the PMT function set in step a); if false, inquire with a new nested IF function, if the frequency is monthly: if true, proceed with the PMT function set in step b), if false proceed with the PMT function set in step c).

For the calculation of the total cash outlay of each loan, it is necessary to multiply the installment just calculated for the total number of payment periods, calculated by multiplying the number of years:
  a) By 2 in the case of six-monthly installments
  b) By 12 in the case of monthly installments
  c) By 4 in the case of quarterly installments

With an IF function, inquire first if the frequency is six-monthly: if true, proceed as in step a); if false inquire, with a new nested IF function, if the frequency is monthly: if true, proceed as in step b), if false, proceed as in step c).

Comment point 2
The function required for the calculation of the final value of each investment plan is the FV function: using this function it is necessary to pay attention to the temporal coherence among the arguments.
In addition to the arguments Pmt (equal to the respective periodic payment) and Type (equal to 0 or omitted as payments are made at the end of period):
  a) In case of quarterly payments, the annual interest rate must be divided by 4 and the number of years multiplied by 4
  b) In case of monthly payments, the annual interest rate must be divided by 12 and the number of years multiplied by 12

Use an IF function to inquire first if the frequency is quarterly:
- If true, proceed with the FV function set in step a)
- If false, proceed with the FV function set in step b)

Comment point 4
After sorting the table according to the final values, from the largest to the smallest, you must use Goal Seek, with the following criteria:
- Set cell: **G2** (the cell with the highest final value)
- To value: 3,500,000
- By changing cell: **E2** (the cell of its periodical payment, to be modified to achieve the defined target)

EXERCISE 4.4 - Cloth Paradise

Tools needed to solve the exercise:
Simple formulas (addition, subtraction, multiplication, division), SUMPRODUCT, PMT functions, chart creation, scenarios, naming cells, Paste command options (Transpose).

EXERCISE 4.5 - Discount on rates

Tools needed to solve the exercise:
Simple formulas (multiplication), IF, PMT functions, Conditional formatting.

EXERCISE 4.6 - Smart Investments Bank

Tools needed to solve the exercise:
FV, IF, AND functions, nested functions.

EXERCISE 4.7 - Garden Center (commented)

Tools needed to solve the exercise:
Subtotal, Conditional Formatting, Remove duplicates command, SUMIF, IF, PMT, AVERAGE, MAX functions, nested functions, scenarios, naming cells, simple formulas (multiplication, division), sorting, Goal Seek, Paste command options (Transpose).

Comment point 1
In general, note that before proceeding with the use of subtotals, you must sort the data in the table. In this specific case, as you are asked to calculate the total amount for each item sold, you need to first sort the data by the column Item.
To answer the second question, it is necessary to use the conditional formatting with formulas, as you are being asked to format item name cells, when a condition occurs in different cells (those relating to the sale price). In the formula to be included in the conditional formatting, it is necessary to pay attention to the use of cell references, partly relative and partly mixed.

Comment point 2
After creating, in the first column of the **Turnover** worksheet, a unique list of the types of trees, it is necessary to use the function SUMIF to calculate, for each center, the total turnover for each type.
Within the formula, it is therefore necessary to place:
- As "Range" the range of cells of the worksheet **Sales** containing different types of trees (constant for all centers).
- As "Criteria" the cell of the **Turnover** worksheet containing the type of tree.
- As "Sum_range", the range of cells of the **Sales** worksheet containing the turnovers (different for each center).

In this case, as well, it is necessary to pay close attention to the use of the references, partly absolute and partly mixed.

To satisfy the second request, it is necessary to use two nested IF functions: you have to inquire if, for each type of tree, the related turnover of a center corresponds to the maximum turnover realized by the three centers.

Comment point 3
First, it is necessary to create the two scenarios required, placing as variable cells of the range **B3:D3**.
At this point it is necessary to assign to each variable cell and each result cell (those of the range **B4:D4**) a meaningful name, and then proceed to the creation of the Scenario summary.

Comment point 4
To calculate the quarterly installments pay attention to the temporal coherence among the arguments. It is therefore necessary to divide by 4 the annual interest rate and multiply by 4 the number of years.
You then have to enter as argument **Pv** the name of cell "Principal", previously assigned, and as **Type** the value 1, as we are calculating advance installments.

Comment point 5
To sort the data with the goal of having in the first place the proposal with the quarterly installment of a lesser amount, pay attention to the fact that the amounts of the installments are negative numbers and, therefore, it is necessary to sort in the "Largest to smallest" order.
Now you have to use the **Goal Seek** tool and draw your attention to the fact that the target value (2,500 euros), is a negative number and, therefore, it should be entered with a minus sign: -2500.

EXERCISE 4.8 - GreenBio

Tools needed to solve the exercise:
PMT, SUMIF, FV functions, Subtotal, Paste command options (Transpose), Goal seek, Scenarios, naming cells.

EXERCISE 4.9 - PhotoMagic (commented)

Tools needed to solve the exercise:
Remove Duplicates command, COUNTIF, AVERAGEIF, SUMPRODUCT, IF functions, Conditional Formatting, nested functions, sorting, chart creation, Subtotal.

Comment point 1
After using the Remove Duplicates command to create a list of unique values, use the function COUNTIF in the column **Number of Models (Brand)**, starting from cell **B2**, to count the number of occurrences of each brand in the list in the worksheet **Warehouse**.
Before copying and pasting the function in the cells below, pay special attention to the references, which must be mixed for the range (with the $ symbol in the column reference) and relative for the criteria.
The above steps should be repeated for the number of models for each size of the LCD screen.

Comment point 2
The first question should be solved through the use, in cell **H53** of the worksheet **Warehouse**, of the SUMPRODUCT function, entering as arrays the two ranges of cells related to the acquisition cost and quantities.
To proceed with the conditional formatting with formulas of cells of the column **Model**, select the entire range of cells you want to format. Subsequently, in the window of the conditional formatting, enter the following formula: **=(H2*I2)> 6500**. It is advisable to write the cell references by hand rather than select the cells, because in the latter case the cells would present automatically the absolute references that would invalidate the result of the conditional formatting if not removed.

Comment point 3
For the calculation of the **Discount %** use a nested IF function within another IF function. First (test of the first IF function) inquire if the margin % is less than or equal to 10%: if true, conclude that the discount rate is 8%. If false, inquire if the margin % is greater than or equal to 20% (test of the second IF function): if it is true, the discount percentage will be 25%. If it is false, the discount percentage will necessarily be equal to 15%.

Comment point 4

Also in this case use a nested IF function inside another if function; first inquire if the price of the discounted product (that you must calculate within the function) is less than or equal to the purchase cost (test of the first IF function): if true, conclude that it is an offer "Underpriced". If false, inquire if the amount present in stock is less than 25 units (test of the second IF function): if true, it is an offer "Until stocks last", if false it is a "Super Offer".

Comment point 5

To calculate the average amount for each producer, use the AVERAGEIF function, setting as **Range** the range of cells that in the sheet **Warehouse** includes brands, as **Criteria** cell **A2** (with relative reference) and as **Average_range** the range of cells that in the spreadsheet **Warehouse** includes the quantities. A similar procedure should be used for the calculation of the average discount %.

Having sorted data in a descending order, on the basis of the number of models and then on the average quantity, select the data useful for the creation of the chart: brand, average quantity, and average discounts. Remember that, in the case of non-contiguous data, it is necessary to select them simultaneously holding down the CTRL key.

When creating the chart, e.g., a column chart, it is likely that, despite the fact that the series **Average Discount** appears in the legend, the relative data is not visible on the chart. This happens because the values of this series are very small compared with those of the series **Average Quantity** and, therefore, the corresponding columns are difficult to see and to select. Hence, you should select the series **Average discount**, display it on the secondary axis and change the chart type to a line chart.

Remember that, after copying and pasting data from the **Warehouse** worksheet to the **Totals** worksheet, before proceeding with the subtotals you should sort the data according to the **Offers** column.

EXERCISE 4.10 - Bright Sun

Tools needed to solve the exercise:

Naming cells, IF, AVERAGEIF, PMT, FV functions, simple formulas (addition, subtraction, multiplication, division), sorting, conditional formatting, scenarios, Paste command options (Transpose), Goal Seek, Remove duplicates command, chart creation.

Comments and functions unit 5

EXERCISE 5.1 - IBAN codes (commented)

Tools needed to solve the exercise:
MID, RIGHT functions.

Comment point 1
The request to extract from each IBAN code the digit related to the CIN code should be met with a **MID** function.
The source text is the IBAN code reported in cell **A2**.
The CIN code, consisting of a single digit, is shown after the two letters representing the nation and after the 2-digit control code.
Using the MID function, we must then specify that the extraction must start from the fifth character of the IBAN code, and that the number of digits to extract is 1.

Comment point 2
Similar to the previous point, the request to extract from each IBAN code the digits related to the ABI code should be met with the MID function.
The source text is again the IBAN code reported in cell **A2**.
The ABI code is reported after the two letters representing the nation, the 2-digit control code, the single digit related to the CIN code.
The extraction must then start from the sixth character of the IBAN code and we have to extract the five digits that compose the ABI code.

Comment point 3
The reasoning is similar to point 2 as we have to use again a MID function. We have to work on the IBAN code in cell **A2**. The extraction must start from the eleventh character of the IBAN code and we have to extract the five digits that compose the CAB code.

Comment point 4
This request has to be met using the function **RIGHT**. We know that the bank account number is related to the last 12 digits of the IBAN code, so we have to work on **A2** and extract 12 characters.

EXERCISE 5.2 - Names (commented)

Tools needed to solve the exercise:
PROPER, LEFT, SEARCH, RIGHT, LEN functions, Data Validation.

Comment point 1
The first point asks you to extract the first name of each person with the first letter in upper case.
The first function to be set is therefore PROPER. The text argument of this function is the result of a function LEFT that works on the full name (cell **A2**) and extracts as many characters as those that precede the space that separates the first from the last name.
This value is obtained with a SEARCH function. In order not to include the space in the extraction, you should subtract 1 character to the result of the SEARCH function.

Comment point 2
The first point asks you to extract the last name of each person with the first letter in upper case. Similar to the previous point, the first function to be set is PROPER. The text argument of this function is the result of a function RIGHT that works on the full name (cell **A2**) and extracts the number of characters of the last name. For the first row, this number of characters is derived from the difference between:
- The overall length of the text string containing the name and surname (cell **A2**)
- The number corresponding to the position of the first space (always in cell **A2**)

The first value is calculated with a LEN function applied to the content of cell **A2**; the second value is obtained with a SEARCH function applied to the same cell (**A2**), where the find_text is a space (" "). The function in cell **C2** is:

=PROPER(RIGHT(A2,LEN(A2)-SEARCH(" ",A2,1)))

Comment point 3
The third point requires the application of Data Validation on the cells of the column **D**, next to each name, so that the user can enter only the validated

values "F" (for females) and "M" (for males). The request is met by creating the validation list in a new worksheet called **Validation List**, then selecting all the cells to be validated (range **D2:D32**), and finally applying the Data Validation command from list, setting the range in the **Validation List** worksheet as the source.

EXERCISE 5.3 - Superstore (commented)

Tools needed to solve the exercise:
Remove Duplicates command, COUNTIFS, SUMIFS, AVERAGEIFS, options of the Paste command (transpose).

Comment point 1
The first point asks you to calculate in a new worksheet called **Products**, for each product sub-category (column **M** in the worksheet **Orders**), the number of orders with a value greater than 500 US dollars (column **E** in the worksheet **Orders**) and shipping cost less than 10 US dollars (column **G** of the worksheet **Orders**).
It should be useful to copy the values in column **M** of the worksheet **Orders** in the new worksheet **Products**, then you have to use Remove Duplicates to clean the list of product subcategories.
The COUNTIFS function to be placed in cell **B2** is the following:

=COUNTIFS(Orders!M$2:M$8400,A2,Orders!E$2:E$8400,"> 500",Orders!G$2:G$ 8400,"< 10")

The first range of criteria (criteria_range1) refers to the product sub-categories (Orders!M$2M$ 8400). The second range of criteria (criteria_range2) refers to the value of the orders (Orders!E$2:E$ 8400), with the criteria2 set ">500" as requested.
Finally, the third criteria range (criteria_range3) refers to the shipping cost (Orders!G$2:G$8400), with the criteria3 set "<10" as specified in the text.

Comment point 2
In order to answer the second point, it is useful to create a table in a new worksheet (**Customers**), with customer segments by columns and regions by rows. To create this table, you can copy the values reported in columns **J** and

K of the **Orders** worksheet, then paste the values in the new worksheet **Customers**, and use Remove Duplicates (for customer segments you should use Paste Special - Transpose).

The values by column (customer segments) and the values by row (regions) represent the criteria on which you can set a SUMIFS function. The sum range is the value of any single order (**Orders!$E$2:$E$8400**).

The first range of criteria (criteria_range1) refers to the regions (**Orders!$J$2:$J$8400**), the second range of criteria (criteria_range2) refers to customer segments (**Orders!$K$2:$K$8400**).

We suggest to use mixed references to indicate the criteria to use, so that the formula in cell **B3** of the **Customers** worksheet can be copied into all the cells of the table.

Comment point 3

The last point requires an AVERAGEIFS function that returns the average order value, for each shipping mode (column **F** of the **Orders** worksheet) and for orders shipped during the first half of 2020 (Column **H** of the **Orders** worksheet).

The average range refers to the values in **Orders!E$2:E$8400**, while the request to consider only on the orders shipped during the first half of 2020 (from 01/01/2020 to 06/30/2020) must be met with 2 different criteria, working on the same range (**Orders!H$2:H$8400** with criteria ">= 01/01/2020" and "<=06/30/2020").

It is important to consider that the criteria set on the dates in this way can work only if the international options of the system in use are set to represent dates as "month/day/year".

EXERCISE 5.4 - Beauty (commented)

Tools needed to solve the exercise:
Pivot table.

Comment point 1

In order to create the pivot table, we should start by selecting the source data in the **Sales** worksheet. Then, we use the **Pivot Table** command available in the **Insert** tab of the Ribbon, making sure that the options suggested are correct.

In the new worksheet wherein the table is hosted, we then have to select the fields that should be presented. In this case: **Units sold** in the Values box (keeping the sum as the function to be applied); **Product** in the Rows box; Period in the **Columns** box.

Comment point 2

To group the list of products by brand, it is enough to insert the **Brand** field before the **Product** field in the **Rows box**.
To show only the brand level of detail, right click on one of the products to select the **Expand/Collapse** option, then the **Collapse Entire Field** command. At this point, to show the details for the brand STARFACE alone, click on the icon with the "+" symbol next to the name.

Comment point 3

To group the months in quarters, the month names just being simple text labels, we should proceed by **manually grouping** the columns. Select therefore the months belonging to the first quarter, then right-click, and select **Group**. Repeat the same procedure for the months belonging to the second quarter, then for those belonging to the following quarters.
To customize the labels, overwrite the existing ones with: First quarter, Second quarter, and so on.

Comment point 4

To filter the values of the table as required, insert the **Category** field in the **Filters** box, then select the option Skincare from cell **B2**.

Comment point 5

To complete the label customization, just overwrite the existing ones.

EXERCISE 5.5 - Europe sales

Tools needed to solve the exercise:
Pivot table, Pivot chart.

EXERCISE 5.6 - Erasmus

Tools needed to solve the exercise:
LEFT, PROPER, RIGHT, LEN, SEARCH, Data Validation, operations on worksheets (Hide).

EXERCISE 5.7 - Vitanic

Tools needed to solve the exercise:
AVERAGEIFS, COUNTIFS functions, Pivot table, Pivot chart.

EXERCISE 5.8 - Office Line

Tools needed to solve the exercise:
CONCATENATE, LEFT, MID, SEARCH, nested functions, Data Validation.

EXERCISE 5.9 - Greenwich Village

Tools needed to solve the exercise:
CONCATENATE, UPPER, LOWER, LEFT, RIGHT, MID, LEN, IF, SUMIFS functions, nested functions, Pivot table, Pivot chart, Remove Duplicates command, Data Validation, conditional formatting.

EXERCISE 5.10 - Black-yellow supporters (commented)

Tools needed to solve the exercise:
CONCATENATE, UPPER, LOWER, LEFT, RIGHT, IF, LEN, SEARCH, SUMIFS, AVERAGEIFS, COUNTIFS functions, nested functions, Pivot table, Pivot chart, Remove Duplicates command, Data Validation.

Comment point 1

This point has to be solved using some nested text functions, which are grouped within a CONCATENATE. The text functions to be used are (following the steps suggested by the text):
- UPPER and LEFT to obtain the first 2 digits of the last name
- RIGHT to obtain the last 4 digits
- LOWER for the gender
- UPPER and LEFT for the first 3 letters of the country
- The dash, that has to be inserted using the quotation marks ("-")

For the last request, that is to insert into the code a different label according to the age of each supporter, you have to use a double IF. The logical test of the first IF checks if the supporter's age is less than 26, as to indicate "YNG" if true.
In case the logical test is false, you will have to check if the supporter's age is greater than 60 using a nested IF function. In case the logical test of this second IF is true (i.e., age greater than 60), the output will be "SEN". Otherwise (i.e. when the age is between 26 and 60), the output "STD" is returned. Thus, the last text argument of the CONCATENATE function is:

IF(E2<26,"YNG",IF(E2>60,"SEN","STD"))

Comment point 2

Point 2 asks you to create a customized message for each supporter. Also, in this case you have to concatenate different text arguments: some of them can be directly taken from the table in the worksheet **Supporters**, whereas others require a manual input following the directions. The function CONCATENATE has to be created as follows:
- The text "Dear "
- The supporter's name, using RIGHT, LEN, and SEARCH
- The text ", you have gained a discount voucher to spend on purchases on our website! For more information please visit our web page at www.yellow-black.com/"
- A text to complete the web link started in the previous step: as the last digits ("it" or "en") depend on the supporter's country, it must be used as an IF function.

It is useful to underline that to answer the second step it has to be used both as a **LEN** and **SEARCH** function nested into a **RIGHT** function.

As you are asked to recall just the supporter's first name (which has different digits according to the content of cells in column **B**), the number of digits to be extracted must be calculated as the difference between the total number of digits that compose the supporter's name (LEN(B2)) and the position (expressed in number of characters) of the space that separates the first name from the last name SEARCH(" ",B2).

Comment point 3

The creation of the pivot table starts with the selection of the data in the worksheet **Supporters** (Supporters!$A$1:$H$767). Then, you have to drag the fields **Age** and **Subscription type** in the areas (respectively) Column Labels and Row Labels. The selection of values is the last step. You can drag the field **Name** in the Values area as to automatically obtain a count of supporters.

To get the age clusters, you have to group the **Age** field, starting from 30 and grouping by 20. In this way, the clusters that Excel automatically creates are: "<30", "30-49" and "50-69".

Then, you have to add the field **Gender** as a detail of the field **Subscription type** and use the field **Country** as a filter of the table. The other requirements are met with an editing on the cells of the pivot table, by manually typing the headers required by the exercise.

The pivot chart can be automatically created from the pivot table.

Comment point 4

The first request is to calculate, in the new worksheet **Purchases**, the sum of incomes coming from supporters with at least one purchase in the year 2015, for each product purchased. You can create the list of products in column **A** of the new worksheet, and then use the SUMIFS function, setting the values in column **A** as the first group of criteria.

It is useful to underline that the second criterion to be used must indicate the function to consider only the rows of column **G** (of the **Online Store** worksheet) other than "None". This is why the criteria argument should be set using "<> None".

To answer the second request, it is necessary to use the function **AVERAGEIFS**, using again the group of criteria in column **A** (product purchased), and the criterion "Italy".

The last request is met by creating a new table in the worksheet **Purchases** that shows the supporters' countries as the criteria on which to set a COUNTIFS function.

Comment point 5

The first request has to be met using Data Validation (list) on the cell range **Online Store!$H$2:$H$1009**. The source list is the one in the worksheet **Gifts** (that has to be hidden later).

The second request has to be met using Data Validation (decimal) on the cell range **Online Store!$I$2:$I$1009**. Validation includes values from 5% to 35%: you have to write 0.05 and 0.35 while setting the range, as the character "%" cannot be used.

Comments and functions unit 6

EXERCISE 6.1 - Two hours (commented)

Tools needed to solve the exercise:
Calculations between hours and between dates, simple formulas (subtraction, multiplication), MAX, MIN, SUM functions.

Comment point 1
To calculate the duration of the training in the hh:mm:ss format, it is necessary, for each row, to subtract the value of the training end time (column **D**) from the training start time (column **C**). In both columns there are the decimal numbers corresponding to fractions of a day: 0 corresponds to 00:00:00 AM, 0,99999 corresponds to 11:59:59 PM. In most cases, Excel, recognizing that you are making calculations between times (due to the hh:mm:ss formatting of cells used for the operation), sets the result cell already in the correct format. If this should not happen, it will be necessary to select the custom format hh:mm:ss.

Comment point 2
To calculate the duration in minutes in decimal format, for each row you must multiply the result just computed in column **E** by 60 and then by 24. This is because we must remember that Excel stores dates and times as numerical values, in which the units correspond to days. For example, 6 hours for Excel are 1/4 of a day and therefore, they are represented in decimal format by the numeric value 0.25. Let us suppose we want to see minutes expressed as integers. Each hour is made of 60 minutes, so 6 hours should be expressed as 360 units of minutes. In order to convert the value 0.25 into 360, we need to multiply it by 60 (number of minutes in an hour), and then by 24 (number of hours in a day), applying at the end an appropriate format (Number or General).

Comment point 3
In this case, the reasoning to be applied is almost identical to the previous one. To calculate the duration in hours with decimal format, given that an hour is 1/24 of a day, it is sufficient to multiply by 24 the difference between the values in column **D** and those in column **C**, already calculated in column **E**.

Comment point 4
To find the difference between the best and the worst training, it is necessary to calculate the longest time in column **E** using the MAX function, and the shortest time also in column **E** using the MIN function, and then subtract the two values. The values of column E are in fact decimal numbers displayed in the format hh:mm:ss. In this case too, Excel should recognize that you are making calculations regarding times, thus it should set the result cell already in the correct format. If this should not happen, it will be necessary to select the custom format hh:mm:ss.

Comment point 5
To get the total duration of the trainings in hours, with minutes and seconds expressed as a decimal number, simply sum up the values in column **G**.

Comment point 6
To calculate the number of days that were necessary to reach the goal of running two consecutive hours, you need to subtract the value in cell **B2** (date of first training) from the value in cell **B34** (date on which you reached 2 hours of continuous running). Each date corresponds to a serial number expressing the number of days passed since 1/1/1900: the difference between the two dates therefore calculates the number of days that have passed.

EXERCISE 6.2 - Timesheet (commented)

Tools needed to solve the exercise:
WEEKDAY, COUNTIFS, AVERAGEIFS, OR, IF, DAYS, DATE functions, custom number formatting, calculations between hours, nested functions, simple formulas (addition, multiplication, division).

Comment point 1
To view the corresponding day, in full, referring to the date in column A, you must enter the WEEKDAY function in column D. The function returns a value ranging between 1 and 7. To display the names of the days you need to select the custom format dddd.

Comment point 2
To calculate the hours worked for each day with minutes and seconds as decimal numbers, you need to add the values in column **B** to those in column

C; the latter ones, however, must be divided by 60. In fact, 30 minutes expressed as a decimal number are equal to 0.5 (hours), and to obtain this number it is necessary to divide the minutes by 60 (30 divided by 60 is equal to 0.5). This calculation shall not be done for all the rows: if the corresponding day is Saturday, Sunday, public holiday or vacation, the text string "None" should appear. To do this you must use the IF formula, with a nested OR function in the test argument, which verifies the occurrence of at least one of the four conditions (Saturday, Sunday, public holiday, or vacation); if one of the conditions is met, the system will return the text "None", otherwise, it will perform the calculation. For example, in row 2, the function is as follows:
=IF(OR(D2=7,D2=1,B2="Public Holiday",B2="Vacation"),"None",B2+C2/60)

Comment point 3
In the **Analysis** worksheet, enter the days of the week from Monday to Friday in cells **A2:A6**. Remember, though, to enter first the corresponding numbers (2 to 6) and then display them with the custom format dddd.

Comment point 4
It is then requested to calculate, in column **B**, the number of times the employee (throughout the entire year of 2020) has worked for more than 8.5 hours for each day of the week. To do so, you must use the COUNTIFS function, as there are two criteria to manage:
- The counting of the number of days
- The counting of the cells in column **E** of the **Hours worked** worksheet with a value exceeding 8.5

Attention should be paid to the fact that, although the days are expressed in full, in reality, they have been inserted in the cells as numbers. Thus, you will need to take this into account when creating formulas.

Comment point 5
In column **C**, it is necessary to calculate the average number of hours worked by the employee as overtime (i.e., daily hours exceeding 8.5) for each day of the week.
In this case, AVERGAIFS function is required. Special attention should be paid to the quotation marks to be used to specify the criterion that allows you to select only the days with working hours exceeding 8.5 hours. Finally, you have to subtract the standard time of 8.5 hours from the daily average value

obtained, as we are interested in calculating only the hours worked as overtime.

Comment point 6

In column **D**, you are required to calculate the cost charged to the client regarding overtime, taking into account the hourly cost reported in cell **B8**: it is a simple multiplication between the values in columns **B**, **C** and the hourly cost in **B8**. The only small pitfall is that, to copy the formula in the cells below, you need to set a mixed reference to cell **B8** by blocking the reference to the row (**B$8**), or using an absolute reference (**$B$8**).

Comment point 7

In cell **B9**, you must calculate the percentage of days of work actually performed by the employee in the months from June to September (included) as the ratio of the number of days, in which the employee worked in the period in question and the total number of days present in the same period. To obtain the first value, you must use the COUNTIFS function specifying three criteria: the two extremes of the period, the condition of a day at work, and the date condition "<>None" verified in column E. The second value (i.e., the total of calendar days of the period in question) shall be calculated using the DAY function with an argument that uses the DATA function to express the two dates. Note that if we were to calculate an interval consisting of a single day, we would not be supposed to enter the same date twice in the DAYS function (otherwise, the result would be zero). For this reason, the range of the days between the months from June to September (included) shall be calculated from May 31 to September 30.

EXERCISE 6.3 - Date check (commented)

Tools needed to solve the exercise:
Data validation, IF, DATE, MONTH, WEEKDAY functions, nested functions, simple formulas (addiction, subtraction, multiplication).

Comment point 1
You must use the Data Validation command selecting the Whole number option, and setting the values between 1 and 31.

Comment point 2
In this case, we are dealing with a different implementation of the function used previously. Indeed, it is requested to select the List option in Data Validation. However, at this point, it is necessary to define the source of data to include in the list. In our case, we shall enter numbers between 1 and 12. It is recommended to create a list of data to be entered in a separate worksheet (in this case it is the **Lists** worksheet, as required by the exercise).

Comment point 3
This case is identical to the one in point 1, with the only difference that the values will range between 1900 and 9999.

Comment point 4
Point 4 can be solved in two steps, as the simplest solution requires first the execution of point 5. Anyhow, the first step is the following. Certainly, we shall use the WEEKDAY function. The problem is that this function, to return a correct value, must be applied to a numerical value that reflects the date resulting from cells **B2**, **B3**, and **B4**. It is, therefore, necessary to merge these cells using the DATE function, which will become the argument of the WEEKDAY function.

Comment point 5
To set a solution for this request, it is necessary to understand the behavior of the DATE function when an incorrect date is entered. If, e.g., we write DATE(2015,2,30) the result would refer to a non-existent date (February, 30). In such case, however, Excel returns the value 3/2/2015. Basically, if the number of the day entered is too large for a month in question, Excel counts the days in excess over to the next month. The lack of consistency in the month (February in the function arguments, March in the result), hence shows that something is not functioning correctly. So we can extract the month from the date with the MONTH function and compare it, with the IF function, to the number entered in cell **B3**. If it is greater, it means that the day entered into the system is not correct.

Comment point 6
The reasoning behind the solution for this request stems from the assumption that in a leap year the month of February ends on 29 instead of 28. Similarly, to what was done in point 5, we can use the DATE function, this time together with the MONTH function, to verify the month of the day on February 29. If

is equal to 2, it means that the day 29 really belongs to the month of February, and that it is a leap year.

EXERCISE 6.4 - Linguistic Certifications

Tools needed to solve the exercise:
DATEDIF, COUNTIF, COUNTIFS functions, simple formulas (subtraction, multiplication, division)

EXERCISE 6.5 - Techno Building

Tools needed to solve the exercise:
TODAY, DAYS, DATEDIF, IF, IFERROR, CONCATENATE functions, simple formulas (multiplication), Data Validation.

EXERCISE 6.6 - Hotel booking (commented)

Tools needed to solve the exercise:
Data Validation, IF, AND, OR, IFERROR, YEAR, MONTH, DAYS, DATE, WEEKDAY functions, nested functions, simple formulas (addition, multiplication), conditional formatting with formula.

Comment point 1
In both cells, it is necessary to use the Data Validation command by choosing the Date option and setting the values greater than or equal to 1/1/2021.

Comment point 2
To calculate the day of the week relating to the check-in and check-out dates it is necessary to use the WEEKDAY function in cells **C2** and **C3** and then change the default cell format to the custom format dddd, in order to transform the number contained in the cells in days written in full.

Comment point 3
To check if the check-out date is before the check-in date, we must use an IF function by setting **B3<B2** in the test argument.

Comment point 4
In cell **A5**, we need to use conditional formatting with formula because the condition must be set on cells different from those where it has to be applied. The formula is the same as the one set in the test argument of the IF function seen in the previous point **B3<B2**: it is important to remember that the conditions in conditional formatting with formula must begin with the "=" symbol.

Comment point 5
The Data validation to be set in cell **B8** must allow integers from 1 to 8. It is also necessary to set the error message as indicated in the exercise text.

Comment point 6
As in the previous point, also in cell **C8** it is necessary to use the Data validation command allowing all the integers between 0 and twice the number entered in cell **B7**: as the maximum number allowed it is therefore necessary to enter the formula **=B8*2**. Also in this case it is necessary to set the error message as indicated in the text of the exercise.

Comment point 7
Use the YEAR function to calculate the year of the check-in date. This number will be used in the following points.

Comment point 8
To calculate the number of days between the check-in and the check-out date in cell **G9** we need to use two IF functions. The first one is necessary in order to return an empty cell when at least one of the cells **B2** and **B3** is empty, that is, when one of the two dates has not been entered. The second IF function, on the other hand, must check if the check-out date is after the check-in date and calculate the number of days between the two dates, using the DAYS function. If the check-out date is prior to the check-in date, the function must return 0 (days), as it would not make sense to calculate a negative number of days. To calculate the number of days between the two dates, the DAYS function has been used and not the simple difference between the two dates because the DAYS function returns an integer, while the subtraction between two dates also takes into account any decimals (representing the hours, minutes and seconds for one or both dates).

Comment point 9
To check if check-in takes place on Friday or Saturday, we need to use the WEEKDAY function which, if the returned_type argument is omitted, returns a value between 1 and 7 where 1 corresponds to Sunday and 7 corresponds to Saturday. In the test argument of the IF function it is therefore possible to proceed in two ways: to use an OR function with two conditions, one to check if the check-in takes place on Friday (= 6) and one to check if it takes place on Saturday (=7); or to check if the day of the week is greater than or equal to 6, that is to Friday or Saturday.

Comment point 10
The calculation of the total amount without additional charges or discounts for the stay for adults and under 15s is done by multiplying the price per night per person by the total number of days and by the total number of people. The IFERROR function is required to ensure that any errors are handled by returning an empty cell.

Comment point 11
To solve the exercise point, it is necessary to calculate the amount of additional charges both for adults and for under 15s using an IF function in each cell of the range to check if the additional charge must be applied. If there is no need to apply an additional charge, the IF functions must return 0. To calculate the additional charge for the month of August, it is necessary to set the test argument of the IF function so that it checks if the check-in date is between 6 and 18 August of the year considered. This is done using an AND function with two conditions: the first condition checks if the date is equal to or after August 6 of the year of the check-in date, the second one if the same date is before or equal to August 18 of the same year. Remember that in Excel it is not possible to set a condition with the mathematical syntax of the type "data =< cell =< date". In both conditions the cell is compared with the two dates calculated using the DATE function, where the year of the check-in date is obtained from cell **G8**, calculated in point 7. Similarly, the additional charge for the check-in which takes place on Friday or Saturday uses what is calculated in cell **G10** at point 9. In all the cells of the range, cell references have been set so that it is possible to write the function in the cells of column **G** and then copy them into the cells of the column **H** without having to rewrite them.

EXERCISE 6.7 - *My friends*

Tools needed to solve the exercise:
IF, AND, YEAR, MONTH, DAY, TODAY, CONCATENATE, TRIM, PROPER functions, nested functions, Conditional Formatting with formula.

EXERCISE 6.8 - *Temporary workers (commented)*

Tools needed to solve the exercise:
Calculations between hours, simple formulas (addition, subtraction, multiplication, division), IF, HOUR, MINUTE, CONCATENATE, DAY, MONTH, YEAR functions, nested functions.

Comment point 1
In cell **B4**, just add the value of cell **B3** to that of cell **C3**. The latter one, however, must be divided by 60 to obtain the decimal value corresponding to minutes: in fact, it is necessary to obtain a value expressed in hours; the minutes must therefore be expressed in the same unit of measurement. The minutes of cell **C3** are then converted to hours by dividing by 60: 30 minutes correspond to 0.5 (hours).

Comment point 2
In this case, just subtract the smallest value (column **A**) from the largest one (column **B**) and multiply the result by 24, for the same reason described in the previous point.

Comment point 3
The difference between the actual time and that agreed on is obtained by subtracting the values in column C from the value in cell **B4**. If the employee has worked less, the difference will then be a positive number. To generate a non-compliance, this difference must be greater than the 6-minute tolerance. Considering that in column **C** and in cell **B4**, we have expressed hours as integers and minutes as decimals, we must transform the 6 minutes into a decimal number. The formula is 6/60 or 0.1.

Comment point 4
The question can be solved by applying the function HOUR to the values of column **C** divided by 24; in fact, while in column **C** integers represent the hours, we must remember that when we use the date/hour functions, integers are

interpreted as days. Therefore, we must transform the hours from column C into days, dividing them by 24.

Comment point 5

The solution is practically identical to the one in the previous point, with the only difference that instead of the HOUR function, you will use the MINUTE function.

Comment point 6

In this case we have to use a simple IF function to return 0 in case of compliance or the difference in minutes in the event of non-compliance. There are two possibilities for the calculation of minutes:

- Subtract the values in column **C** from the value in cell **B4** and then multiply the result by 60 or
- Divide the values in column **F** by 60 (to have the minutes in decimals), add them to the values in column **E**, and then subtract the result from the value in cell **B4**. Finally, multiply the result by 60, as the value obtained represents the minutes in decimal format, while it is necessary to have minutes ranging between 0 and 60.

In theory, the two possibilities should be identical, while in practice, the second is preferable as the first one returns minutes in decimal numbers while the second returns only integers (subject to exceptions due to system rounding-ups). This is because the HOUR and MINUTE formulas in columns **E** and **F** apply rounding-ups that eliminate decimal numbers.

Comment point 7

In this case, it is necessary to apply the CONCATENATE function within the IF function, as you must first check whether there is any non-compliance. Furthermore, it is necessary to subdivide the date in column **A** using the YEAR, MONTH, and DAY functions (alternatively, you could use the TEXT function, a topic of unit 9).

Due to possible inaccuracies in the rounding performed by Excel in previous calculations, it could happen that for some dates the result would show an offset in minutes with many decimal places. In such case, the problem could be resolved by using a ROUND function (another topic of unit 9).

EXERCISE 6.9 - Payments (commented)

Tools needed to solve the exercise:
IFERROR, LEFT, SEARCH, IF, DATE, WEEKDAY, AND, OR, YEAR, MONTH, DAY, HOUR, MINUTE, CONCATENATE, UPPER functions, nested functions, simple formulas (addition, subtraction, multiplication), custom number formatting, Conditional Formatting.

Comment point 1
As the second name is separate from the first name by a space, you can proceed as follows:
- Find where the space is located, in terms of characters, using the SEARCH function.
- The result then can be used within the LEFT function to extract only the letters that match the first name. However, be careful: it is necessary to decrease the result of the SEARCH function by one unit, as the letters of the name end one character before the position of the space.

However, in the case of individual names, the approach just mentioned would return an error, as the formula would not find the space character. It is therefore necessary to insert the foregoing within an IFERROR function, which in case of error, will simply return the value of column **A**.

Comment point 2
Regarding the report that payment has been made, this can be solved with an IF function that, on finding the word "PAID" in column **F**, returns the wording "Already paid!". In the event that payment has not yet been made, it is necessary to distinguish in between the two cases (purchase made before March 15, 2020 and purchase made after March 15). Here too, you can use the IF function and set it to add 90 days to the value of column **D**, when the purchase date is before March 15, 2020, or else set it to add 120 days to the value of column **D**.

Note: to express the value of March 15, 2020, in the formula you must use the DATE(2020,3,15) function that allows Excel to treat the date as a number and therefore to compare it to the values of column **D**.

Comment point 3
To extract the day of the week from a date, simply use the WEEKDAY function for the data in column **G**. In some cases, however, the formula would

return an error, as for payments already made, column **G** contains the wording "Already paid!". You can solve this situation in two ways:
- The IF function combined with the "Already paid!" condition in column **G** or
- The IFERROR function applied to payment deadline date

In both cases, the return value must be an empty cell (indicated by "").

To make sure that the name of the week in full (Monday, Tuesday etc.) appears in the cells of the **Day** column, you need to apply the custom format dddd. To ensure that Saturdays and Sundays are formatted automatically in bold, with a dark blue font character and a light blue background color, it is necessary to apply Conditional Formatting, taking into account that the values in the **Day** column are numbers from 1 to 7, representing the weekdays (displayed in the just set dddd format). It is then possible to proceed in two ways:

- Applying twice the Conditional Formatting on the same range of cells, setting the cells of DAY column equal to the value of 1 (for Sundays) in the first instance, and to the value of 7 (for Saturdays) in the second instance.
- Applying Conditional Formatting with formula, verifying jointly the condition (using the OR operator) as follows: OR = (H2=1, H2=7).

Comment point 4

To fulfill the request of point 4, you have to enter in **New Discounted Amount**, a new column, a function that can return different results depending on the time of purchase and on the fact of payment already made.

From the description it is clear that we are in front of a nested IF function, as different alternatives must be managed. In particular, there are three alternatives and therefore two IF functions (one within the other) will be needed. You can start by checking if the payment has been made: if column **F** (or **G**) shows that payment has already been made, then the formula should return the value "Send voucher". In case this condition has not been verified, you need to insert another IF function, setting the following condition: if the HOUR function applied to the cell of column E returns a value greater than or equal to 23 and the MINUTE function (applied to the same cell) returns a value greater than 10, then a 15% discount (i.e., 85% of the value in column **F**) must be applied, otherwise a 5% discount (i.e., 95% of the value in column **F**) shall be applied.

Comment point 5

To prepare a message according to the provided indications, it is essential to concatenate several text strings using the CONCATENATE function (or "&" operator) as follows:

- The opening courtesy formula is a simple text string, which however, must include the separation space from the string that will follow.
- To obtain all-uppercase sequence of Cleaned Name and Last Name (separated by a space), the UPPER function has been applied to the concatenation of the cells in columns B and C. To avoid further complication of the formula, the "&" concatenation operator has been used.
- The text "you can spend this voucher of $ 20 by" has been treated as a single argument of the CONCATENATE function, without forgetting the spacing and the punctuation at the beginning and the end of the string.
- The deadline date has been finally inserted by decomposing the Date of purchase present in column D and adding one unit to the year component.

EXERCISE 6.10 - Stationery (commented)

Tools needed to solve the exercise:
UPPER, CONCATENATE, LEFT, RIGHT, MID, SEARCH, WEEKDAY, SUMIFS, COUNTIFS, AVERAGEIFS functions, simple formulas (addition, multiplication), custom number formatting, Pivot table, Pivot chart, Data Validation, Remove Duplicates command, and calculations between hours.

Comment point 1
The answer to the first question involves the use of the UPPER function (rendering the entire string to be created in capital letters), within which the CONCATENATE function shall be used (needed to combine all the parts that make up the ID code). Within this latter, in addition to fixed text arguments, such as slashes, we have to use different functions: the LEFT function to extract the first character of the article type, the RIGHT function to extract the last character of the article type, the SEARCH function, inserted in the MID function, to be able to extract the first character of the second word of the Item. More specifically, the syntax of this last part is the following:

MID(C2,SEARCH (" ",C2)+1,1). Notice that the "+1", after the SEARCH function, is required to extract the letter following the space that the SEARCH function has found.

In order to respond to the second part of the requests from point 1 and to calculate the day of the week related to each sales date, it is necessary to use the WEEKDAY function and then change the default format of the cell with a customized one such as dddd, so as to convert the number in the cells into days written in full.

Comment point 2

The pivot table to be created must compare the quantity sold by Item and by Sale date and time: given that the size to be analyzed is made up by the quantities sold, you must drag the Quantity field in the Values area of the pivot table. The Item field may instead be entered into the Column Labels while the Sale date and time field can be dragged into the Row Labels. The decision of which field to display in a row and which in a column depends only on evaluations related to the layout (it is usually better to have many rows and a few columns).

To solve the subsequent requests for customization of the pivot table, you should remember that the values of pivot tables can be grouped in two ways: by selecting the cells that you want to group and then selecting the Group command from the menu that appears, when you right-click with the mouse; or - in case the data are of the numerical type, as are the dates and hours in Excel - by right-clicking on one of the values and then selecting the Group command. You will be asked then to choose the desired type of grouping, based on the type of data available.

To create the pivot chart, it is sufficient to position the cursor inside the pivot table and then use the Pivot Chart command.

Comment point 3

Point 3 of the exercise is solved using the Data Validation command: after having selected the range of cells to be prepared (in our case B2:B4), select the Data Validation command, which opens a dialog box with three tabs. On the Setting tab you must set the decimal value ranging between 0 and 1, while on the Error Alert tab, it is necessary to set the Stop style and then enter the message title and text.

Comment point 4

The calculation of the amount of each order issued can be done by multiplying data of columns **C** and **F**.

To calculate the total turnover for each product type, considering only the sales made in the first 10 days of the month, it is necessary to use the SUMIFS function, because there are two criteria to manage: the product type and the sales date. The formula is as follows:

=SUMIFS(G$15:G$454,D$15:D$454,A2,A$15:A$454,">=03/01/2020",A$15: A$454,"<=03/10/2020")

It should be noted that the condition "ranging between" is managed as a union of two conditions "greater than or equal to" and "less than or equal to": in this case it is therefore necessary to set the conditions "greater than or equal to 03/01/2020" and "less than or equal to 03/10/2020".

The list of the products marketed by the company in March can be obtained by copying the values in column **E** of the **March sales** worksheet, pasting them in column **A** of the **Analysis** worksheet and then using the Remove Duplicates command. To calculate the number of orders, the total turnover and average turnover, it is then necessary to use the COUNTIFS, SUMIFS, and AVERAGEIFS functions. All formulas are based on the data indicated in the **March Sales** worksheet. Please note that in these functions all the criteria including a comparison operator must be put between quotation marks.

Comment point 5

In this case, it is necessary to subtract the values of column **A** from those of column **E**, and then multiply by 24. As explained in other exercises, Excel uses days as the unit of measure for managing dates and time: integers are therefore days, while decimals are fractions of a day. To change an integer (days) into hours, you need to multiply it by 24 (hours in a day).

It is furthermore requested to calculate, in a table to be created in the same worksheet, the number of individual products sold (not the sum of quantities) for each day, whose shipping time was less than 100 hours, and the number of those whose shipping time was equal to or greater than 100 hours. The request can be carried out using the COUNTIFS function. To count the days, refer to the values in column **B** of the **Online sales** (Day column) worksheet, while for the delivery time, refer to column **F**. The optimal choice regarding the criteria is to write them as table headers (the days on the rows, written as numbers and then formatted with custom format dddd; and shipping time as the column header), using then in the final formula references to the related cells.

Comments and functions unit 7

EXERCISE 7.1 - Rocky Sports (commented)

Tools needed to solve the exercise:
VLOOKUP, AVERAGEIFS functions, Data Validation.

Comment point 1
The request to return the name of the area agent next to each store in the **Stores** worksheet must be carried out using the VLOOKUP function, which allows to look for a value in the first column of another table and returns a value corresponding to the one sought, placed in another column. The elements shared by the tables of the **Stores** and **agents** worksheets are the values of the Country column: the VLOOKUP function must therefore be set to look for the value of a nation in the first column of the table leaf agents. Once you find the Country, the function will return the name of the correspondent, which is on the same line, in the second column.

Note that the cell reference in the value argument of the VLOOKUP function in cell **D2** of the **Stores** worksheet is relative, to allow copying the function downward. The cell references in the table_array argument, instead, are mixed (they could also have been absolute) because it is necessary that the coordinates of the table of the **Agents** worksheet do not adjust to the new position when the function is copied in the cells below. Finally, the range_lookup argument has been set to the FALSE value because it is necessary that the match between the value sought (value argument) and the value found in the first column of the table in the Agents worksheet (table_array argument) is exact.

Comment point 2
To calculate the commissions that Rocky Sports has to pay to the agents for the turnover achieved in the assigned area, it is necessary to multiply the turnover of each store by the correct commission rate. The turnover of each store is already present in the **Stores** worksheet, whereas the commission rates to be used for the calculation are in the **Commission rates** worksheet and must be returned using the VLOOKUP function.

The table of the **Commission rates** worksheet does not contain all the possible turnover values in its first column, but just some of them, sorted in an ascending order, which represent the lower bounds of different numerical ranges, as shown in the following figure.

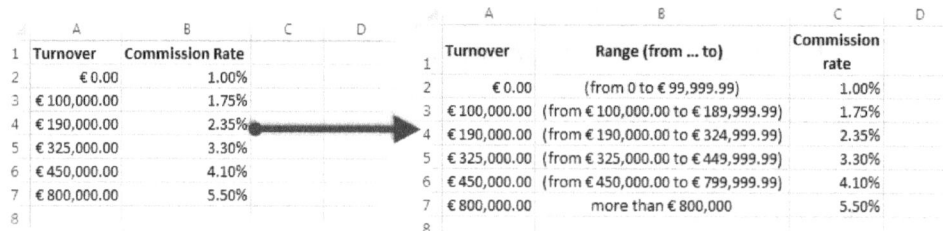

When the searched values are numerical, they are sorted in an ascending order and represent the bounds of a numerical range (from-to), it is necessary to use the VLOOKUP function imposing an approximate match (TRUE value in the range_lookup argument).

Therefore, to calculate the commission to be paid by Rocky Sports in cell **E2**, we must multiply the turnover of the Cracow 2 store (cell **B2**) by the commission rate corresponding to 471,441.57 euros. We use the VLOOKUP function to look for the turnover value (cell **B2**) in the first column of the table in the **Commission rates** worksheet, which then returns the corresponding value of the second column. Note the formula present in cell **E2** of the **Stores** worksheet: the arguments value, table_array and range_lookup have been set so that the function looks for the turnover value in the first column of the Commission rates table and returns the corresponding value of the second column.

The range_lookup argument has been set with the TRUE value because the values in the first column of the table in the **Commission rates** worksheet are not continuous and represent the lower bounds of different numerical ranges (as shown in column **B** of the previous figure). In these cases, it is necessary to use the TRUE value to set an approximate match, because if the VLOOKUP function does not find the exact value, it returns an error.

Comment point 3

The request of the third point of the exercise is to create a drop-down list in the cell, from which it is possible to choose the name of one of the countries where the Rocky Sports stores are. After creating the new **Average** worksheet and the heading in cell **A1**, it is necessary to set a Data Validation in cell **A2**. The validation criteria must be set selecting the List option, which allows limiting data entry in the cell to the values in the list of countries of the **Agents** worksheet. About the settings of the Data Validation command, note that in the Source box a range that considers only the cells with the names of countries has been inserted, thus excluding the heading and all the other empty cells of the first column of the **Agents** spreadsheet.

Comment point 4

On the basis of the country selected, in cell **B2** of the **Average** worksheet, we must calculate the average commission to be paid by Rocky Sports when the store turnover has been greater than 500,000 euros.

The average of the commissions should be calculated when two conditions are met: the country selected in cell **A2** and the turnover greater than 500,000 euros. In order to perform the calculation, it is necessary to use the AVERAGEIFS function, set as follows:

- In average_range argument insert the values of the Commission field (column **E** of the **Stores** worksheet)
- In criteria_range1 argument insert the values of the country field (column **C** of the **Stores** worksheet) and in the criteria1 argument the reference to cell **A2**, which contains the name of the country selected from the drop-down list
- In criteria_range2 argument insert the values of turnover (column **B** of the **Stores** worksheet) and in criteria2 argument the criterion ">500000"

About the AVERAGEIFS function, note that the cell references are relative in all the arguments that contain cell ranges, because the function does not have to be copied downwards or in other cells. Moreover, the condition set in the Criteria2 argument was properly enclosed in quotation marks: in this regard, it should be remembered that in the AVERAGEIFS function the criteria including a comparison operator followed by a number must always be enclosed in quotation marks.

To complete the fourth point of the exercise, it is also necessary to ensure that when it is not possible to calculate the average commission (e.g., because the stores of a country have not reached the 500,000 euros of turnover) the function shows a dash as a result in cell B2.

In the solved file an IFERROR function has been used, so that in case the AVERAGEIFS function returns an error (Value argument), a dash is shown (value_if_error argument).

EXERCISE 7.2 - Property evaluation (commented)

Tools needed to solve the exercise:
IF, OR, TODAY, DATEDIF, VLOOKUP functions, nested functions, operations on worksheets (Hide), worksheet protection, workbook protection.

Comment point 1
Based on the data available about a property, it is possible to answer the questions of point 1 by doing the following:
a) The exact age of a property to the current date (the one when the file is opened and used) is calculated using the DATEDIF and TODAY functions. It has to be noted that DATEDIF function is available in Excel to guarantee compatibility with older software, and it expects the use of parameters only with the English syntax (where: year = y, month = m, day = d). Therefore, to calculate in **B4** the difference in years between the date of construction and today, we have to write: =DATEDIF(B3,TODAY(),"y"). To ensure that cell B4 is blank when in B3 the date is missing, the formula should be completed as follow: =IF(B3="","",DATEDIF(B3,TODAY(),"y")).
b) To determine the value per square meter, it is necessary to use the VLOOKUP function such that the value per square meter corresponding to the range where the actual years of age belong is returned. Using the table available in the **Property age** worksheet, and making sure that the resulting cell is blank when the input value is missing, in cell **B5** the following formula should be used: =IF(B4="","",VLOOKUP(B4,'Property age'!A3:B6,2,TRUE)). Note, the use of the parameter TRUE (fourth argument of the lookup function) so as to get the value corresponding to the range where the years of age belong, not being ensured the exact correspondence with one of the values in the table of the Property age worksheet. In this case, it has to be remembered the importance of sorting the table in the **Property age** worksheet in ascending order by years (column **A**).
c) The initial estimate of the property is given by the product of the square meters time the value per square meter just calculated. Also in this case the output cell should be blank if the input cell is empty. Therefore, the formula in **B6** should be: =IF(B5="","",B2*B5).

d) The improving or worsening rates in percentage terms have to be calculated, in cells **C9:C12**, using the same lookup approach (VLOOKUP) adopted in the previous steps. However, this time it is important to consider that the value (among those available in the **Parameters** worksheet) exactly corresponding to the code entered in column **B** of the table in which the corrective rates are calculated has to be returned. For this reason, the fourth argument of the lookup function has to be FALSE (or 0):
=IF(B9="","",VLOOKUP(B9,Parameters!A2:C5,3,FALSE)).
The formula, initially inserted in **C9**, will then have to be rewritten in the cells below, changing every time the references to the correct table among those in the **Parameters** worksheet.

e) Calculating the improving or worsening rates in euros, given by a simple multiplication of the initial estimate with the correction rate in percentage, the use of the OR function ensures that the cell remains blank in case even just one of the cells of origin contains no data:
=IF(OR(B$6="",B9=""),"",$6B*C9). After inserting the formula in **D9**, paying attention to the correct use of the $ symbol, you can perform the calculations in the cells below by copying and pasting the content in cell **D9**.

f) After the calculations above, the final estimate of the property in cell **D13** is given by the arithmetic sum of all the amounts in euros that have been previously calculated: =SUM(B6,D9:D12).

Comment point 2

To protect the **Evaluation** worksheet, ensuring that in cells **B2:B3** and **B9:B12** is possible to enter the data, you need to change the setting of these cells, making them **Not** Locked. Please note that in the default settings of the Format Cells menu, the security option Locked is originally preset on all cells. Before activating the protection of the worksheet (Protect Sheet command), it will therefore be necessary to uncheck the case of the Locked option for those cells that need to be editable.

Comment point 3

To hide the **Property age** worksheet, it is necessary to select the Hide command, for instance, from the context menu that you get by clicking with the right key of your mouse on the label with the name of the worksheet. The same applies to the **Parameters** worksheet.

Comment point 4

Activating the Protect Workbook command (keeping the standard settings) each change to the structure of the workbook will be prevented, including the possibility to show worksheets previously hidden.

EXERCISE 7.3 - Copy shop

Tools needed to solve the exercise:
Data validation, operations on worksheets (Hide), IFERROR, VLOOKUP, IF, AND, OR functions, nested functions, simple formulas (multiplication), worksheet protection, workbook protection.

EXERCISE 7.4 - Paper and related (commented)

Tools needed to solve the exercise:
IF, AND, RANK.EQ, DAVERAGE functions, nested functions, Data validation command, Conditional formatting, operations on worksheets (hide), workbook protection.

Comment point 1

The solution of the first problem requires the use of the IF function with the RANK.EQ function and the AND function nested. The IF function is the outer function, and it is the one that allows to define the different results to the occurrence or absence of certain conditions (in this case related to the price of the products). As the possible results are three, you will need to nest another IF function within the outer IF. The logic of the function is as follows:
=IF(check whether the product is one of the five most expensive, if true the result is "premium product", if false: IF (check whether the product is between the 6th and the 10th most expensive, if true: result is "top product", if false the result is an empty cell))

To check if the product is one of the five most expensive you must use a function RANK.EQ. The function RANK.EQ, in fact, returns the position of a value in a list (depending on the direction selected in the third argument of the function, "1" can match the more or less expensive product). To identify the five most expensive products, therefore, you can use the following syntax, which is the test argument of the outermost IF:

RANK.EQ(D2,D$2:D$39,0)<= 5

The value "0", in the third argument of the RANK.EQ function (order), indicates the direction of the function: in this case, it is decreasing (i.e., the result "1" corresponds to the highest value).
For products from the sixth to the tenth, however, you can use two functions RANK.EQ within an AND function (position >=6 and at the same time <=10). The complete function will be:

=IF(RANK.EQ(D2,D$2:D$39,0)<=5,"premium product",IF(AND(RANK .EQ(D2,D$2:D$39,0)>=6,RANK.EQ(D2,D$2:D$39,0)<=10),"Top product",""))

Alternatively, you can also use a single function RANK.EQ, which identifies the products with rank>11: the case excluded, in this way, would be the one related to the products from the 6th to 10th.

Comment point 2
The second step requires the use of conditional formatting, with a rule that includes a formula. The format, in fact, should not be applied to the cells that contain the reference values (column Premium/top), but to the cells of the column Product ID. The formulas to be included in the two rules of conditional formatting, after selecting the cells to format (**A2:A39**), are as follows:
=E2="Premium product"
=E2="Top product"

Comment point 3
In this case, you need to set a Data Validation criterion of the List type on cells from **B2** to the bottom of column **B**. A selection of such cells can be made by conveniently selecting cell **B2**, then pressing the key combination CTRL+SHIFT+down Arrow (twice). Once you select the cells and choose the Data Validation command, you can set as a reference the list of values already available in the **Lists** worksheet. The exercise also asks you to specify an error message of the type Interruption (always from the Data Validation dialog box, in the Error Alert tab).

Comment point 4

To hide the **Lists** worksheet, simply click with the right mouse button on the corresponding tab and use the Hide command. Once you have done this, you can protect the structure of the workbook (Protect Workbook command) and enter the required password.

EXERCISE 7.5 - Purchasing Department

Tools needed to solve the exercise:
IF, VLOOKUP, SUMIF functions, simple formulas (subtraction), Conditional Formatting, creation of a mixed chart and with two axes.

EXERCISE 7.6 - DoReMi

Tools needed to solve the exercise:
Simple formulas (addition, subtraction, multiplication, division), VLOOKUP function, workbook protection, creation of mixed chart with two axes.

EXERCISE 7.7 - Thinkstore

Tools needed to solve the exercise:
Data validation, IF, VLOOKUP, IFERROR functions, simple formulas (addition, subtraction, multiplication), operations on worksheets (hide), worksheet protection, workbook protection.

EXERCISE 7.8 - Print Service

Tools needed to solve the exercise:
TODAY, IF, VLOOKUP functions, Data validation, simple formulas (addition, subtraction, multiplication), hide worksheets, worksheet protection, workbook protection.

EXERCISE 7.9 - European University

Tools needed to solve the exercise:
VLOOKUP, DATEDIF functions, Pivot table.

EXERCISE 7.10 - Consulteam

Tools needed to solve the exercise:
Data validation, CONCATENATE, IF, VLOOKUP, OR functions, simple formulas (addition, multiplication), operation on worksheets (hide), worksheet protection, workbook protection.

EXERCISE 7.11 - Candidates selection

Tools needed to solve the exercise:
TODAY, DATEDIF, VLOOKUP, IF, AVERAGE, COUNTIFS, AVERAGEIF, SUMIFS, COUNT, MAX, nested functions, creation of a mixed chart with two axes, operation on worksheets (Hide), worksheet protection, workbook protection.

EXERCISE 7.12 - MagicWood

Tools needed to solve the exercise:
VLOOKUP, SUM, RANK.EQ, AVERAGEIFS, IFERROR functions, unit normalization, time units normalization, conditional formatting, Pivot tables, Remove Duplicates command.

EXERCISE 7.13 - Phone calls (commented)

Tools needed to solve the exercise:
VLOOKUP, IF, LEFT (or MID), WEEKDAY, MATCH, AVERAGEIFS, nested functions, Pivot table, Data validation, worksheet protection, Remove duplicates command function, workbook protection.

Comment point 1

The range_lookup argument of the VLOOKUP function entered in the new Destination/Operator column of the **Calls** worksheet has been set with the value FALSE to force an exact match between the values sought and found. The field in common between the two tables (Phone number) contains in fact textual values made of numbers and text characters (asterisks), so it would make no sense to set an approximate match, possible only when the values of the first column of the table set in the table_array argument are numeric and sorted in an ascending order.

In the Landline/Mobile column of the **Calls** worksheet, we used the IF function to check if each call was directed to a landline number or to a mobile number. The test argument of the IF function is the following:

LEFT(E2,3)="393"

In practice, the IF function checks whether the first three characters starting from the left correspond to "393": if so it is a call to a mobile operator, otherwise to a fixed operator. As the first two characters of all the numbers in the list are the same ("39"), we could have achieved the same result also using the MID function in the test argument of the IF function to see if the third character was equal to "3": MID(E2,3,1)="3".

Comment point 2

The duration of each phone call was calculated as the difference between the ending time of the call and its starting time. To view the results in the hh:mm:ss format, we need to set a Time format in the cells of the Call Duration column.

The calculation of the cost of each phone call in the Cost of Call column is made using a first IF function to identify calls to landline number from those going to mobile number, and a second IF function to consider different pricing based on the day of the week of the calls to mobile numbers. The syntax of the function in cell **I2** is the following:

=IF(G2="Landline",0.15,IF(WEEKDAY(B2,1)<=3,0.0015*H2*24*60*60,0.002*H2*24*60*60))

There are two issues to note: the first one concerns the test of the second IF function (WEEKDAY(B2,1)<= 3), made possible by the fact that the days of the week Sunday, Monday, and Tuesday correspond to the numbers 1, 2, and

3. If the days were different, it would be necessary to use an OR function, and to set in its arguments various **WEEKDAY** functions.

The second issue to consider concerns the calculation of the cost of phone call: as the cost is calculated per second, to calculate the cost of the phone call, we need to multiply the cost per second by the duration of the phone call in seconds. The duration in cell **H2**, however, is expressed in days, so to calculate it is necessary to normalize the duration of the call, changing the unit of measurement from days to seconds by multiplying by 24 (hours per day), for 60 (minutes per hour), and again for 60 (seconds per minute).

Comment point 3

The table of the **Discounts** worksheet contains the discount rates on the cost of calls on the basis of different length intervals: each hour in the table represents the lower bound (the starting time) of each time interval. Furthermore, the values to be searched are numeric (remember that times are decimal values that express a fraction of a day), and the values of the first column of the **Discount** worksheet are sorted in an ascending order. Therefore, the VLOOKUP function used to return in the **Calls** worksheet the different discount rates is set with the value TRUE in the range_lookup argument.

The pivot table is set with the **Starting time** field in the Columns area, with the **Landline/Mobile** and **Destination/Operator** fields in the Rows area and the **Discounted cost** field in the Values area. The grouping of the **Starting time** field was done by selecting the value hours in the grouping criteria of the Group dialog box.

Comment point 4

Cell **A2** of the new **Control** worksheet has been set with a data validation with the list option: the cell references to the origin of the list are relative, but they could also be absolute or mixed, as the cell should not be copied to other positions. However, it is important to remember that, unless otherwise stated, in setting the origin of the Data Validation command only the cells containing the values must be selected, excluding from the references the table headings and the empty cells below the list.

The VLOOKUP function has been set with the value FALSE in the range_lookup argument because the values to look for are textual (made of text characters and numbers). In the col_index_num argument, the MATCH function has been used to return the number of the column with the discounted cost in the table of the **Calls** worksheet. To use the MATCH function effectively, the searched value must be equal to the heading of the field for which the number of column is needed (in this case "Discounted cost"). So, the MATCH function has been set to search for the value of the **B2** cell in the range of cells with the headings of the table of the **Calls** worksheet, with an exact match.

It should be remembered that to properly protect the **Control** worksheet it is necessary to first prepare the cells using the Format Cells command: in this case the options Locked and Hidden must be selected for all the cells of the sheet, except for cell **A2** in which they should not be selected.

Comment point 5

After creating the list of destinations using the Remove Duplicates command on the values of the Destination/Operator field copied in the **Cost Jan 2021** worksheet, we must use the AVERAGEIFS function to calculate the average cost of calls sustained by Luxury Car Rental. The request to consider only the phone calls made in the month of January 2021 means that we should set a criterion of the type "between": this type of criterion has to be divided into two simple conditions such as "equal to or greater than" and "equal to or less than" using two pairs of range-criteria arguments. In this case, it is therefore necessary to set a criterion as ">=1/1/2021" and the other one as "<= 1/31/2021", both on the range **Call!B$2:B$8134**. The AVERAGEIFS function must then be inserted in the value argument of the IFERROR function.

EXERCISE 7.14 - Box Office Star

Tools needed to solve the exercise:
CONCATENATE, LEFT, MID, RIGHT, IF, YEAR, VLOOKUP, MATCH, IFERROR, DATEDIF, TODAY, SUMIFS, COUNTIFS, AND, RANK.EQ functions, conditional formatting, data validation, subtotals, Remove duplicates command worksheet protection.

EXERCISE 7.15 - Sunshine Events (commented)

Tools needed to solve the exercise:
VLOOKUP, DATEDIF, TODAY, IFERROR, CONCATENATE, RIGHT, LEFT, YEAR, DAY, MONTH, SUMIFS, AVERAGEIFS functions, nested

functions, percentage calculation, Pivot table, conditional formatting, Data Validation.

Comment point 1

The range_lookup argument of the VLOOKUP function entered in the new column Description of the **Events** worksheet has been set with the FALSE value to set an exact match between the values sought and the values found. In this case, it has to be noted that the values to be sought (Ticket Category column) are textual, therefore it should not be possible to use the TRUE value in the range_lookup argument.

The calculation of the number of days between the present day and the day before each event was performed using the following function:
=D2-1- TODAY()
In particular, it should be noted that we used the TODAY function to calculate the present date dynamically.

Comment point 2

The pivot table was created with only the fields **Ticket category** (Column area), Event date (Rows area) and **Tickets sold** (Values area). Later the following operations were performed:

- The **Event date** has been automatically grouped by months
- The **Genre** field was added in the Rows area, under the **Event date** field already present in the area, to show the details of the event genre for each month
- The field **City** was added in the Filter area
- A numeric format with thousands separator and no decimal places was applied to the values of the **Tickets sold** field (command Number format in the Value field settings dialog box) to improve data readability and organization

Comment point 3

In order to return in the **Events** worksheet the values of the table of the **Margins** worksheet, we need to use the VLOOKUP function. Note that the TRUE value was used in the range_lookup argument to set an approximate match between the values sought (Ticket price field in the **Events** worksheet) and the ones found in the first column of the table set in the table_array argument (Ticket price field in the **Margins** worksheet). This setting is correct because both the data searched and those present in the first column of the table of the **Margins** worksheet are numeric; also, these are not continuous and have already been sorted in an ascending order.

The VLOOKUP function has been put in the Value argument of the IFERROR function so that the text "N.A." replaces an error message when the ticket price of an event is missing. Note that in this case, it would have not been possible to use the IF function to obtain the same result.

The calculation of the turnover margin in euros earned by Sunshine Events for each ticket category of event was made by multiplying the margin for each ticket category by the number of tickets sold. To avoid that the formula returns an error when there is no ticket price, we used the IFERROR function, but in this case we could have also used the IF function. For example, it would have been correct to use one of the following functions in cell **M2**:

=IFERROR(F2*I2*L2,"N.A.")
=IF(F2="","N.A.",F2*I2*L2)
=IF(F2="N.A.";"N.A.";F2*I2*L2)

Comment point 4

To create the required ID code we need several text, date, and time functions. The function used in cell **A2** of the **Events** worksheet is the following:

=MAIUSC(CONCATENATE(RIGHT(YEAR(D2),2),"-",G2,LEFT(B2,3),"-",LEFT(C2,3),DAY(D2),"/",MONTH(D2)))

Date and time functions are required because any date in Excel corresponds to a serial number, so the text functions do not allow extracting parts of a date from a cell, but only a few digits from the corresponding serial number.

The validation of the cells of the Rating column has been set by selecting all the cells of the column corresponding to each event (**O2:O493** range), then setting a decimal type data validation (between 1 and 10) and the customized error message.

Comment point 5

The list of genres can be created quickly by copying all the values of the Genre field of the Events worksheet in the first column of the **Calculations** worksheet, and then using the Remove Duplicates command.

The SUMIFS and AVRAGEIFS functions are necessary to calculate the total margin and the average percentage for the events organized in the month of

July, and have been set such that each one has two conditions to verify the date. It is worth recalling that it is not possible to enter in these functions criteria of type "between" (in this case "between 07/01/2021 and 07/31/2021"), but it is necessary to divide them in two conditions such as "equal to or greater than" and "equal to or less than". Therefore, both functions have two couples of range-criteria arguments, both set up on the cells of the **Event date** field of the **Events** worksheet, the first one with the criterion ">=7/1/2021" and the other one with the criterion "<=7/31/2021".

The last request of the exercise requires the use of conditional formatting, with a rule that includes a formula. The format, in fact, should be applied to the cells of the Ticket Code column, but the conditions must be verified in other columns (Tickets available and Event date). The formula to be included in the conditional formatting rule, after selecting the cells to format (A2:A493), is the following:

=AND(H2>=500,D2>=DATE(2021,7,21))

The DATE function is necessary for Excel to correctly compare the reference to the cell with the event and control dates (7/21/2021). When both the conditions are true the AND function returns TRUE and the formatting is applied to the cells of the Ticket Code field; when the AND function returns FALSE because one or both the conditions are false, the formatting is not applied.

Comments and functions Unit 8

EXERCISE 8.1 - Students (commented)

Tools needed to solve the exercise:

Recording a macro.
Comment
To carry out this exercise, you must record a macro that follows the requests step by step. The result is contained in the **Format_and_sort** macro in the **Exercise 8.1 - Students solved.xlsm** file.
As a good practice, the first two actions to perform when recording a macro that must act on a specific worksheet (to be done even when the file contains a single worksheet!) are: 1) the selection of the worksheet by clicking on its tab, 2) the selection of a cell in the worksheet - typically the one at the top left (A1). This produces the following instructions:

    Sheets("Students").Select
    Range("A1").Select

These two instructions allow VBA to always operate on the correct worksheet, even if new worksheets are added to the file later.
The selection of the table headers (the range **A1:G1**) can be done in various ways; depending on the method you are using, the recorder produces different instructions. Using the method "select cell A1 - hold down the shift key - select G1" you get the instruction in the solved file:

    Range("A1:G1").Select

Using the Method "select cell A1 - hold down the shift key - press the Ctrl key and the right arrow simultaneously" [Command key for Mac] you get this code:

    Range(Selection, Selection.End(xlToRight)).Select

which represents a generalization of the previous one because it makes the selection (.*Select*) of the range of cells (*Range*) that starts from cell **A1** (the *Selection* we have from the instruction in the previous row) and arrives at the last non-empty cell (*Selection.End*) by moving to the right (*xlToRight*), then to cell **G1**.

So this instruction would also apply if you add extra columns to the right of the table, or delete some of them, as long as no empty cells are left; the selection *Range("A1:G1")*, on the other hand, is fixed: by varying the size of the table in the Excel sheet, the VBA code does not update automatically.

Sheets and Range are typical Excel objects that allow VBA to understand which sheet and which cell or range of cells it has to work with. A trick to learn how to read the dot notation of VBA's instructions like "Object.Action" is to read them from right to left, to understand what you want to do (action, e.g. *.Select*) on which object (e.g. *Range*).

Selection.Font.Bold = True

This instruction modifies a property/attribute/characteristic of the *Selection* object (which now coincides with the range **A1:G1**): it activates the bold, setting the *.Bold* feature of the *.Font* to True.

To sort the table by increasing values of the **Name** column, you must first select a cell in that column (better not to use the header):

Range("B2").Select

The instructions from *ActiveWorkbook.Worksheets("Students")...* to *End With* are those related to reordering the table. We can note that:
- First it deactivates any possible sorting (*SortFields.Clear*) from the **Students** sheet contained in the active Excel file (*ActiveWorkbook*), and then adds (*.Add*) the sorting we want
- Having selected a cell within the table as the active cell allows VBA to understand / deduce what the overall dimensions of the table are (*Range("A2:G201")*)
- since the range starts from row 2, the selection does not contain the column headings of the table (*Header = xlNo*)
- the order is ascending (*Order:=xlAscending*)

- it sorts by rows (*Orientation = xlTopToBottom*)
- *Key:=Range("B2")* indicates which column (la **B**) to use

These are many parameters ... nobody learns them by heart! Typically, those who work with VBA make a lot of small macro recordings to extract the code snippets, articulated like this, which they then paste and integrate into the overall macro.

A neat way to complete / close a macro code is to select the first cell on the top left (**A1**) of the sheet that we want to be the active one when the program is finished. It is a conventional choice, but from a logical point of view it works like bringing the shopping cart back to the front door of the supermarket, instead of abandoning it somewhere. For this reason, it is advisable to close the macros with this action, even when not explicitly indicated:

Range("A1").Select

EXERCISE 8.2 - Tickets (commented)

Tools needed to solve the exercise:

Recording a macro, assigning a macro to a shape.

Comment

The highlights of the **Format** macro contained in the solved file are the following:

- Since the table is very long, instead of using the mouse wheel to reach the last row of the table (row **493**), it is better to use the system "click on the first cell in the column you are interested in (**B2**) and then press CTRL + SHIFT + DOWN ARROW "[Command with the Mac], obtaining the following instruction:

Range(Selection, Selection.End(xlDown)).Select

- Depending on which font color you have chosen (one of the Theme Colors, rather than one of the Standard Colors or More Colors...), your code may slightly differ from the resolved one

- The *With – End With* structures that VBA automatically creates are a way to write the dot notation in a more compact way, avoiding to keep writing the initial part common to all the lines; therefore this code:

With Selection.Interior
  .Pattern = xlSolid
  .PatternColorIndex = xlAutomatic
  .ThemeColor = xlThemeColorAccent3
  .TintAndShade = 0.399975585192419
  .PatternTintAndShade = 0
End With

is equivalent to writing:

Selection.Interior.Pattern = xlSolid
Selection.Interior.PatternColorIndex = xlAutomatic
Selection.Interior.ThemeColor = xlThemeColorAccent3
Selection.Interior.TintAndShade = 0.399975585192419
Selection.Interior.PatternTintAndShade = 0

- To obtain a non-repetitive code when you need to reorder a table by more than one column at the same time, as in this exercise, it is better to use the Custom Sort feature in the Home tab of the Ribbon
- The empty lines within the code were added manually, at a later time, to divide it into logical blocks that facilitate reading and understanding, they are not inserted by the recorder. Adding them is a highly recommended good practice
- Any shape or image can be combined later with a macro using the Assign macro... instruction from the object's context menu. It is also possible to add descriptive text (i.e. the name of the macro or a description of it) to the shape

EXERCISE 8.3 - Product list (commented)

Tools needed to solve the exercise:

Recording a macro, assigning a macro to a button.

Comment

The highlights of the **Sort** macro contained in the solved file are the following:
- When the macro has to operate on a specific sheet and there are multiple sheets in the file, a trick to correctly record the selection of the sheet and the first active cell in it, is to start recording by having the active cell in a different sheet (e.g., start the recording from cell **B2** of the **Macro** sheet); in this way you are forced to select the correct sheet and cell
- Since the first cell at the top left is given by the union of cells **A1:D1**, the *Range("A1:D1")* is directly recorded
- The actions of "copy the contents of the selection to the clipboard" (i.e. in the temporary memory of the operating system) and "paste the contents of the clipboard" translate into *Selection.Copy* and *ActiveSheet.Paste*
- It is important to recognize and remember the following instruction

Application.CutCopyMode = False

because it is the one that deletes the contents of the clipboard:
when you copy or cut something in Excel, the dashed border remains flashing around the copied / cut selection; to eliminate the unattractive effect (as well as empty the clipboard) it is useful to add this instruction at the end of the macro, if you have made a copy or cut and VBA has not already added it for us
- In Excel worksheets you cannot have "holes", i.e. numbers that jump when deleting rows-columns-cells. For this reason the *Selection.Delete* statement (and inside *Selection* now there is row **1** of the **Macro** sheet) is followed by *Shift: = xlUp*, which is used to make VBA understand that it must renumber all subsequent lines by subtracting the number of deleted lines, then making them "slide up"
- Note that while Bold and Italic are characteristics of characters (Font) that can only be present or absent (therefore True or False), there are different types of Underline; the simplest was used in the solved file: *xlUnderlineStyleSingle*
- In VBA all constant values/elements starting with xl, such as xlUp, xlToRight, xlUnderlineStyleSingle, are Excel specific values

- To automatically adapt the width of the columns to their content, use the Adapt column width function in the Format drop-down menu of the Home tab in the Ribbon (you will get the *Selection.Columns.AutoFit* statement)
- The type of button required in the exercise is found in the Insert drop-down menu, in the Controls group of the Developer tab, and is the first in the top left. Beware that although the command button in the third line looks the same aesthetically, the functioning of the Form Controls elements is different (much simpler) than the ActiveX Controls (which we will not use). With the buttons, the macro is assigned during the creation of the button itself. To customize the button name, use the Edit text function from the context menu

EXERCISE 8.4 - Stores (commented)

Tools needed to solve the exercise:

Recording a macro, assigning a macro to a button, simple VBA editing.

Comment

The highlights of the **Format** macro contained in the solved file are as follows:
- While the background/fill of the cell (*Interior*) is only one, the individual borders are eight in total; for this reason, by asking to apply the standard border "Thick bottom border", only *Borders(xlEdgeBottom)* has parameters set, all the other borders have *LineStyle = xlNone* which is the default and therefore those are instructions that can be removed from the macro (deleted) but it is not mandatory to do so
- Even if we had the operating system set to Italian and the exercise request was to apply the Italian standard currency format (i.e. Euro), VBA would still record the following instruction

Selection.NumberFormat = "$ #,##0.00"

with currency symbol $ and English separator format (decimal point and thousands separator comma) because VBA always follows British notations. It is the Italian Office settings of our machine that shows us the symbol and punctuation in the Excel file consistent with the local operating system settings.

The highlights of the **Delete_formats** macro contained in the solved file are as follows:
- When selecting an entire sheet (using the triangular button at the top left between the buttons of column A and row 1), VBA does not use the usual *Range* type object, which is used to represent single cells or ranges with traditional coordinates letter-number, but an object of type *Cells* that represents the set of all single cells identified with the numeric coordinates rowNumber,columnNumber (as in traditional mathematics). This is an extremely useful notation that we will review in other exercises.
Here the *Cells.Select* instruction, without specifying the coordinates of a single cell, means "select all the cells of the sheet"
- To delete only the formatting and not the contents of the cells, you need a special feature found in the Clear drop-down menu of the Home tab

EXERCISE 8.5 - Household linens

Tools needed to solve the exercise:

Recording a macro, assigning a macro to a button.

EXERCISE 8.6 - Arithmetic (commented)

Tools needed to solve the exercise:

Recording a macro, assigning a macro to a button.

Comment

In the **Addition** macro, the selection of multiple non-contiguous cells is represented by VBA by two statements:

Range("A2,A7").Select
Range("A7").Activate

The *.Select* identifies the list of cells by separating them with commas, so *Range("A2:A7")* with a colon means all the cells between A2 and A7, while *Range("A2,A7")* means "only the cells present in the list".

The *.Activate* tells VBA which of the two is the active cell in the selection, the last one we selected.

Another new notation is the one that VBA uses to write in the code the formulas we write in the cells:

$$ActiveCell.FormulaR1C1 = "=R[-6]C[-1] + R[-6]C[1]"$$

It writes in the active cell (which now is **D10**) a formula using the *R1C1* notation: we are used to the notation with letters for columns and numbers for rows, but for programming languages using letters is not easy (from A to Z, and then from AA to ZZ, and then from AAA to XFD). For this reason the recorder uses the RowNumber_ColumnNumber notation which is traditionally used in mathematics (e.g., matrix algebra).

Cells **C4** and **E4** also have cell references transformed into the R1C1 notation, but with a bit more reasoning. Instead of considering them in absolute terms (Row4Column3 and Row4Column5), VBA sees them as displacements from cell **D10**. Therefore, **C4** becomes R[-6]C[-1] because it is 6 rows above and 1 column to the left of **D10**, while **E4** becomes R[-6]C[1] because it is always 6 rows above but in 1 column to the right of **D10**.

The formulas we write in the cells of the worksheet are considered textual values by VBA, which is why they are written between quotation marks (pay attention to the = symbol which must be inserted between quotation marks too).

By analyzing the macro code of the other three arithmetic operations, you can see that, if desired, you could avoid registering them: it is sufficient to copy the **Addition** macro within Module1 and then change its name and the mathematical operator used in the formula.

Selection.ClearContents

The Delete (or Canc) key on your keyboard only clears the contents of the cells and not the formatting, which is exactly what you need in this case.

EXERCISE 8.7 - Airbnb (commented)

Tools needed to solve the exercise:

Recording a macro.

Comment

By testing the macro with the 2020 data file, it can be seen that if the automatic selection system of the **price** column (CTRL/Command + SHIFT + down arrow) was used during the recording, then the currency has been correctly applied up to bottom even in the case of a longer table:

Range("E2").Select
Range(Selection, Selection.End(xlDown)).Select
Selection.NumberFormat = "[$£-en-GB]#,##0.00"

because the *Selection.End(xlDown)* statement makes VBA calculate which is the last full cell in the table.

However, the reorder does not work correctly: the last 2,000 rows of the 2020 table are not taken into consideration. By checking the code, you can see that the recorder has "frozen" the cell reference of the table that reorders to the range **A2:H9001**:

ActiveWorkbook.Worksheets("Airbnb - London").Sort.SortFields.Add2 Key:=Range(_
"H2:H9001"), SortOn:=xlSortOnValues, Order:=xlDescending, DataOption:= _
xlSortNormal
With ActiveWorkbook.Worksheets("Airbnb - London").Sort
.SetRange Range("A2:H9001")

To generalize this code, it would be necessary to manually modify the program, creating a local variable in which to save the actual size of the table each time the macro runs.

EXERCISE 8.8 - Filtered data (commented)

Tools needed to solve the exercise:

Recording a macro, assigning a macro to a shape.

Comment

The problems in registration that prevent you from trying to create the **Data** sheet more than once in the file (because from the second attempt onwards the program goes – rightly - into run-time error), can only be overcome by intervening directly on the VBA code. You need to change these lines of code:

Sheets.Add After:=ActiveSheet
Sheets("Sheet1").Select
Sheets("Sheet1").Name = "Dati"

eliminating the reference to the standard name *"Sheet1"* (crystallized in the code), as proposed later in Exercise 8.17.

EXERCISE 8.9 - Deliveries (commented)

Tools needed to solve the exercise:

Recording a macro, assigning a macro to a button.

Comment

As in the previous exercise, it is necessary to manually modify a part of the recorded code to avoid problems in the macro test phase (from the second attempt to use the macros the program goes into run-time error). In this case the lines to be modified are:

Graph_create
ActiveSheet.Shapes("Chart 1").IncrementLeft -375.6
ActiveSheet.Shapes("Chart 1").IncrementTop 48.6
ActiveSheet.Shapes("Chart 1").ScaleWidth 1.21, msoFalse, msoScaleFromTopLeft

Graph_delete
ActiveSheet.ChartObjects("Chart 1").Activate

which all refer to the graphic object called "*Chart 1*", which exists with that name only the first time the chart is created: by recreating a new chart, this will be called *"Chart 2"* for VBA. For this reason, the error you get says "The element corresponding to the specified name was not found", because VBA looks for something called *"Chart 1"* that no longer exists in the file.

EXERCISE 8.10 - Subtotals

Tools needed to solve the exercise:

Recording a macro, assigning a macro to a button.

EXERCISE 8.11 - Table (commented)

Tools needed to solve the exercise:

Recording a macro, assigning a macro to a button, simple VBA editing.
Comment
The exercise aims to highlight once again the difference between using:
- user-defined and therefore static cell ranges (*Range("A1:C1")*, *Range("A1:C6")* etc.)
- rather than "dynamic" ranges, i.e. identified by VBA once the user has set the starting point

Range("A1").Select
Range(Selection, Selection.End(xlToRight)).Select
Range(Selection, Selection.End(xlDown)).Select

This increases the generalization of the code, making it more flexible in correctly handling cases not explicitly foreseen by the programmer.
In the **Delete_formats** macro it is necessary to insert the instruction that returns the width of column **B** to the original size because otherwise, after the first execution of the **Format** macro, it would no longer be restored: remember that the clear instructions (all, formats etc.) do not restore default row heights or column widths.

To check or modify the macro assigned to a button (or to a shape or image) simply use the Assign macro... command from the contextual menu.

EXERCISE 8.12 - Worksheet protection (commented)

Tools needed to solve the exercise:

Recording a macro, assigning a macro to a button, simple VBA editing, InputBox.

Comment

Some clarifications:
- To be sure that the macro can operate on any sheet, just do not select any of them during the registration and, when using it, make the sheet you want to protect the active one before launching the macro. Given the characteristics of the macro, it would make more sense - in a professional context - to save it locally on your machine and combine it with an icon on the Quick Access Toolbar or on the Ribbon
- The cell attributes *.Locked = True* and *.FormulaHidden = True* are applied to all the cells of the sheet (*Cells.Select*) to be sure not to skip any, using the instructions in the most generalized way possible (so avoid limiting to the range **B6:C33** only)
- As a matter of IT security, if a password is set while recording the macro, the password is not entered in the code; that's why it does not appear in our registration
- Working in *Option Explicit* mode within VBA, in order to use a local variable (a container in the computer memory in which to temporarily park a value, without writing it in an Excel cell), it must first be dimensioned, i.e. explicitly assign a name and a data type

Dim myPwd As String

Is the instruction to create the **myPwd** variable, which is enabled to contain text type values (*String*)
- To ask the user for a value (here the password he/she wishes to use), use the *InputBox* function which displays a dialog box with a field for

entering data and with two buttons, OK and Cancel, to send the data to VBA or close the window

myPwd = InputBox(" _ text that explains to the user what we are asking him/her _ ")

The argument of the function is the text we want to appear in the window. The contents of the window must be assigned to the variable, which has already been initialized, using the assignment operator = in this way:

container_name = what_we_want_to_put_inside

- In the solved file, to improve the readability of the *ActiveSheet.Protect* instruction, its parameters have been wrapped (one per line), reentering them to make it clear that they are part of the outermost upper line:

ActiveSheet.Protect _
  DrawingObjects:=False, _
  Contents:=True, _
  Scenarios:=True, _
  AllowFormattingCells:=True, _
  AllowFormattingColumns:=True, _
  AllowFormattingRows:=True, _
  AllowFiltering:=True, _
  Password:=myPwd

To wrap an instruction in VBA use the combination "blank + underscore".
To use the password requested from the user, the *Password* parameter must be added to the list of *.Protect* features. Note the use of the symbol :=, instead of the simple =, to assign the value on the right to the parameter written on the left.

EXERCISE 8.13 - Chart axis (commented)

Tools needed to solve the exercise:

Recording a macro, assigning a macro to a button, simple VBA editing.
Comment
Some clarifications about the code:
- to build a chart it is not enough to choose the type (first instruction), but you must also pass the data to it (second instruction):

    ActiveSheet.Shapes.AddChart2(240, xlXYScatterSmooth).Select
    ActiveChart.SetSourceData Source:=Range("Curves!$B$5:$C$26")

    Note that the indication of the range of cells to be used includes the name of the worksheet in which they are ("*Curves!$B$5:$C$26*") written with the classic syntax of absolute references of Excel formulas. This is because the chart is not physically part of the **Curves** worksheet (it is a *Shapes* type object placed on top) and because the data could belong to a different worksheet than the one in which the chart is
- the *ActiveSheet.Shapes* instructions concern any movements and resizing of the chart that you may have made during the registration phase and are relevant to a specific chart (the first that was done in the workbook, therefore in the solved one is "*Chart 1*"); to guarantee the generality of the code without complicating it, it is better to firstly eliminate them
- to transform the maximum value of the vertical axis of the graph from a constant value set by the program (180) to a value dependent on the data (which must therefore change if the data is changed), it is necessary for VBA to retrieve the value written in cell **C3**:

    Range("C3").Value

    The content of the cell is the *.Value* attribute of the *Range* object. Since **C3** contains the formula for calculating the maximum, every time the macro is launched it uses the updated/corrected value of the maximum.

EXERCISE 8.14 - Table template (commented)

Tools needed to solve the exercise:

Recording a macro, simple VBA editing, iterative structures.

Comment

The exercise intends to introduce the concept of replication of the same code several times: you want to perform the same type of actions on all the sheets in the workbook, without creating unnecessary repetitions. The macro must also function correctly regardless of the number of sheets present.

All the actions to be performed on a single sheet are recorded in the **Macro_Original**, thus constituting the block of code to be repeated several times.

We now need a programming structure capable of taking into consideration all the sheets in the folder, one at a time, to apply the same code block for all. That iterative structure in VBA is the *For Each... Next* loop, which works as follows:

For Each ws In ActiveWorkbook.Worksheets
  instruction_block to repeat
Next ws

For every single sheet (*ws*) belonging to the set of sheets of the active workbook
   Do these actions
Then move on to the next sheet until you've taken them all into account

ActiveWorkbook.Worksheets is the set of all the sheets in the active workbook (reading the dot notation from right to left!). We need a generic name to indicate the single sheet: here we chose **ws**, but **sheetK** could have worked just as well. However, we must remember that before we can use a name in VBA we must present it to him / let him know / define it / declare it by specifying what type of objects it belongs to, or rather what type of objects it may contain:

Dim ws As Worksheet

It is like saying: dear VBA, let me introduce you **ws** which is a worksheet object.

Before executing the block, within the *For Each*, the sheet **ws** must be selected or made active; the following instructions are alternatives to each other:

ws.Activate
ws.Select

Since the **Macro_Original** is already fine on its own, it is actually useless to copy it back into the **Macro_Modified**. As a best practice in the VBA Modules, you avoid leaving redundancies, i.e. many macros very similar to each other: it is done here for purely didactic purposes. What you do in reality is to break down a big problem into many smaller and easier to build, manage and update sub-pieces (top-down approach to programming and problem solving). For this reason, a more efficient solution than the exercise is this one:

Sub Macro_Modified( )
  Dim ws As Worksheet
  For Each ws In ActiveWorkbook.Worksheets
    ws.Activate

    Macro_Original   ' it calls the specific macro without rewriting the code
    ' after it has run it, VBA automatically returns here
  Next ws
End Sub

Since the macro is nothing more than a "named" code fragment, that is "with a name", we can use the name *Macro_Original* to tell VBA that when it gets to that instruction it must execute that macro, then go back and continue with the remaining *Macro_Modified* statements.

EXERCISE 8.15 - Alternate rows (commented)

Tools needed to solve the exercise:

Recording a macro, simple VBA editing, InputBox, conditional expressions, iterative structures.

Comment

The exercise aims to show how increasingly sophisticated programs can be created by nesting different types of programming structures. Below we analyze the **Macro_Modified** code.

The first data you need is the number of lines that the user wants to format:

n_rows = InputBox("Enter the number of rows to format")

Since the answer must be saved in a variable, this must first be created by assigning it the integer type:

Dim n_rows As Integer

We want to repeat the row formatting for all rows from 1 to the one indicated by the user. We therefore need not an object crossing loop (*For Each ... Next*), but a simple counter loop (*For ... Next*), where the variable **i** is the counter that subsequently assumes all the integer values from 1 to **n_rows** with an increment equal to + 1 (including extremes):

For i = 1 To n_rows
... code to be defined
Next i

Again, in order to use the variable **i** it must first be defined. Typically, all the declarations are gathered together at the beginning of the macro.

Dim i As Integer

Not all rows need to be formatted, only even-numbered ones. We therefore need a simple conditional structure (*If ... Then ... End If*), nested inside the *For*, that allows VBA to scan all the lines, to check if the identifying number of the line, our variable **i**, is even and only in this case do something. When the condition is false all the internal block is skipped, so no formatting is applied to the row.

>   *If (i Mod 2) = 0 Then*
>   *... code to be defined*
>   *End If*

>   If conditionToTest is true   then
>   Do something
>   End of the block

To understand if a number is even, it is sufficient that the remainder of its division by 2 is equal to zero. In VBA, the mathematical operator that calculates the remainder of the division is **Mod**, while the relational operator of equality is the single equal (=). In programming languages such as Python, to avoid ambiguity with the assignment operator, instead, a double equal (= =) is used, but **VBA** in this is a little less scrupulous.

Within the code block of "what to do if the tested condition is true" we will enter the code recorded in the original macro. But to format the row it must first be selected. We must therefore generalize for the case of row **i** the specific instruction for row **2** recorded previously: *Rows("2:2").Select*

>   *Rows(i & ":" & i).Select*

The string representing line **i** is obtained by concatenating with the operator & the value of **i** and the colon symbol.

The formatting instructions are at the same indentation level as the *Rows...* instruction.

>   *Selection.Font.Bold = True*
>   *With Selection.Interior*
>   *.Pattern = xlSolid*
>   *.PatternColorIndex = xlAutomatic*
>   *.ThemeColor = xlThemeColorAccent4*
>   *.TintAndShade = 0.799981688894314*
>   *.PatternTintAndShade = 0*
>   *End With*

As usual, for a neat operation of the macro, at the end we make **A1** the active cell.

EXERCISE 8.16 - *Sales chart (commented)*

Tools needed to solve the exercise:
Recording a macro, assigning a macro to a button, simple VBA editing, MsgBox, conditional expressions.

Comment
The exercise shows an example of application of the *Select Case* conditional structure, which is used in place of the sequential conditional structure *If... ElseIf... ElseIf...* when the different conditions to be tested are actually different possible values contained in the same object or variable. In our case, depending on the content of cell **G2**, we want to make VBA do different actions.

The code obtained with the sequential conditional structure illustrated below is more inefficient from a computational point of view than the use of the *Select Case*, but it is not formally wrong. It is definitely more verbose to write and less self-evident to read:

If Range("G2").Value = "Column" Then
   ActiveSheet.ChartObjects("Chart 1").Activate
   ActiveChart.ChartType = xlColumnClustered

ElseIf Range("G2").Value = "Line" Then
   ActiveSheet.ChartObjects("Chart 1").Activate
   ActiveChart.ChartType = xlLine

ElseIf Range("G2").Value = "" Then
   MsgBox "Attention, no type of chart selected!", vbExclamation

Else ' all other possible values
   MsgBox "Impossible case, as data validation has been applied to G2", vbExclamation

End If

In the *Select Case* structure the condition to be tested is implicit:

Select Case   Range("G2").Value

   Case "Column"
      ActiveSheet.ChartObjects("Chart 1").Activate
      ActiveChart.ChartType = xlColumnClustered

   Case "Line"
      ActiveSheet.ChartObjects("Chart 1").Activate
      ActiveChart.ChartType = xlLine

   Case ""
      MsgBox "Attention, no type of chart selected!", vbExclamation

   Case Else   ' all other possible values
      MsgBox "Impossible case, as data validation has been applied to G2", vbExclamation

End Select

Basically it is like saying:

   Look at the value contained in   variableInTest
     If it is equal to XXX
       Do this
     If it is equal to YYY
       Do that
     If it is equal to ZZZ
       Do this other
     If it is a different value from the previous ones
       Do something else
   End of the block

Since data validation has been applied to cell **G2**, it is not actually possible to enter values other than "Line", "Column" and empty cell. Therefore, the use of *Else* in both cases here illustrated is superfluous. However, it is a good practice of coding in general, when using conditional structures to try to predict and manage all possible cases, also providing for the management of cases, which are not imaginable by the programmer.

The *MsgBox* function in VBA has the same role as *print* in Python: it allows you to show something to the user (a text, a result etc.). It opens a window that is much more customizable than an *InputBox*.

EXERCISE 8.17 - Add worksheets (commented)

Tools needed to solve the exercise:
Recording a macro, assigning a macro to a button, simple VBA editing, MsgBox, conditional expressions.

Comment
To carry out this exercise it is necessary to create a macro (**InsertWorkSheet_OneSheet**) that adds a new worksheet to the current workbook, in the last position, with a given name. The problem is to find a generalized way to identify which is the last sheet in the folder, while the opportunity given by **VBA** is the ability to take advantage of dot notation to write a single instruction that does everything it takes.

The sheets in the folder in VBA can be identified, as well as by their name, e.g. *Sheets("My Sheet")*, also with their location:

    Sheets(1)   first
    Sheets(5)   fifth

Therefore, to identify the last one, it is enough to know how many sheets there are (at that moment) in the workbook. The *Sheets* object has various properties, one of these is "how many sheets is it made up of": *Sheets.Count*

    Sheets.Add After:=Sheets(Sheets.Count)

This instruction creates a new worksheet at the end (far right side). To give it the name we want, we use the *Sheets(number).Name* property to give the correct name to what is by now the last worksheet:

Sheets(Sheets.Count).Name = "name we want to use"

Dot notation allows you to concatenate the two instructions into one:

Sheets.Add(After:=Sheets(Sheets.Count)).Name = "name we want to use"

This instruction was then used in the **InsertWorkSheet_Modified** macro. Below we analyze the checks to be made by VBA so that the macro complies with the delivery of the exercise:
- the macro must read the active selection in the worksheet: it is therefore necessary to work with the *Selection*
- you must check that only one cell has been selected: among the properties of the *Selection* object there is the one that counts how many cells have been highlighted (*Selection.Cells.Count*), this counter must be equal to 1
- once you have checked that only one cell has been selected, it must not be empty: use the *Selection.Value* property to check that the content is not an empty string ("")
- once these two checks have been successfully completed, the contents of the cell can be used as the name of the sheet (possibly saving it, as in the solved version, in a local variable, **ws_name**) inside the previously created concatenated instruction

To manage a structure of subsequent conditional checks, instead of nesting many *If... Then... End If* inside each other, it is computationally more efficient to use the sequential conditional structure *If... Then... ElseIf... Then...* in this way:

Check if it is more than one cell then
    Bring up an appropriate message
Otherwise check if the cell is empty then
    Bring up an appropriate message
Otherwise

Create the sheet
End of the block

It is not possible to use the *Select Case* structure in this exercise because looking at the code we see that the two necessary tests are different from each other:

If Selection.Cells.Count > 1 Then
   MsgBox "More than one cell has been selected", vbCritical

ElseIf Selection.Value = "" Then
   MsgBox "An empty cell has been selected", vbCritical

Else
   ws_name = Selection.Value
   Sheets.Add(After:=Sheets(Sheets.Count)).Name = ws_name

End If

The error messages to be shown to the user are simple *MsgBox* windows with the white X in the red circle, the error symbol (the *vbCritical* parameter), instead of the exclamation point in the yellow triangle which is the attention/warning symbol (*vbExclamation*).

To avoid the automatic error signaling that a sheet with that name already exists when selecting cell **B3**, you can add an additional check (before the *Else*) that the *Selection* is not that cell:

ElseIf Selection = Sheets("Customer list").Range("B3") Then
   MsgBox "The table title has been selected", vbCritical

Since the problem is not represented by the cell **B3** in any sheet, you can use the dot notation to specify in one go the couple sheet and cell you want: *Sheets("Customer list").Range("B3")*

The **InsertWorkSheet_Final** macro with this change is the one assigned to the button in the solved file.

EXERCISE 8.18 - Sales pivot (commented)

Tools needed to solve the exercise:
Recording a macro, simple VBA editing, conditional expressions, iterative structures, parameters.

Comment

In the file **Exercise 8.18 - Sales pivot solved.xlsm** it is possible to find both the original recording of point 1 of the exercise (**Macro1**) from which to obtain the necessary instructions, and the **Macro_Original** which performs all the actions for the specific Middle Region. The latter is generalized so that it can be applied to any Region in this way:

    Sub Macro_Modified(region_name As String)

    ' selection of the starting sheet
       Worksheets("Pivot").Select

    ' filtering the pivot table against the value contained in the region_name parameter

    ActiveSheet.PivotTables("PivotTable2").PivotFields("Region").ClearAllFilters

    ActiveSheet.PivotTables("PivotTable2").PivotFields("Region").CurrentPage = region_name

    ' creation of the sheet at the end of the workbook
       Sheets.Add(After:=Sheets(Worksheets.Count)).Name = region_name

    ' copy
      Sheets("Pivot").Select
      Range("B4:F9").Select
      Selection.Copy

    ' paste only values
      Sheets(region_name).Select

Selection.PasteSpecial _
  Paste:=xlPasteValues, _
  Operation:=xlNone, _
  SkipBlanks:=False, _
  Transpose:=False

End Sub

The **region_name** macro parameter has been created and it is sized in the initial *Sub* statement, where it is specified that it is of type text (*String*). Where in the **Macro_Original** we found the specific reference "Middle", now we find the **region_name** parameter, which works totally as a local variable.

Before creating the sheet, it is necessary to verify that it is not already present, therefore it is necessary to compare the **region_name** with the names of all the existing sheets and, only if it is not already used, proceed to the creation of the new sheet.

To simplify the algorithm, a support variable is introduced, **create_ws** of the Boolean type, which initially assumes a True value. The support variable **create_ws** will be the one that "activates" the creation of the sheet. If the name already exists in the workbook, **create_ws** will be set to False. Since the comparison (a simple *If*) must be repeated for all the names, we can insert this code in a *For Each* loop that considers all the sheets of the file, one at a time:

Dim create_ws As Boolean
create_ws = True

Dim ws As Worksheet

For Each ws In ActiveWorkbook.Worksheets
  If ws.Name = region_name Then
    create_ws = False
  End If
Next ws

Finally, the abstract concept "create the sheet if not already present" takes the form of the use of a simple *If* structure that performs creation only when the **create_ws** support variable contains the value True:

```
If create_ws Then
    Sheets.Add(After:=Sheets(Worksheets.Count)).Name = region_name
End If
```

In the overall macro, **Create_sheetsAndTables**, the specific macro (**Macro_Modified**) is called three times, each time assigning the name of a different Region.

```
Sub Create_sheetsAndTables()

    Macro_Modified ("North")
    Macro_Modified ("Middle")
    Macro_Modified ("West")

    Sheets("Pivot").Select
    Range("A1").Select

    ActiveSheet.PivotTables("PivotTable2").PivotFields("Region").ClearAll Filters
        Application.CutCopyMode = False

End Sub
```

The macro also contains the final instructions required by the exercise, which must be executed only once at the end of the program.

Note that **Macro_Modified** does not appear in the list of macros in the file, accessible from the View tab or the Developer tab. This is because macros that take input arguments, like this one, are subroutines / subprograms that cannot be executed by themselves, because VBA would not know where to get the values to assign to the input parameters.

EXERCISE 8.19 - *Insert rows (commented)*

Tools needed to solve the exercise:
Recording a macro, simple VBA editing, Worksheet events, parameters.

Comment

To solve this exercise, it is necessary to record a macro that inserts a row in a random position in the worksheet. The result is contained in a macro called **Macro_Original**, in the **Exercise 8.19 - Insert rows solved.xlsm**.

Sub Macro_Original( )

Dim row_number As Integer

row_number = ActiveCell.Row

Rows(row_number & ":" & row_number).Select
Selection.Insert Shift:=xlDown,
CopyOrigin:=xlFormatFromLeftOrAbove

End Sub

ActiveCell is the active cell object, *ActiveCell.Row* is its row coordinate.
This macro was been copied and renamed to **InsertRow**; was then modified to make the variable **row_number** its input parameter:

Sub InsertRow(row_number As Integer)

Rows(row_number & ":" & row_number).Select
Selection.Insert Shift:=xlDown,
CopyOrigin:=xlFormatFromLeftOrAbove

End Sub

To make the macro be associated with a double click of the mouse (= by double clicking on the sheet, the macro is executed), the events of the Worksheet object must be used. Instead of writing code in Module1, we must write it in Sheet1: inside the VBA editor, in the VBAProject Project window, double-click on 'Sheet1 (Data)', located within the "Microsoft Excel Objects" folder.

In the window for the code that opens, it is necessary to select in the drop-down box on the left (located at the top, just below the menu bars) the item Worksheet. Code for an event is automatically generated (usually **Worksheet_SelectionChange**). This event is not the one to be used for the solution of the exercise and should be ignored for now. In the drop-down box on the right, select the **Worksheet_BeforeDoubleClick** item. Even in this case the code for the management of this event is generated (the event triggered by the double click of the mouse on the worksheet **Data**) characterized by input parameters set by VBA.

Private Sub Worksheet_BeforeDoubleClick(ByVal Target As Range, Cancel As Boolean)

End Sub

Within the Sub **Worksheet_BeforeDoubleClick** it is necessary to call the **InsertRow** procedure, passing as a parameter the row number of the cell on which the double click was made. This value is obtained from the Target parameter, which represents the active Range at the moment when the double click was made. The complete code is as follows:

Private Sub Worksheet_BeforeDoubleClick(ByVal Target As Range, Cancel As Boolean)
   InsertRow (Target.Row)
End Sub

Completely remove the **Worksheet_SelectionChange** event code (or any other event generated automatically while you were searching for the correct event in the drop-down boxes).
At this point it is possible to test the automatic insertion of a new row by double clicking in the **Data** sheet.
Event-triggered macros also do not appear in the list of macros in the file (accessible from the View tab or the Developer tab).
Note that if you add a new sheet to the folder and try to double click on it, no new row is inserted. This is because the macro **Worksheet_BeforeDoubleClick** is defined *Private*, which means that VBA sees it only if the active sheet is **Data**. All the macros written in the Modules, on the other hand, have global

visibility: for this reason within an Excel work session we can see and run all the macros in the currently open files, not just those in the active one.

EXERCISE 8.20 - Stock Exchange (commented)

Tools needed to solve the exercise:
Recording a macro, simple VBA editing, InputBox, MsgBox, Chart object, conditional expressions, Error Handling.

Comment
To solve this exercise, the following steps must be performed:
a) Record a macro for copying and formatting a time series
b) The code should then be generalized to work with any stock exchange index, according to the user's selection
c) Record a macro to modify the time series (Open/High etc.)
d) Merge the code of the second macro into the first one
e) Modify the code obtained so that the series can be selected by the user

First, it is necessary to proceed with the macro for copying and formatting data:
a) Record a macro for copying and formatting one stock exchange index (e.g., **DJI**) within the **Chart** worksheet. The macro is available in the solved exercise, by the name **Macro_Original**. To obtain a similar code, the column **A** in the **DJI** worksheet must be selected, copied, and pasted in the column **A** in the **Chart** worksheet.
b) Without stopping the recording, select the column A in the Chart worksheet (which contains the data that have just been pasted) and activate the feature available in Excel 'Text to columns', in the Data tab. Text to columns must be configured as follows:
   - Delimited
   - Delimiter comma (,)
   - In the advanced features, the separator for decimals must be set to a comma and the separator for thousands must be set to a period (point)
c) It is finally necessary to sort column A, which contains the dates of the time series, in an ascending order.
d) Stop the Macro Recorder!

e) Associate the macro to a button in the Chart worksheet.

The chart of one of the series should be visible at this point (the chart is already located in the worksheet).

If those cells that contain preexisting data have not been deleted yet, the macro should be modified by inserting the code for cells clean up (columns A to G):

Columns("A:G").ClearContents

As the macro explicitly refers to the DJI worksheet, it will be necessary to ask the user the name of the worksheet from which data must be copied. This operation can be performed through the creation of the **index_name** variable, populated through the *InputBox* function, which requires user's action.

Dim index_name As String
index_name = InputBox("Select Stock Exchange index")

It is then necessary to test whether the user has actually inserted a value for the stock exchange name. If not, the user must be notified with a message and the macro executing stopped:

If index_name = "" Or series_name = "" Then
    MsgBox "Warning: the stock exchange name has not been inserted!", vbCritical
    Exit Sub
End If

The exercise requires that the user also choose the column of values to be displayed in the chart. Even in this case, it is necessary to declare a variable and use the *InputBox* function, adding the check that the variable does not contain an empty string:

Dim series_name As String
series_name = InputBox("Scegli la serie (High/Low/Close/...)")

If series_name = "" Then

> MsgBox "Warning: the series name has not been inserted!", vbCritical
> Exit Sub
> End If

Before proceeding with the selection of the sheet and the copy of the data, we insert the error management to prevent the program from crashing if the user has entered incorrect or non-existent names for the index or for the series to be displayed in the chart:

> On Error GoTo ErrHandler

At the end of the procedure, the label **ErrHandler** and the error handling code must be defined (i.e. what VBA should do instead of showing the standard run-time error window). Before defining the label, however, the execution of the procedure should be stopped, so that the code for error handling is not executed in case the inserted data are correct:

> ...
> Exit Sub
>
> ErrHandler:
>
> MsgBox "Warning, an error occurred: the Stock Exchange index or the series do not exist!", vbCritical
>
> End Sub

Error handling here simply consists of a message to the user, performed through the *MsgBox* function. Note that **ErrHandler** is an absolutely arbitrary name, we could have used any other name, e.g. BadError.

In the exercise, it is stated that the worksheet has already been set with some named ranges. Verifying their names, it can be noted that for each series (Open, High, Low, Close, Volume, AdjClose) there is a named range for the heading (e.g., Open_name) and a named range for the whole data series (e.g., Open). Therefore, it is possible to ask the name of the series, then use this name entered by the user to make VBA understand which data to use in the graph.

It is then necessary to record a macro that changes the series of the chart (data and name). The macro is the following:

```
Sub Macro_ChangeSeries_Original()
    ActiveSheet.ChartObjects("Chart 1").Activate
    ActiveChart.FullSeriesCollection(1).Select
    ActiveChart.FullSeriesCollection(1).Name = "=Chart!$B$1"
    ActiveChart.FullSeriesCollection(1).Values = "=Chart!$B$2:$B$22"
End Sub
```

The code of this macro must be copied within the first macro, just before its end.
To conclude you must substitute:
- "=Chart!$B$1" with "=Chart!" & series_name & "_name" (the name of the series corresponds to the Column headings, and the named Range that is in the Column headings ends with _name)
- "=Chart!$B$2:$B$22" with "=Chart!" & series_name
- Save the file and test the macro.

Comments and functions unit 9

EXERCISE 9.1 - Hot deals (commented)

Tools needed to solve the exercise:

RAND, IF, INT, VLOOKUP, ABS, AVERAGE functions, nested functions, Paste command options (Values).

Comment point 1
The discount rates can be calculated using the RAND function, which generates random numbers between 0 and 1. The RAND function generates a new number at any change that takes place in the workbook, so to fix the results of the function it is necessary to copy and paste the results of the functions using the Values option.
The calculation of the correct discount rates can be performed using two IF functions. In cell **H3**, the function is the following:
=IF(B3<=0.3,0.3,IF(B3>=0.9,0.9,B3))
It should be noted that it would not have been possible to use the RAND function nested in the IF function because the result could have been less than 30% or greater than 90% anyway. Consider the following function:
=IF(RAND()<=0.3,0.3,IF(RAND()>=0.9,0.9,RAND()))
As we can see, the last RAND function avoids the control of the test argument of the IF function, and its result can be any number between 0 and 1.

Comment point 2
To round down the product prices to the nearest integer, it is possible to use the INT function entering the reference to the cell containing the number to be rounded down in the number argument.

Comment point 3
In order to calculate the discount rates rounded down to the nearest integer, we need to use the VLOOKUP and INT functions: the first one is used to obtain the correct discount rate from the **List** worksheet (corresponding to the ID of each product), and the second one to round down to the nearest integer.
In cell **H2** of the **List** worksheet, the function is the following:
=INT(G2-G2*VLOOKUP(A2,Discount!A$3:H$311,8,FALSE))

Comment point 4

The Historical worksheet contains the discount rates variation between each time interval and the previous one in the last 48 hours: to calculate the average variation, we must use the AVERAGE function, putting in the number argument all the cells containing the price variations of each product for each time interval. To calculate the absolute value of the result of the AVERAGE function, we must use the ABS function.

EXERCISE 9.2 - Blue Vision (commented)

Tools needed to solve the exercise:

RATE function, HLOOKUP function, SUMPRODUCT function, NPV function, IRR function.

Comment point 1

In the Debt worksheet, we have the residual balance, duration in years, and quarterly payment of each of the four mortgages. With these three variables available, it is possible to calculate the interest rate of each of the four mortgages using the RATE function.

The setting of the function is very similar to that of the PMT function, and it is worth remembering that in the RATE function, as in all financial functions, it is important to maintain the temporal coherence between all the values entered. In this case, having a quarterly installment, the rate function is set to return a quarterly interest rate. Having to calculate the annual interest rate, we need to multiply the result of the RATE function by 4.

To calculate the annual cost of each debt, we must multiply the quarterly payment of each mortgage by the number of quarters in one year. The HLOOKUP function allows searching the name of each mortgage in the first row of the table with the mortgages features and, once the correct mortgage is found, it returns the corresponding value placed in one of the rows below. The quarterly payment is in the fourth row of the table, so the row_index_num must be set to 4. Finally, note that the cost of the line of credit has to be entered by hand in the cell.

The weight of the annual cost of each debt compared with the total cost is calculated by dividing the annual cost of each debt by the annual cost of all the debts. The formula in cell **C9** is the following:

=B9/SUM(B$9:B$13)

The interest rate of each debt in cells **D9:D13** is shown using another HLOOKUP function. Compared with the function used previously, the annual interest rate is in the fifth row of the table, then the row_index_num argument must be set to the value 5.

To calculate the weighted average rate, it is necessary to multiply the interest rates of each debt by the corresponding weight, and then add all the results. The SUMPRODUCT function allows performing the whole calculation setting in the array1 and array2 arguments the reference to the ranges containing the interest rate values and the weights.

Comment point 2

The calculations of the net present value and the internal rate of return are performed using the NPV and IRR functions, after copying the interest rate in the cell **B14** of the **Projects** worksheet with a link at the cell **B15** of the **Debt** worksheet.

In fact, the interest rate is necessary to set up the first argument of the NPV function (rate); in the value argument, we must put the reference to the range containing the cash flows. The syntax of the NPV function for the first project is the following:

=NPV(B14,B3:B10)

The cell range set in the NPV function is the same that has to be set in the IRR function.

EXERCISE 9.3 - Gold (comment)

Tools needed to solve the exercise:

CONVERT function, ROUND function, nested functions, simple formulas (multiplication, division), HLOOKUP function, Data tables, FV function, PV function.

Comment point 1

The conversion between two units of measurement can be done quickly, in many cases, using the CONVERT function. The syntax of the function requires the unit abbreviations to be included in the arguments as text, between quotation marks (""); also, first we must enter the unit of the value to be converted, and then the unit in which the value has to be converted. It should also be remembered that the abbreviations of the available units are displayed during the manual entry of the function in the cell; as an alternative, the complete list of units can be found in the Help.

The request to round the amount of gold in ounces to two decimal places can be met using the ROUND function: the CONVERT function is entered in the number argument, and in the num_digits argument we need to enter "2" to force the rounding to the second decimal place. The function in cell **D2** is the following:
=ROUND(CONVERT(C2,"g","ozm"),2)

Comment point 2

To calculate the value (in euros) of the amount of gold held by Mr. Nowitzki, we must first multiply the amount of gold in ounces by the price of gold in dollars/ounce (D2 * B2), then convert it into euros by dividing the result of the previous formula by the EUR/USD exchange rate. To use the values of the EUR/USD exchange rate available in the **Exchange rates** worksheet, it is necessary to use the HLOOKUP function, searching for the year in the first row of the table of the **Exchange rates** worksheet and returning the corresponding exchange rate available in the second row of the same table.

Comment point 3

The data tables allow to analyze more hypotheses simultaneously, evaluating the result of a function as the two inputs change. In this case, the formula to be analyzed is the one that calculates the value of gold (in euros) of Mr. Nowitzki, while the two inputs are the gold price (USD/ounce) and the amount of gold in grams held.

Provide the area within the **Gold** worksheet with the different values to be assigned to the two inputs: e.g., enter in cells **I1:Q1** the values of the variable price of gold (from 1,000 to 1,800, with increments of 1,00 USD/ounce), and in cells **H2:H9**, the values of the variable grams of gold (from 3,000 to 4,400, with increments of 200 grams). Then, create in cell **H1** a link to the cell containing the function to be tested: it is necessary to consider the 2014 data, so in this case it is the cell **E12**.

After selecting the entire area **(H1:Q9)** and then Data table command, we must set cell **B12** as Row input cell and cell **C12** as Column input cell, which are the two inputs of the function to be considered.

Comment point 4

The data already available in the **Investments** worksheet allow using the functions directly to calculate the future value and the present value of the investment in the cells **B5** and **B6**. The syntax of the two functions is the following:

=FV(B3/12,B2*12,B1,,1)
=PV(B3/12,B2*12,B1,,1)

In both cases, to respect the temporal consistency, we had to divide the interest rate by 12 and multiply the duration of the investment by 12, converting everything to monthly values. Note that both functions return a positive result that represents a stream of incoming cash, unlike the monthly payment, which is negative because it represents a cash outflow.

Comment point 5

The analysis of the present value of the investment is performed following the same steps we have already seen in the solution of point 3, creating the area with the different values to be assigned to the two inputs, the monthly payment and the interest rate. The formula to use is the one of the present value of the investment (cell **B6**), while the cells to be set as Row input cell (monthly payment) and Column input cell (interest rate) are cells **B1** and **B3**. It should be noted that to be consistent with the formula to analyze, it is necessary to enter negative values for the "monthly payment" input.

EXERCISE 9.4 - Personal loan (commented)

Tools needed to solve the exercise:

PMT, PPMT, IPMT, IRR functions.

Comment

The calculation of the monthly installment of the loan can be done with the PMT function: pay attention to the temporal consistency of the data used in the function (duration in months and annual interest rate).

The creation of the amortization schedule involves several steps and the PPMT and IPMT functions to calculate the principal payment and the interest payment corresponding to each installment. In particular, the syntax of the PPMT and IPMT functions in cells **C13** and **D13** is the following:

=PPMT(B$4/12,A13,B$3,B$2,,0)

=IPMT(B$4/12,A13,B$3,B$2,,0)

It should be noted that even in this case it is necessary to maintain the temporal consistency between the arguments of the functions, using the monthly interest rate (B$4/12 in the rate argument). Moreover, in the "per" argument we used the identification number of each installment.

To calculate the effective annual interest rate of the loan we can use the IRR function, but first we need to prepare a list of all the cash flows. Actually, in the values argument of the function, it is possible to enter only a single range of cells, in which the order of the values is used by Excel to understand the order of cash flows. This is why, in the first cash flow we also considered the costs of the preliminary credit check and the multi-risk insurance.

EXERCISE 9.5 - *New car*

Tools needed to solve the exercise:

PMT, IRR, NPV functions, simple formulas (sum, multiplication), Conditional Formatting.

EXERCISE 9.6 - *Gluten-free products*

Tools needed to solve the exercise:

INT, HLOOKUP, VLOOKUP, ABS functions, simple formulas (multiplication), percentage variation calculation, advanced filter.

EXERCISE 9.7 - *Condo fees*

Tools needed to solve the exercise:

ROUND, CONVERT, VLOOKUP, COUNTIF function, IF, SUM, nested functions.

EXERCISE 9.8 - Car purchase

Tools needed to solve the exercise:

Simple formulas (addition, subtraction, multiplication, division), Conditional Formatting, Data tables, PMT, IF, MIN, CONCATENATE, ROUND functions, options of Paste command (Values), Goal seek.

EXERCISE 9.9 - Promotional campaign (commented)

Tools needed to solve the exercise:

Solver add-in.

Comment

The situation described in the text of the exercise presents a complex optimization problem, with the following characteristics:
- An output to optimize, setting it to an exact value
- A series of input to be varied to optimize the result
- Many constraints to observe

In order to solve this kind of complex problems, it is necessary to use the Solver. In this case, the objective cell is the one with the six-month net cash flow (**B22**), which must be set at the value of 50 million. You are asked to find which combination of monthly prices and cost per KW·h over the maximum consumption allows to achieve a given cash flow, so that the variable cells are both the ones with the monthly price of each type of contract (cells **B3:D3**) and the ones with the cost of the KW·h over the maximum consumption (cells **B6:D6**).

The Solver constraints must be set as follows.
- The cells with the cost of the KW·h over the maximum consumption must be equal to or less than 0.6 (**B6:D6** <= 0.6)
- The maximum price of the three contracts has to be equal to or less than the prices specified in the text; as the specified prices are different, it is necessary to set three different constraints (**B3** <= 100, **C3** <= 180 e **D3** <= 230)
- The monthly price of each contract has to be an integer (**B3:D3** = integer)

Finally, it should be remembered that it is possible that the result given by the Solver is not the only possible result, and the values found by the Solver could also be different from the ones of the solution proposed, depending on the algorithm chosen to search for the solution and the options selected.

EXERCISE 9.10 - German course

Tools needed to solve the exercise:
TRIM, VLOOKUP, IF functions, Solver add-in.

EXERCISE 9.11 - Overtime

Tools needed to solve the exercise:
Solver add-in.

EXERCISE 9.12 - Home video

Tools needed to solve the exercise:
Componente aggiuntivo Risolutore.

EXERCISE 9.13 - Hotel Eden (commented)

Tools needed to solve the exercise:
Operations with dates, VLOOKUP, HLOOKUP, IF, AND, OR, DATE, IFERROR, AVERAGEIFS, SUMIFS, PMT, IPMT, PPMT, NETWORKDAYS functions, nested functions, Conditional formatting, Pivot tables, macro recording.

Comment point 1
The days of stay for each customer have been calculated as the difference between the check-out and check-in dates.
The calculation of the season in which each customer will be staying at the Hotel Eden has been found using the VLOOKUP function with the

range_lookup argument set with the value TRUE: the values to look for are in fact numeric and not all the values are available in the first column of the table in the **Prices** worksheet, but only those that indicate the lower bounds of as many ranges.

For the calculation of working days it is necessary to use the NETWORKDAYS function. The start and the end dates to be considered are identified thanks to MIN and MAX functions, referring to the cell range that contains the check-in dates.

Comment point 2

To calculate the bill that each customer has to pay for his/her stay, it is necessary to multiply the daily cost per person by the number of people and by the number of days of stay. The last two values are already available in the **Reservations** worksheet, whereas the daily cost per person is available in the **Prices** worksheet: the HLOOKUP function allows us to search for the type of service in the first row of the table of the **Prices** worksheet, but to find the value of the row_index_num we must use an IF function with a second nested IF function that evaluates the line number corresponding to the season. In this case, the function must have 2 as a result if the season is "Low", 3 if the season is "Medium", otherwise 4. The function in cell **L2** is the following:
=G2*J2*HLOOKUP(H2,Prices!D$2:F$5,IF(K2="Low",2,IF(K2="Medium",3,4)),FALSE)

The bill that each customer has to pay must be calculated by using the IF function with an AND function in the logical_test argument, which determines whether all the three conditions are true at the same time. The third condition requires an OR function to ensure that the customer's age is equal to or less than 30 years or equal to or greater than 55 years.

Comment point 3

The calculation of the total days of stay of customers with age between 30 and 55 years must be performed using an AVERAGEIFS function, remembering that criteria of the type "between" must be divided into two criteria of the type "equal to or greater than" (">=30") and "equal to or less than" ("<=55") using two pairs of range-criteria arguments. Then, it is necessary to use the IFERROR function so that when the AVERAGEIFS function returns an error, the formula return the text "N.A.".

To calculate the total bill for customers with check-in date in March 2016 it is necessary to use a SUMIFS function. Also, in this case we must use two pairs of range-criteria arguments to divide the criterion "check-in date in March 2016" into the criteria ">=3/1/2016" and "<=3/31/2016".

Comment point 4

After calculating the mortgage monthly installment with the PMT function, we must calculate the total interests paid and the principal paid pack in the first 3 years. IPMT and PPMT functions allow us to calculate the interests paid and the principal paid pack in a single mortgage installment, so to calculate the total amount we need to repeat the calculation for each installment of the first three years (36 monthly installments).

Comment point 5

The pivot table has been set initially with the fields Service in Columns area, Check-in date field in the Rows area, and Discounted bill field in the Values area.

When customizing the pivot table, it should be noted that:
- After grouping by months the values of the Check-in date field, it is possible to sort them manually, moving the "dec" value in the desired position
- To group correctly the Age field, it is necessary to set the value 18 in the From box and 78 in the To box of the Group dialog box, grouping by 10 years

During the macro recording the format "dddd dd mmmm" has been applied to the values of the Check-in date creating a new custom format.

EXERCISE 9.14 - TechMind contest

Tools needed to solve the exercise:

RANDBETWEEN, VLOOKUP, ROUND, IF, DATEDIF, TODAY, CONCATENATE, TEXT, SUMIFS, IFERROR, AVERAGEIFS functions, nested functions, Conditional Formatting, advanced filters, creation of a mixed chart with two axes.

EXERCISE 9.15 - Pluriplast

Tools needed to solve the exercise:

Simple formulas (multiplication, division), **VLOOKUP, DATEDIF, IF, NETWORKDAYS, SUMIFS, AVERAGEIFS, IFERROR** functions, nested functions, Advanced filter, Solver add-in, Pivot table, Pivot chart, macro recording.

Comments and functions unit 10

EXERCISE 10.1 - Payroll office (commented)

Tools needed to solve the exercise:

Templates.

Comment point 1

To create a template of expense statement simply insert headers, expenditure items, and the totals in an Excel file, starting from a blank workbook (file **Exercise 10.1 - Expense report solved.xltx** shows an example). Once you create the file, save it as a template by choosing the Save As command, then the type of file Excel Template (.xltx).

Comment point 2

To use one of the existing templates in Excel, just use the New command, then draw on the extensive collection of models available. You can look for a template for a given area, e.g., by writing "invoice" in the search box of the templates.
Then, choose one of the available ones. By choosing a model, a new workbook based on the model will be created. Once you have customized the file, you can save and close it. The file **Exercise 10.1 - Invoice solved.xlsx** shows an example.

EXERCISE 10.2 - Sport shoes (commented)

Tools needed to solve the exercise:

Working with groups of worksheets, operation on worksheets (copy, rename), SUM, MAX, VLOOKUP functions, SUM function with 3D references, linking cells.

Comment point 1

You are required to use the SUM function to calculate totals. As the three worksheets are the same, it is possible to speed up operations working with a group of worksheets, i.e., executing exactly the same operation simultaneously on multiple sheets. It is a risky procedure, as it allows you to edit worksheets that are not visible in the foreground at a certain time.

For operations that should be performed in the same cells of different worksheets, it is possible to use it to speed up operations. In this case, for instance, it is possible to perform the sums required simultaneously in all the three worksheets, instead of rewriting or copying from one worksheet to another.

To work with a group of worksheets you need to select tabs together in the corresponding workbook. In this case, you must therefore select the tabs corresponding to the three worksheets in the file. To do this, you can hold down the CTRL key and click on the tabs of the two sheets different from the one displayed in the foreground.

Alternatively, show the first of three sheets, then hold down the Shift key and click the last tab. Once selected, the three worksheets in a group (in the title bar [Group] will appear next to the file name) any operation that is performed on the worksheet in the foreground is automatically performed on other selected worksheets, in the same cells.

You can then insert the header Total in cells **F1** and A9, then calculate the row totals (SUM function in **F2**, then copied to **F7**) and column totals (SUM function in **B9**, then copied to **F9**).

At this point, it is important to remember to deselect the group of worksheets; otherwise, all further operations on one will be replicated on the others: if this is not what we want, we risk making a mess in the workbook!

Comment point 2

Inserting a new worksheet that is an exact copy of another can be done in two ways. First, inserting a new worksheet, then copying and pasting the content that should be reported. Second, (to be more sure of actually copying the entire contents of the worksheet and to do more quickly) you can use the "Move or Copy" command found by clicking the right mouse button on the tab of the worksheet you want to copy.

By choosing the option "Create a copy", you produce an exact copy, in all respects, of the source worksheet. At this point, you can rename the worksheet thus obtained by calling it **Europe Total**, and then delete the contents of cells **B2:F7**.

Comment point 3

To effectively solve this question, you can use the three-dimensional sum (or 3D sum), that is a SUM function that includes the values present in the same cells in different worksheets. The result we want to achieve in each cell of the table, in the worksheet **Europe Total**, in fact corresponds to the sum of the values in the same cells of the worksheets Spain, France, and Italy. For instance, in cell **B2** of the worksheet **Europe Total**, we will get as a result the sum of the values in cell **B2** of the worksheet **Spain**, **B2** of **France**, and **B2** of **Italy**.

Remember that to indicate a cell of a worksheet other than the one in which you are writing the formula, you need to use the syntax Name of the worksheet!Cell reference (e.g., **Spain!B2**).

The three-dimensional sum avoids specifying any single reference shortening the formula syntax. The SUM function may in fact be written as follows, and return a correct result:

=SUM(Spain!B2,France!B2,Italy!B2).

Or you could simply write an addition formula:

=Spain!B2+France!B2+Italy!B2.

In this case, however, and even more so all cases in which the cells to be added are numerous and you look for a more effective syntax, it is possible to insert references to cells as a range, in this way: **Spain:Italy!B2** (i.e. "cell **B2** of all the worksheets between the sheet Spain and the sheet Italy"). The 3D sum will be: =SUM(Spain:Italy!B2). You can enter it manually, or open the parentheses of the function, select the sheets by clicking the first (the one whose tab is more to the left, in this case Spain), and then hold down the Shift key and click the last (the rightmost one, in this case Italy), select cell **B2**, then close the parentheses, and press Enter.

Once you have the result in cell **B2**, you can copy the formula to the other cells of the table, both to the right and downwards, so you get all the desired results.

Comment point 4

The question is solved with a simple MAX function, which can be placed below the table: =MAX(F2:F7).

Comment point 5

The question requires the use of a VLOOKUP, but contains a small "trap", which is a special case requiring a non-conventional solution. VLOOKUP makes it possible to search for a value in the first column left of a table, and returns a value corresponding to that sought by another right-most column (which is precisely this column is defined in the Index argument of the function).

The first constraint (search in the first column on the left) can be circumvented in special cases by selecting, in the table_array argument, only some of the columns of the original table of which the first is one in which we must look for the value.

In this case, for example, the value to look for is the one calculated at the previous point (maximum sales). This value is in column **F**, which then must be the first column of table_array.

The second constraint of VLOOKUP instead is more difficult to get around, and in this case requires an unconventional solution (although in reality such a problem could be solved by using other functions such as INDEX and MATCH).

The value we want to be returned by VLOOKUP is the type of product, but this information is located in a leftmost column of the first column of table_array.

There is no way to indicate the function to return a value from a column to the left, then a solution may be to replicate the column values that we are interested in the next position with respect to the search column. In this case, we can e.g., use cell links in column **G**: in **G2** we enter =A2, then copy into the cells below. At this point, the argument table_array of VLOOKUP will include the cells in **F** and **G**, and the index will be 2, thus:
=VLOOKUP(B12,F2:G7,2,0).

You may the hide column **G**, so you will not see the values that have served only to get the desired result. Clearly, such a solution can be used only when we are certain that the table does not require the inclusion of other values in column **G** and that the fact of hiding it does not represent a problem for the integrity of the data or for the correct calculations.

EXERCISE 10.3 - Budget (commented)

Tools needed to solve the exercise:

Compare and merge workbooks, SUM function, comments, Track Changes command.

Comment point 1

To compare and merge two workbooks in Excel, it is necessary to have two files, both shared: the first is the original document, while the second one is the same document that was later modified, e.g., by adding values or formulas. In this case, the two documents are the file **Exercise 10.3 - Budget.xlsx** (the original workbook) and the file **Exercise 10.3 - Budget Paris.xlsx** (the original document with data on the budget of the Paris office added).

It is therefore possible to compare the two files and merge the contents of the revised document to the content of the original document: open the file **Exercise 10.3 - Budget.xlsx** and use the "Compare and Merge Workbooks" command (if the command is not visible in the ribbon, activate it by using the Customize Ribbon command).

Remove the sharing of the workbook using the Share workbook command, and finally save.

Comment point 2

The total costs for each quarter for Milan and Paris has been calculated using the SUM function.

Comment point 3

To insert a note in cell **B1**, it is necessary to select the cell, then use the New comment command, and type the message in the comment box.

To make sure that the comment is always visible, we must select the cell containing the comment, and then use the "Show/Hide comments" command.

Comment point 4

To activate and track the changes, we must use the command Highlight changes: to allow Excel to highlight the changes made by any person and at any time, it is then necessary to choose the option All in the boxes When and Who in the Highlight changes dialog box.

After the Ok to this operation, we need to save the workbook to let Excel start tracking the changes.

EXERCISE 10.4 - District competition (commented)

Tools needed to solve the exercise:

IF, AND functions, nested functions, macro recording, assigning a macro to a shape.

Comment point 1

The overall score is calculated by adding up the test score to the corresponding points to the conditions indicated by the exercise:

- An IF to assess whether the district is New York, and assign accordingly 10 points, otherwise 0
- An IF with AND for evaluating whether the date of birth is between 1/1/1970 and 12/31/1979. The IF in fact does not allow direct comparison with a date written in the function arguments, then a possible solution is to write the date (or dates, as in this case) in a cell in the worksheet and refer the comparison of the IF function to that cell. An alternative, without typing the dates in the worksheet is to use the DATE function in the arguments of the IF function

EXERCISE 10.5 - Admission office

Tools needed to solve the exercise:

DCOUNTA, DAVERAGE functions, comments, chart creation.

EXERCISE 10.6 - Distributors

Tools needed to solve the exercise:

Compare and Merge Workbooks, IF, DSUM functions, nested functions, chart creation, workbook sharing.

EXERCISE 10.7 - Car dealer

Tools needed to solve the exercise:

TODAY, MONTH, VLOOKUP, SUM, COUNTIF, SUMIF, IF, ROUND functions, sorting, chart creation, Remove duplicates command, nested functions, simple formulas (multiplication).

EXERCISE 10.8 - Fruit and vegetables

Tools needed to solve the exercise:

Data validation, simple formulas (addition, subtraction, multiplication), SUM, VLOOKUP, IF functions, nested functions, worksheet protection, macro recording, assigning a macro to a shape.

EXERCISE 10.9 - Albert Einstein

Tools needed to solve the exercise:

AVERAGE, IF, CONCATENATE, LEFT, LEN, RIGHT, TODAY, COUNTA functions, nested functions, Conditional Formatting, operations on worksheets (rename), macro recording, assigning a macro to a shape, WordArt, grouping objects, chart creation, chart options, inserting comments, protecting file from opening.

EXERCISE 10.10 - SEFCO (commented)

Tools needed to solve the exercise:

VLOOKUP, HLOOKUP, SUMIFS, COUNTIFS, DSUM, DAVERAGE, DMAX, DMIN, RANK.EQ functions, Conditional Formatting with formulas, Comments, workbook sharing, creation of mixed chart with two axes.

Comment point 1
To calculate the new price of each product based on the formula shown in the text of the exercise, we must use the **VLOOKUP** and **HLOOKUP** functions.

The first one is needed to return the increase rate based on the list price from the table of the **New price** worksheet; the second one is needed to return the discount rate based on the quantity sold from the table of the **New price** worksheet.

It should be noted that in both functions, as the formula for the calculation of the new price must be copied into the cells below, it is necessary to use mixed or absolute references to lock the range of cells inserted in the table_array argument.

In addition, the value TRUE must be inserted in the range_lookup argument in both functions because the values to be searched in the two tables of the **New price** worksheet are numeric, not continuous, and already sorted in an ascending order.

To set properly the conditional formatting on the values of the Product ID field, we must use a formula: actually, the commands of the Top/Bottom rules category cannot be used because the values to be formatted are not in the same column where the condition has to be verified. The syntax of the formula to use as the conditional formatting rule is the following:

=RANK.EQ (F2,F$2:F$301,0)<=50

It should be noted that to set the condition of the above formula, the order argument of the RANK.EQ function has been set with the value 0 to have the results in a descending order: this way the new price with the smallest value will be in the last position (corresponding to the highest number, i.e., 300), whereas the new price with the higher value will have the first position (1).

Comment point 2

The SUMIFS and COUNTIFS functions are needed to calculate the number of products with the list price between 1,000 and 5,000 euros, and the total quantity sold last year for products with price between 1,000 and 5,000 euros, both for each type of product. It should be noted that the same result could have been calculated using the database functions, setting the appropriate criteria area.

Comment point 3

After creating the chart with the data of the **Totals** worksheet, move the series "Products with price between 1,000 and 5,000" on the secondary axis and change the chart type of the series. Then, customize the chart using the "Add graphic element" to create a meaningful title to the chart and remove the legend, the options of each axis to set the maximum value and display the data in thousands, the options of the chart plot area to set the **Exercise 10.10 - Valve.png** image as background.

Comment point 4

The use of database functions provides the setting of a criteria area where the conditions on the same line are linked by the logical operator AND, whereas the conditions on different rows are linked by the logical operator OR. It should also be remembered that when we have to set two or more conditions on the same field, it is necessary to duplicate the headings of the field names in the criteria area. In the criteria areas of database functions, we can look at both situations.

Comment point 5

Use the "New comment" command to enter a comment in the cell with the heading Product ID, then use the "Show/Hide comments" command to ensure that the comment is always visible.

Finally, use the "Share Workbook" command and allow Excel to highlight the changes made by any user.

Comments and functions unit 11

EXERCISE 11.1 - Premium Bonds

Tools needed to solve the exercise:
TODAY, COUPPCD, COUPDAYBS, COUPDAYS, YIELD, COUPNCD, IFERROR, XIRR functions, simple formulas (addition, subtraction, multiplication, division), conditional formatting.

EXERCISE 11.2 - Coupon&Coupon

Tools needed to solve the exercise:
TBILLYIELD, XIRR, TODAY functions, simple formulas (addition, subtraction), conditional formatting.

EXERCISE 11.3 - FRN

Tools needed to solve the exercise:
VLOOKUP, YEAR, COUPPCD, COUPDAYBS, COUPDAYS, COUPNCD, XIRR functions, simple formulas (addition, subtraction, multiplication, division), conditional formatting.

EXERCISE 11.4 - Reverse floater

Tools needed to solve the exercise:
COUPPCD, COUPDAYBS, COUPDAYS, COUPNCD, VLOOKUP, IF, YEAR, XIRR functions, simple formulas (addition, subtraction, multiplication, division).

EXERCISE 11.5 - Capital budgeting

Tools needed to solve the exercise:
NPV, IRR, XNPV, XIRR, VLOOKUP, YEAR, SUM functions, data tables.

EXERCISE 11.6 - Super leasing

Tools needed to solve the exercise:
PMT, PPMT, IPMT, IF functions, simple formulas (addition, multiplication), data validation, worksheet protection.

EXERCISE 11.7 - Stock performance (commented)

Tools needed to solve the exercise:
Data import from text file, AVERAGE, MEDIAN, STDEV.S, VAR.S, MIN, MAX, KURT, SKEW functions, simple formulas (addition, subtraction, multiplication, division), Data analysis Add-in, chart creation and customization.

Comment point 1
Data in the **Exercise 11.7 - Stock.txt** file are delimited by a tab, have the comma as a decimal separator, the point as thousands separator, and the dates set with aaaa-mm-dd format. To import data in the Stock worksheet, use the Get External Data/From Text command: to import them correctly, it is necessary to set the tab as a separator (step 2), that the separators used in the file are the comma as decimal separator and the point as thousands separator (Advanced option in step 3), and that the Date field is set with the format "AMD" (step 3).

Comment point 2
To avoid display errors in the chart, it is advisable to create the chart starting from the selection of the Adj close field cells, and only later to set the Date field as horizontal axis labels (sometimes the dates, being numbers, are considered by Excel as a second series).

Comment point 3

The functions to use to create the descriptive statistics are AVERAGE, MEDIAN, STDEV.S, VAR.S, MIN, MAX, KURTOSIS, SKEW: in all the function only one argument must be set, specifying the cell range to be used. The text of the exercise specifies that data at our disposal are a sample of all the historical quotes: for this reason, the function STDEV.S and VAR.C have been used instead of STDEV.P and VAR.S, useful when data represent the entire population.

Comment point 4

The Data analysis tool (installed and enabled in the Excel Options) allows selecting many of mathematical and statistical analysis tools. After selecting the worksheet where the data are located to be analyzed (in this case the Stock worksheet), use the Data analysis command in the Data tab, then select the Descriptive Statistics tool. In the Descriptive Statistics window, it is necessary to set the input range ($E$2:$E$6814 corresponding to the values of the Adj Close field select the cells "Grouped by columns" option, specify that the output should be produced in a new worksheet, and select the Summary statistics option. Data are saved in a new worksheet, to be renamed according to the instructions.

Comment point 5

The simple moving average is the arithmetic mean of the values to use: as each value represents the stock price on a particular day, the average is calculated, with the AVERAGE function, using 30 values in the case of the 30 days simple moving average and 90 values in the case of the 90 days simple moving average.

Comment point 6

Also, for this chart it is advisable to set the values of the Date field later, as the horizontal axis labels.

EXERCISE 11.8 - Stock analysis

Tools needed to solve the exercise:

Data import from text file, AVERAGE, STDEV.S functions, simple formulas (addition, subtraction, multiplication, division), chart creation and customization.

EXERCISE 11.9 - Regression

Tools needed to solve the exercise:
Data import from text file, VLOOKUP, IFERROR, AVERAGE, STDEV.S, COVARIANCE.S, CORREL, SLOPE, INTERCEPT, RSQ functions, chart creation and customization.

EXERCISE 11.10 - Market Analysis (commented)

Tools needed to solve the exercise:
COUPPCD, COUPDAYBS, COUPDAYS, COUPNCD, IF, XIRR, XNPV, VLOOKUP, IFERROR, AVERAGE, MEDIAN, STDEV.S, KURT, SKEW, SLOPE, INTERCEPT, RSQ functions, simple formulas (addition, subtraction, multiplication, division), Conditional Formatting, Goal seek, data import from text file, chart creation and customization.

Comment point 1
To calculate the yield to maturity of the two bonds, the XIRR function has been used in both cases instead of the YIELD and TBILLYIELD functions. In fact, the YIELD function does not calculate correctly the yield to maturity when the cash flows do not occur at regular intervals (in this case the purchase date is different from any coupon maturity date). In addition, the TBILLYIELD function can be used only for zero coupon bond with maturity date shorter or equal to 1 year.

In both cases, it is necessary to create the dates and cash flows table because the XIRR function needs ranges containing cash flows and the respective dates. For the zero coupon bond, we only need two cash flows: the first one is equal to the purchase price, whereas the second one is equal to the face value (always 100). For the fixed rate bond, first it is necessary to calculate the accrued interest to calculate correctly the first cash flow (equal to the purchase price plus the accrued interest), and then calculate all the other dates and their respective cash flows.

The accrued interest is equal to the coupon value (which in this case is semi-annual) multiplied by the days as the last coupon and divided by the days between a coupon and the other. For the calculation, three functions were used: COUPPCD (to automatically calculate the payment date previous to the purchase date), COUPDAYBS (to calculate the days between the date of the last coupon and the purchase date), and COUPDAYS (to calculate the days between the coupon and the other). In all cases, the "Actual/360" basis has been used.

In the case of the fixed rate bond, coupon dates (all but the first one, equal to the purchase date) have been calculated with the formula (cell **A23**):

= IFERROR(COUPNCD (A22,$B$4,2,2),"")

The COUPNCD function calculates automatically the next coupon date and the IFERROR function leaves the cells empty in case of evaluation of a bond with different values and a shorter maturity.

Cash flows have been calculated (all but the first one, equal to the purchase price plus the accrued interest) with the formula (cell **B23**):

=IFERROR(IF(A23=$B$4,$B$6+$B$9,$B$9),"")

The formula controls if the coupon date is equal to the bond maturity date: if the condition is true, the face value is summed to the coupon value, if it is false only the coupon value is shown. Also in this case the IFERROR function leaves empty all the cells not corresponding to a date.

Comment point 2

The XNPV function calculates the net present value of a series of cash flows (at least one must be negative) corresponding to a series of dates. At first, the result of the function is equal to -68,202.17 euros, which corresponds to the present value of all cash flows discounted at 3.45%.

Using Goal seek, we found the annual discount rate for which the internal rate of return would be equal to 100,000 euros.

Comment point 3

Data from the **Exercise 11.10 - Stock.txt** and **Exercise 11.10 - Index.txt** are separated by tab, have the comma as decimal separator and the point as thousands separator, and have the dates set with aaaa-mm-dd. To import correctly the data with the Get External Data/From Text command, it is necessary to specify that the separators used in the file are the comma as decimal separator and the point as thousands separator and that the Date field is set with the format "AMD".

The simple moving average of the index quotes has been calculated using the AVERAGE function and setting a range of 50 values.

Statistics in the **Index** worksheet have been calculated using the AVERAGE, MEDIAN, STDEV.S (imported data are a sample), KURT and SKEW, set with the range including all the Adj Close field values (F2:F2527).

Comment point 4

After copying the values of Date and Adj Close fields of the **Index** worksheet in columns A and B of the **Analysis** worksheet, it is necessary to use a function to return, for each date, the price of the Alpha stock. The values can be returned using the VLOOKUP function, which searches for each date in the **Stock** worksheet and returns the corresponding value in the Adj Close field:
=IFERROR(VLOOKUP(A2,Stock!A$2:F$2596,6,FALSE),C3)
The IFERROR function is needed to avoid that when a certain date is not available, the value of the Alpha stock an error message is shown. In this case, the missing value is replaced by the quote of the previous day.

Comment point 5

The slope, the intercept, and the R-squared of the linear regression between the Alpha stock and the index have been calculated using the functions SLOPE, INTERCEPT, and RSQ: in all the functions, the quotes of the Alpha stock have been set as dependent variable (y) and the quotes of the index as independent variable (x).
To show the formula of the regression line on the chart, create a scatterplot, then insert a linear trendline, and in the Format trendline tab select the "Show equation on chart" option.

Comments and functions unit 12

EXERCISE 12.1 - Turnover

Tools needed to solve the exercise:
INDEX, MATCH, IFERROR functions, data validation.

EXERCISE 12.2 - Orders

Tools needed to solve the exercise:
INDEX, MATCH, IFERROR functions, data validation, Paste command options (Transpose).

EXERCISE 12.3 - Gifts

Tools needed to solve the exercise:
Data validation, COUNTIF, AND, SUM, ISNUMBER, LEN, SUBSTITUTE functions.

EXERCISE 12.4 - Product IDs

Tools needed to solve the exercise:
Data validation, LEFT, AND, OR, LEN functions.

EXERCISE 12.5 - Countries and offices

Tools needed to solve the exercise:
Data validation, INDIRECT, OR, WEEKDAY, TODAY functions.

EXERCISE 12.6 - Variable period

Tools needed to solve the exercise:
Data validation, SUM, OFFSET, MATCH functions.

EXERCISE 12.7 - Choose your category

Tools needed to solve the exercise:
Data validation, VLOOKUP, MATCH functions, chart creation.

Comment point 1
In cell I1, it is necessary to use the data validation to create a drop-down menu in the cell. In the Source box of the Data validation tool, it is possible to specify the references to a range of cells with the list of values to be used; as an alternative, it is possible to specify the values entering them in the Source box, separated by a comma and without the equal sign at the beginning. In this case, it is necessary to be careful and write the values in the Source box exactly as they can be found in the table: a slight difference in the values (e.g., a space at the end of a value) would lead to an error.

Comment point 2
Cell **E1** is set to show the value selected in cell **I1** (=I1). It is possible to use different functions to show the values of the category selected in **I1** in the cells of the **E** column. In the Products worksheet, the VLOOKUP and MATCH functions have been used. In cell E2, the function is the following:
=VLOOKUP(A2,A$2:D$11,MATCH(E$1,A$1:D$1,0),FALSE)
The function is set to search for the product in the first column of the table and return the value corresponding to the field selected in cell **E1**. The MATCH function is necessary to return the exact number of the column in which the value searched by the VLOOKUP function can be found and which must be returned: entering the number of the column in the col_index_num argument of the VLOOKUP function, it would be necessary to change the value of the column each time a new value is selected in cell **I1**.
As an alternative to the VLOOKUP and MATCH functions, we could have used other functions. In particular, in cell **E2**, we could have used the IF, INDEX, and MATCH functions or the OFFSET and MATCH functions:
=IF($E$1=$B$1,B2,IF($E$1=$C$1,C2,D2))

=INDEX(A2:D2,1,MATCH(E$1,$A$1:$D$1,0))
=OFFSET(A2,0,MATCH(E$1,$A$1:$D$1,0))

Comment point 3
The chart has been created by selecting the values of the A and E columns at the same time, and then selecting a column chart. When the value selected in cell **I1** changes, the values of column **E** also change, and so those shown in the chart.

EXERCISE 12.8 - Chart with bands

Tools needed to solve the exercise:
IF function, form control setting (checkbox), chart creation and customization.

EXERCISE 12.9 - Scroll bar

Tools needed to solve the exercise:
OFFSET function, form control setting (scroll bar), chart creation and customization.

EXERCISE 12.10 - Dashboard (commented)

Tools needed to solve the exercise:
VLOOKUP, MATCH functions, conditional formatting, chart creation and customization, options of the Paste command (Paste as linked picture).

Comment point 1
The drop-down menus in cells **C4**, **F4**, and **C13** have been created with the data validation tool from a list: in all the three cases, the Country list can be found in the **Control** worksheet. In order to accelerate the setting of data validation, we could also have assigned a name to the range of cells of the **Control** worksheet with the list of Countries (e.g., "countries") and used it as the data validation tool in place of the references to the range

(**Control!$A$8:$A$38**). Also in cell **F13**, data validation has been used, but with a different list from the **Control** worksheet.

The text "Value in 2008" in cells **C5**, **F5**, **C14**, and **F14** has been calculated using the following formula:

="Value in "&Control!$B$4

As an alternative, it would have been equally correct to use the CONCATENATE function. It is important to note that to set the reference year, we used an absolute reference in cell **B4** of the **Control** worksheet. This way, if we decided to use a new reference year for the dashboard, we would change only the value in the **Control** worksheet.

Comment point 2

The values corresponding to Gdp, public debt, public debt/Gdp ratio and population of the selected Countries must be calculated using the VLOOKUP function: this way every time that a different Country is selected, Excel returns the right value, without having to change the function settings.

The function used in cell **C6** is the following:

=VLOOKUP(C4,Gdp!$A$4:$M$44,MATCH(Control!$B$4,Gdp!$A$3:$M$3,0),FALSE)

Note that the value searched for by the function is the one in cell **C4** (selected Country) and that the MATCH function has been used to return the number of column in which the desired reference year can be found: this value has been entered as a reference to cell **B4** of the **Control** worksheet, so that if the reference year changes, the values automatically update.

As each requested value can be found in a different worksheet, it was not possible to create a function in cell **C6** and then copy it downwards. But, once you set the functions of the first selected Country (**C6:C9**) using absolute references where needed, it was possible to copy the cells in the **F6:F9**, **C15:C18**, and **F15:F18** cell ranges.

Comment point 3

In the **I6:I9**, **I15:I18** and **I24:I27** cell ranges, the names of the Countries selected in cells **C4**, **F4**, **C13**, and **F13** have been shown using a cell reference. Gdp, public debt-gdp, and population values of the selected Countries have been calculated using once again the VLOOKUP and MATCH functions. In both cases, we used mixed cell references to set the function once in the first

cell in the top left corner and then copied it in all the other cells. The function used in cell **J6** is the following:
=VLOOKUP($I6,Gdp!$A$3:$K$37,CONFRONTA(J$5,Gdp!$A$3:$M$3,0), FALSE)
The result of the function in cell **J15** (calculation of the public debt-gdp ratio) has been divided by 100, because in the **Debt-gdp** worksheet we have integer numbers representing percentage values.

Comment point 4
To create the tables with the list of the Countries sorted by their public debt-Gdp ratio in the **Calc2** and **Calc3** worksheets, we copied first the Country list from the **Control** worksheet. Then, also in this case the VLOOKUP and MATCH functions have been used to always return values updated to any possible change of the reference year.
To cells of both tables (cells with the values), a conditional formatting has been applied (data bars). Finally, the two tables have been sorted.

Comment point 5
The last point of the exercise has not difficult requests: charts have been created without special settings and then moved into the **Dashboard** worksheet. The area **B1:F18** of the **Calc1** worksheet has been copied and pasted as linked image to permit its automatic update if the values change. Finally, tables of the **Calc2** and **Calc3** worksheets have been pasted as pictures.

Authors

Massimo Ballerini is Course Director of Computer science and lecturer in other Information and Communication Technology courses at Università Bocconi. He is a contract lecturer at Politecnico di Milano and he has been lecturer and research fellow at Bicocca University, IULM University and other educational institutes. As a professional, he is a consultant for international companies operating in the fields of digital technologies for media.

Alberto Clerici is the Director of IT Education Center and Language Center at Università Bocconi. As a lecturer and consultant, he has worked with several universities and major training companies in the Information Technology field. He is author of several ICT books.

M. Chiara Debernardi is an Academic Fellow for Computer science course and teaches statistical software and coding in extracurricular courses at Università Bocconi. She deals with consulting and corporate training in the field of Business Intelligence, Big Data and Machine Learning.

Davide Del Corno has been for several years an Academic Fellow for the Computer science course and for the extracurricular course of Excel Advanced at Università Bocconi. He heads the Property Management and Development function at Fondazione Patrimonio Ca' Granda.

Maurizio De Pra is Course Director of Computer science and lecturer in other courses in the area of information technology and office automation at Università Bocconi. Senior lecturer in computer science and finance, he has worked for major Italian insurance and banking companies. He is author of books and publications on various technical topics.